Covid-19 Pandemic and Economic Development

"With the Pandemic still around us, the countries and firms around the world are seeking to devise a more resilient socio-economic systems and business models. This book offers a timely and effective idea for such endeavor in diverse sectors and areas in India, Punjab in particular."

—Keun Lee, *Vice Chairman, National Economic Advisory Council (NEAC) for the President of Korea and Professor of Economics, Seoul National University, Seoul, South Korea*

"A timely response of a group of scholars manifested in a most comprehensive, yet highly insightful, exposition of the multi-dimensional manner in which COVID 19 pandemic has impacted Punjab economy and the plausible way forward. While this volume is inspirational for scholars from India and abroad, it is an indispensable read for anyone, especially policy makers, concerned with the pandemic and the economy."

—K. J. Joseph, *Director, Gulati Institute for Finance and Taxation (GIFT), Thiruvananthapuram, India*

"This collection of policy briefs evaluates a broad range of issues affecting the Punjab economy, all in the context of the COVID-19 pandemic. The contributions are short and readable, and many provide updates on the impacts of the pandemic, not easily available elsewhere. All the writers have a deep engagement with Punjab and its economic situation. The book will be very valuable for policymakers and scholars."

—Nirvikar Singh, *Distinguished Professor of Economics, University of California, Santa Cruz, USA*

Sukhpal Singh · Lakhwinder Singh ·
Kamal Vatta
Editors

Covid-19 Pandemic and Economic Development

Emerging Public Policy Lessons for Indian Punjab

palgrave
macmillan

Editors
Sukhpal Singh
Centre for Management in Agriculture
Indian Institute of Management Ahmedabad
Ahmedabad, Gujarat, India

Lakhwinder Singh
Commerce, Management and Economics
Khalsa College
Punjabi University
Patiala, Punjab, India

Kamal Vatta
Department of Economics and Sociology
Punjab Agricultural University
Ludhiana, Punjab, India

ISBN 978-981-16-4441-2 ISBN 978-981-16-4442-9 (eBook)
https://doi.org/10.1007/978-981-16-4442-9

This Palgrave Macmillan imprint is published by the registered company Springer Nature Singapore Pte Ltd.
The registered company address is: 152 Beach Road, #21-01/04 Gateway East, Singapore 189721, Singapore

Preface

The Covid-19 pandemic has claimed 2.7 million human lives worldwide by March 26, 2021 and an additional 21 million suffering from the infection. India lost 160983 human lives with 421032 active cases at this time. Punjab has emerged as one of the worst affected states in terms of infection and the fatality rate. When we look back, a year ago on March 24, 2020, the Government of India announced the lock down and Government of Punjab also imposed 24X7 curfew. That decision, in the initial days, was taken by the citizens very seriously and all kinds of movement of humans, goods and services was stopped. The poorer sections were the worst affected as they failed to access the bare minimum necessities of life as their daily earnings were gone. They were the first ones to start flouting the restrictions in search of food. When they stepped out from their homes, the police treated them harshly. The vernacular press and social media came handy to raise alarm both of the plight of the poor and the high handedness of the police. However, the Government then allowed the regular flow of essential goods and services and also provided packets of essential items to the poor households through police and local political leadership.

Then, the migrants turn came. The migrants started walking barefoot along with their family members including small children to go back to their villages. The lockdown created a bigger crisis of human existence. It was soon realized that longer period lockdown has devastated the economy and employment opportunities. The Government of

Punjab appointed a Committee under the Chairpersonship of Montek Singh Ahluwalia on April 25, 2020 to assess the losses and also to suggest the roadmap for the revival of the crisis ridden Punjab economy. The crisis of Punjab economy has remained under discussion and debate for a long period of time and substantial amount of policy documents, research articles and books published bear testimony to it. The Centre for Development Economics and Innovation Studies (CDEIS), Punjabi University made a unique contribution in terms of organizing workshops and conferences involving various stakeholders on the crisis of Punjab economy. As the lockdown and restrictions started easing, there was urge to again discuss the state of affairs of Punjab economy and also provide alternative pathways to rejuvenate the Punjab economy. From the platform of CDEIS, we (the undersigned) invited scholars to contribute a policy brief each in their area of expertise on the Punjab economy and we received an overwhelming response. We received more than twenty policy briefs on which various daily newspapers published stories. This interest in the policy briefs and the editors' desire to make the policy briefs available to larger academic community and policy makers in one place encouraged them to bring together all the policy briefs in the form of a book. Palgrave Macmillan response for the proposed publication was very encouraging. We are grateful to Ms. Sandeep Kaur and her team for bringing out this volume in this difficult time of Covid-19 pandemic quickly and in a timely manner.

The CDEIS has provided all the possible support and a stimulating intellectual environment. The credit of making this a happening place goes to the supporting staff. We are highly obliged and express our gratitude for the unfailing help of Mr. Baltej Singh Bhathal and Mr. Gurdeep Singh. They have carried out all the work with a smiling face. The colleagues in the CDEIS have remained a source of inspiration and intellectual stimulus and deserve our heartfelt appreciation. We are grateful to Professors Anita Gill, Kesar Singh Bhangoo, Jaswinder Singh Brar, Anupma Uppal, Rakesh Kumar Khurana and Parmod K Agarwal for their continued encouragement and selfless help. The contributors of this volume have smilingly borne with the demands of the editors and the publisher in terms of meeting the deadlines and doing several rounds of revisions. Their enthusiasm encouraged us to expand the scope of the volume covering most aspects of the state economy and its developmental domain ranging from agriculture to agro-markets, MSMEs, health, education, services, farm labour, gender, marginalized caste workers, migrants, philanthropy, diaspora, fiscal issues, federalism and governance. We express our gratefulness to the contributors for their intellectual input. We hope that this volume will receive the needed attention from various relevant quarters and create genuine interest at various levels for more engagement with the developmental issues of the state. More importantly, we sincerely hope that the book will help the public policy makers to plan and build a better world for the wellbeing of the citizens of Punjab and similarly situated people anywhere in the world.

Ahmedabad, India — Sukhpal Singh
Patiala, India — Lakhwinder Singh
Ludhiana, India — Kamal Vatta

Contents

Contributors

Ashapurna Baruah National Institute of Technology (NIT), Hamirpur, Hamirpur, India

Jatinder S. Bedi Institute for Development and Communication (IDC), Chandigarh, India

Shruti Bhogal Centers for International Projects Trusts (CIPT), New Delhi, India

Amarjit Bhullar University of Northern British Columbia, Prince George, BC, Canada

Sandeep Dixit Centers for International Projects Trusts (CIPT), New Delhi, India

Angrej Singh Gill Panjab University Rural Centre, Kauni, Sri Muktsar Sahib, India

Sucha Singh Gill CRIID, Chandigarh, India

Adam S. Greens McDonald Institute for Archaeological Research, University of Cambridge, Cambridge, UK

Varinder Jain Institute of Deveploment Studies, Jaipur, India

Shailly Kedia The Energy and Resources Institute, New Delhi, India

Deepak Kumar Punjabi University, Patiala, India

Anuja Malhotra National Institute of Public Finance and Policy, New Delhi, India

Swati Mehta Punjab School of Economics, Guru Nanak Dev University, Amritsar, India

Kamlesh Narwana Panjab University Rural Centre, Kauni, Sri Muktsar Sahib, India

Rita Pandey National Institute of Public Finance and Policy, New Delhi, India

Cameron A. Petrie Department of Archaeology and McDonald Institute for Archaeological Research, University of Cambridge, Cambridge, UK

Gayatri Prabhakar Institute for Development and Communication (IDC), Chandigarh, India

Varinder Sharma Institute for Development and Communication (IDC), Chandigarh, India

Manjit Sharma Department of Economics, DAV College, Chandigarh, India

Pushpak Sharma Department of Economics, Panjab University, Chandigarh, India

Baldev Singh Shergill Guru Kashi College, Punjabi University, Punjab, India

Indervir Singh National Institute of Technology (NIT), Hamirpur, Hamirpur, India

Lakhwinder Singh Commerce, Management and Economics, Khalsa College, Punjabi University, Patiala, Punjab, India

Sukhpal Singh Centre for Management in Agriculture, Indian Institute of Management Ahmedabad, Ahmedabad, Gujarat, India

Sukhpal Singh Punjab Agricultural University, Ludhiana, Punjab, India

Pritam Singh Oxford Brookes University, Oxford, UK

Sukhwinder Singh Public Health Foundation of India, Gurgaon, India

Naresh Singla Department of Economic Studies, School of Social Sciences, Central University of Punjab, Bathinda, India

Shinder S. Thandi Department of Global Studies, University of California, Santa Barbara, CA, USA

Kamal Vatta Department of Economics and Sociology, Punjab Agricultural University, Ludhiana, Punjab, India

Satish Verma Centre for Research in Rural and Industrial Development (CRRID), Chandigarh, India

Abbreviations

APMC	Agriculture Produce Market Committee
AQ	Air Quality
ASER	Annual Status of Education Report
ASHA	Accredited Social Health Activist
BAAC	Bank for Agriculture and Agricultural Cooperatives
BAME	Black, Asian and Minority Ethnic
BPL	Below Poverty Line
CAG	Comptroller and Auditor General
CAs	Commission Agents
CBSE	Central Board Secondary Education
CCI	Cotton Corporation of India
CFA	Contract Farming Act
CGSSD	Credit Guarantee Scheme for Subordinate Debt
CHC	Community Health Centre
CMIE	Centre for Monitoring Indian Economy
DAFW	Department of Agriculture and Farmers' Welfare
DBT	Direct Benefit Transfer
ECLGS	Emergency Credit Line Guarantee Scheme
ELC	Emergency Line of Credit
FCI	Food Corporation of India
FLFPR	Female Labour Force Participation Rate
FPOs	Farmer Producer Organizations
GM	Genetically Modified
GNP	Gross National Product
GoI	Government of India
GoP	Government of Punjab

GSDP	Gross State Domestic Product
GST	Goods and Services Tax
GSVA	Gross State Value Added
HYV	High-Yielding Varieties
IFS	Institute of Fiscal Studies
ILO	International Labour Organization
IMF	International Monetary Fund
MARKFED	State Agricultural Co-operative Marketing Federation
MDF	Marketing Development Fund
MGNREGS	Mahatma Gandhi National Rural Employment Guarantee Scheme
MSMEs	Micro Small and Medium Enterprises
MSP	Minimum Support Price
NBFCs	Non-Banking Financial Companies
NCGTC	National Credit Guarantee Trustee Company or corporation?
NGOs	Non-Government Organizations
NHS	National Health Service
NPA	Non Performing Assets
NRIs	Non-Resident Indians
NSDM	National Skill Development Mission
NSSO	National Sample Survey Organization
OAEs	Own Account Enterprises
ONS	Office of National Statistics
PACS	Primary Agricultural Credit Society
PAU	Punjab Agricultural University
PCMY	Producer Consumer Market Yard
PDS	Public Distribution System
PHC	Primary Health Centre
PHE	Public Health England
PMJDY	Pradhan Mantri Jan Dhan Yojana
PSF	Price Stabilization fund
PUNSUP	Punjab Civil Supplies Corporation
RBI	Reserve Bank of India
RTE	Right to Education
SC	Scheduled Caste
SDGs	Sustainable Development Goals
SDP	State Domestic Product
SGPs	Self-Help Groups
SGST	State Goods and services Tax
SHC	Subsidiary Health Centre
SLBC	State Level Bankers' Committee
SOM	Soil Organic Matter
TIGRRESS	Transforming India's Green Revolution by Research and Empowerment for Sustainable Food Supplies

UHC	Universal Health Coverage
UK	United Kingdom
USA	United States of America
WHO	World Health Organisation

List of Figures

Employment Participation of Rural Women in Punjab: A Need for Policy Retrospect

COVID-19 Pandemic and the Service Sector in Punjab: An Assessment of Impact and Policies for Revival

List of Tables

Impact of COVID-19 Lockdown on Punjab Agriculture

Need for Innovations in Crop Residue Management in Punjab: Lessons from the COVID-19 Pandemic

Making Punjab's Urban Informal Sector More Resilient While Securing Livelihoods During Post-COVID-19 Times

Implementation of Emergency Credit Line Guarantee Scheme (ECLGS) in Punjab: An Assessment of Performance of Scheduled Commercial Banks

Employment Participation of Rural Women in Punjab: A Need for Policy Retrospect

COVID-19 Pandemic and the Scheduled Caste Workers in Rural Punjab: A Need for Structural Transformation

Livelihood of Agricultural Labourers in Punjab: Emerging Policy Issues

COVID-19 and Health Care Services in Punjab: Consequences and Challenges

Making 'Quality Education Accessible' to All: Policy Perspective on School Education in Punjab

COVID-19 Pandemic and the Service Sector in Punjab: An Assessment of Impact and Policies for Revival

Covid-19 Pandemic and Sustainability of Punjab Economy

Sukhpal Singh, Lakhwinder Singh, and Kamal Vatta

1 Introduction

The COVID-19 pandemic and its unprecedented spread posed very high risk to human life and disrupted the economic and social life globally. A sudden upsurge in the infection and its threat to life forced the governments across countries to take stringent measures including lockdowns and almost completely the economic activity. After originating in China the virus first spread to Europe and North America. The state of Indian Punjab due to its historical links and substantial presence of diaspora in

S. Singh
Centre for Management in Agriculture, Indian Institute of Management Ahmedabad, Ahmedabad, Gujarat, India
e-mail: sukhpal@iima.ac.in

L. Singh (✉)
Commerce, Management and Economics, Khalsa College, Punjabi University, Patiala, Punjab, India
e-mail: lakhwindergill@pbi.ac.in

K. Vatta
Department of Economics and Sociology, Punjab Agriculture University, Ludhiana, India
e-mail: kmlvatta@yahoo.com

S. Singh et al. (eds.), *Covid-19 Pandemic and Economic Development*,
https://doi.org/10.1007/978-981-16-4442-9_1

these countries fearing the transmission of disease, started early vigil on the travellers coming to Punjab to contain the spread of corona virus.

With the Indian government announcing the lockdown on March 24, the Punjab government imposed curfew along with lockdown to completely prohibit any movement of the population. As the economic activity came to a halt, the poor and vulnerable sections of the society were most adversely affected and struggled to fulfil their basic needs. The vernacular press reported high handedness of the police and the genuine demands of the marginalized sections of society. The impact of this was that the government allowed philanthropist agencies to serve food but also geared up to provide some basic services to the marginalized and while resurrecting image of police, they were asked to deliver food kits at the doorsteps of the marginalized sections of the society. The lockdown was initially successful to contain the spread of the COVID-19 but as soon as the unlocking process started, the spread of the disease was again on the rise. The Covid-19 deaths have approached to 0.1 million and the infection rate has been rising in India. In Punjab, the daily reported infections were flattening since September 21, 2020 and the death rate was three per cent, which seems to be on the higher side. The trends of rising infection and higher fatality rate continue to point to the risk and uncertainty to human life. This also continued to have a high degree of uncertainty with respect to economic activities. Even in early 2021, the state witnessed another wave of Covid-19 infections along with states like Maharashtra, Gujarat and Kerala.

The incidences have severely disrupted the economy, both in terms of the demand and supply. The first quarter GDP growth rates for the financial year 2020–2021 showed a grim picture. Indian economy shrunk by 23.9 per cent compared with the first quarter of 2019–2020. It is the highest decline across all countries of the world. Somewhat similar trends in the SDP are expected in the state of Punjab. The nature of economic downturn was quite different compared with the earlier crisis faced by the global economy. This has engaged scholars to assess the nature of the crisis and possible public policy resolution (Jain and Singh, 2020; Lee, 2020). During the pandemic times, a well-informed debate on the future course of capitalist economic development has taken place with the emergence of one-sided consensus that the state-led economic development is the way forward. The private sector of the economy has shied away from the responsibility in this difficult time and has demanded government support to make up for its business losses. The major ingredient of this debate was revival of economic development process with human face and preservation of the nature and natural environment, that is, sustainable development. But in reality, the state has turned more liberal providing more space to the private economic activities and amending rules and regulation that allows restructuring of the capital. There has been a substantial disruption to the international transactions, institutional arrangements and employment. The assessment of the loss to the GNP has been made by various agencies such as IMF. The revival of economic activities was predicted by various agencies under some assumptions but the revival is relatively very slow and tardy because the Covid-19 spread remains unabated in the absence of any effective medical treatment.

Punjab government has set up a Committee to suggest roadmap for revival of the state economy during post-Covid-19 period which submitted its interim report in July 2020 (Singh, 2021) and is expected to submit the final report anytime soon though it has missed the December deadline. Punjab's economic development was under stress prior to the occurrence of this pandemic. The rate of growth had decelerated over a long period of time (Singh and Singh, 2002). Punjab had been a leading state in terms of per capita income till the end of twentieth century and thereafter, it started lagging behind and slipped to 9th rank among the major Indian states. The state is also lagging behind in terms of SDGs and ease of doing business (Iqbal and Misra, 2020). This indicates that Punjab economy has been suffering from governance and investment deficiencies from the last three decades but recent pandemic has further deepened the recessionary tendencies. The fiscal policy of the state government, the only instrument in the hand of the state government, has remained nearly dysfunctional in the past three decades. The emergence of high debt-GSDP ratio and relatively slow pace of tax collection is an indicator of governance failure. Even the newly established GST tax system has reduced the capacity of the state to independently take decisions regarding raising tax revenue. However, the promise of the Union government of India to compensate the loss in revenue seems unrealized as the Union government asked the state governments to borrow. In fact, the revenue raising capacity of the state government has been undermined due to several reasons apart from the current GST system. As a consequence, the state government has reduced expenditure on capital formation and social sectors such as health and education. The COVID-19 pandemic further exposed the weaknesses of health infrastructure pointing to the need for immediate restructuring and revamping. Therefore, it is pertinent to estimate the loss of economic activity caused by the lockdown and subsequent disruptions in order to plan the economic revival more rationally.

Public policy plays an important role in the revival of economic activities especially in the time of depressed economic environment. The agricultural sector has recorded very low or negative growth rates of the crop sector in the state income. Farmers and agricultural labourers are neck deep in crisis due to fall in income and rise in the cost of production. Consequently, there is emergence of high degree of indebtedness and suicides (Singh et al., 2020). The economic transformation of the Punjab economy is moving on a slow pace (Singh and Singh, 2016) and Punjab has overstayed in agriculture. The industrial sector of the economy is predominantly small scale. It is usually based on social capital and household savings (Banerjee, 2005) but the scale of production continues to remain small. This sector has failed to emerge as an engine of growth of the Punjab economy. The productive sectors of the economy have not been able to keep the pace of performance for the desired level of economic transformation. The rejuvenation of the Punjab economy in the post-COVID-19 is urgently needed to give hope to the economic actors of production to regain the past glory and also to attain the path of economic transformation. The aim of this book is to provide concrete public policies for the revival and rejuvenation of the Punjab economy. These policy measures may also be useful for other Indian states to revive their economic development process. This book contains twenty two chapters exclusively written by scholars working on Punjab economy to understand the status of the economy and proposes a strategy of rejuvenating its development process. The coverage includes governance issues, agricultural sector, agricultural markets, industrial sector, service sector, labour, diaspora, gender, environment, state revenue, centre-state relations and public policy. These contributions are organized in the following six sections keeping in view the thematic unity.

2 Covid-19 Pandemic and Sustainability of Agriculture

Indian agriculture, especially Punjab agriculture, has shown resilience during the period of Covid-19 pandemic and witnessed positive rate of growth even in the first quarter of the financial year 2020–2021 when stringent restrictions of lockdown were under operation. The state of Punjab with the highest crop productivity levels has always contributed significantly to the national food security. This aspect further strengthened during the lockdown period. However, the crisis of Punjab agriculture is multidimensional in nature. The simple income statistics of agricultural sector has shown that the crop sector within the sector has shown a declining trend (GoP, 2021). The livestock sector has recorded a positive rate of growth. The rising cost of cultivation is rendering the small and marginal holdings economically unviable causing a high degree of indebtedness (Singh et al., 2020). The intensive agriculture has led to the depletion of natural resources such as groundwater, air, etc. As a result, both the income and environment in Punjab are undergoing a severe sustainability challenge. The six chapters included in this section provide an in-depth analysis of the state of affairs of Punjab agriculture and also strive to provide future pathways.

In Chapter 2 entitled 'Agriculture Sustainability in Punjab: A Way Forward', Sukhwinder Singh examined the sustainability challenges for the agriculture sector. The author has argued that Punjab is an agriculturally strategic state of India. However, its agricultural sector is currently passing through a critical phase where the natural resources are depleting, yields are stagnating and farm incomes are falling. A continued reliance on wheat and rice (paddy) production and overdependence on underground water resources have raised questions about the sustainability of Punjab agriculture. The current cropping patterns, which are heavily dependent on wheat and rice, are highly intensive with low diversity potentially undermining overall agricultural sustainability of the state. From a policy perspective, crop diversification policies in Punjab need to be more practical and pragmatic providing alternative sets of crops to farmers which can economically compete with wheat and rice. In the post-COVID-19 phase, Punjab government might consider promoting rural agribusiness, i.e. food processing, fine-tuning the current agricultural marketing systems and rationalizing the current regime of subsidies to farm sector for improving the overall agricultural sustainability in Punjab.

It is curious to know that how agricultural sector of Punjab has been impacted during the period of lockdown in Punjab. Kamal Vatta, Shruti Bhogal, Camron A Petrie, Adam S Green and Sandeep Dixit in Chapter 3 entitled 'Impact of Covid-19 Lockdown on Punjab Agriculture' have assessed the impact of lockdown on agriculture. The authors have examined the impact of lockdown at the time of wheat harvesting faced with immediate shortages of labour and machinery and challenges for effective procurement. A few months after wheat harvesting, sowing/transplantation of kharif crops such as cotton, maize and paddy required multiple times more labour force and posed serious challenges to farmers across the state. The authors made an assessment, which is based on telephonic/personal survey of 120 farmers.

From the empirical evidence and analysis, the authors concluded that despite considerable challenges, farmers adopted different strategies to address labour shortages and marketing challenges as influenced by their holding size, financial resources and access to local information networks. Marginal and small farmers increased the use of family labour, while medium and large famers showed an increased use of machinery. The cost of cultivation, harvesting and marketing operations have gone up and the authors suggested that the government should reduce this burden by financial support. To ensure sustainability of agriculture in the future, the authors suggested a three-pronged strategy. One, strengthening the role of agro-machinery service centres in the state in the public as well as in private sector to ensure timely, cost-effective and easy availability of farm machinery. Two, strengthening of supply chains for quality seeds by active participation of various stakeholders such as Department of Agriculture and Farmers' Welfare (DAFW), farmers' cooperatives, FPOs, etc. Three, strengthening of supply networks at the local level by involving village Panchayats, farmers' cooperatives and local traders. The focus should be on meeting the local demand effectively. The government may devise incentive mechanisms for strengthening such networks.

The intensive agriculture in north India produces lot of biomass. The biomass management practices have been the cause of air pollution. The paddy stubble, when it is wet, burning in the winter generates huge quantity of toxic gases. The quantity of paddy stubble generated alone in Punjab is 30 million tons (GoP, 2021) and out of it 25 million tons have been usually put on fire. This creates a health hazard, decreased visibility on the roads and turns to an air and surface transport hazard. The lockdown period has reduced substantial amount of environmental pollutants. But the revival of the economic activity has again brought us back to similar or even worse conditions of air quality. In Chapter 4 entitled 'Need for Innovations in Crop Residue Management in Punjab: Lessons from the COVID-19 Pandemic', Rita Pandey, Shailly Kedia and Anuja Malhotra have examined the situation arising out of crop stubble burning. The authors are of the opinion that the spread of Covid-19 has put constraints on the health care infrastructure and additional pollution caused air quality deterioration due to stubble burning in Punjab further increases the stress multiplier. The authors have suggested short to medium term practical solutions such as making food production in north India more resource efficient and resilient to environmental and climate change.

The Covid-19 shock has disrupted global and local supply chains. It has added to food insecurity of the households especially the poor and vulnerable households. Amarjit Bhullar, in Chapter 5 entitled 'Farm Gardens: A Promising Approach to Enhance Food Security and Sustainability', has argued that local food production such as farm gardens plays an important role in solving the problem of food insecurity and sustainability. He has argued that the farm gardens are an integral part of local food systems and the agricultural landscape of many developing countries has endured the test of time. The farm gardens have five intrinsic characteristics: (1) are located at own farm; (2) contain a high diversity of plants; (3) production is supplemental rather than the main source of family consumption and income; (4) occupy a small area and (5) are a production system that the poor can easily enter at some level. Punjab farmers were accustomed to produce not only a variety of food grains but also the vegetables, fruits, eggs, meat and milk for domestic use. But now with the exception to wheat, rice and milk, most of the farming families are dependent on the market for supply of other food items required for nutritional adequacy such as vegetables, fruits, eggs, meat and the other food grains. The result is nutritional inadequacy, higher expenditure and lack of access to fresh and quality food. Farmers have enjoyed the economies of scale by producing wheat and rice but have forgone the economies of scope.

Bhullar further argued that the COVID-19 has provided an opportunity to think and revive the system of self-production of food items. Punjab Agricultural University has developed plans for home gardens with potential to produce fruits and vegetables around the year, but adoption has failed to pick due to lack of policy support. A policy framework for large-scale adoption of farm garden plans with estimates of comprehensive assessment of financial and institutional resources is required. The author has provided a strategy and policy steps to ensure the success of the farm gardens.

Agricultural markets are lifeline of agriculture. The way they are being provided, reformed and regulated gives hope for the sustainability of agriculture. However, the three farm acts passed during the initial phase of the

Covid-19 spread have been contested by the farmer organizations with a view that these laws will erode the sustainability of agriculture and will adversely affect the Indian consumers. Sukhpal Singh, in Chapter 6 entitled 'Reforming Agricultural Markets in Punjab in the Context of Union Farm Acts for the Post-Covid-19 Recovery', has analysed the status and implications of agricultural markets reforms for Punjab agriculture. Singh has argued that the reforms in agricultural markets in India are long due, is not disputed, though the nature of such reforms is under question. This was evident from the way the perishable produce farmers experienced losses during the COVID-19 pandemic though the wheat procurement was smooth due to the fact it was procured by state agencies, by and large, in Punjab. Punjab has either lagged or has taken adverse steps which were not in tune with the Indian trend in agricultural market reforms. Recently, when the Union government enacted new Acts on two major state domains i.e. on agricultural trade area outside the APMC market yards/sub-yards and, on contract farming, Punjab again has amended these Acts at its own level to provide for Minimum Support Price (MSP) for wheat and paddy across all channels which are not forwarded by the Governor to the President of India for his approval for them to be made into a law. At the same time, before the Union Acts came in, Punjab had not followed the model APLM Act (2017) and the Model contract farming Act 2018. Its legislation (APLM Act, 2107 with rules framed in 2020) was not in tune with the Model APLM Act 2017 and it is not willing to implement the new union Acts as well. In this context, a comprehensive review of the state of agricultural markets and agricultural market policy and regulation for their potential role in agricultural market development is provided. The author examines the Union model APLM (2017) and APLCF&S (2018) Acts and amended Punjab APLM Act, 2017, Punjab's contract farming Act of 2013, as well as the two recent Union Acts (The Farmers' Produce trade and commerce Act, 2020 and the Contract farming Act, 2020) for their implications for Punjab as well as the relevance and significance of Punjab's amendments to the central Acts. Finally, the author suggests an agricultural market reform map for Punjab and mechanisms for bringing about desired type and level of agro-market development in the state in tune with globalization and the needs of the state's farmers in the light of focus on post-COVID-19 agricultural recovery.

In Chapter 7 entitled 'Impact of Covid-19 Pandemic on Dairy Industry in Punjab: Major Concerns and Policy Options', Naresh Singla has examined the dairy industry of Punjab. The author put forward the idea that the livestock sector continues to drive rural livelihoods and contribute significantly to the agricultural economy of Punjab. Within livestock sector, milk accounts for about 80% of the total value of output of livestock. In the recent times, dairy sector has undergone rapid growth and structural shifts in terms of establishment of dairy cooperatives, producer companies and private dairy companies, which are seen as one of the several pathways to diversify and boost the rural income and livelihoods in crisis ridden agrarian state of Punjab. Singla has argued that imposing of lockdown and curfew disrupted all the economic activities and created disruptions in agriculture and allied sectors with serious implications for food production and farmer incomes. The author explored how the dairy sector in Punjab was, particularly the milk producers, affected due to the outbreak of COVID-19 and how did the milk producers and the state government respond to COVID-19 pandemic to ensure sustainable dairy-based livelihoods which would also work in the post-COVID-19 period. The findings reveal that there was a decline in milk sales and procurement, increase in cost of dairy production, rise in animal health issues resulting in low milk productivity as veterinary services and dairy input supplies were affected due to the outbreak of COVID-19. The author has suggested public policy measures that can meet challenges from such pandemic outbreaks to make the dairy enterprise a win–win situation for all the stakeholders.

3 Covid-19 Pandemic and Small Scale Industry of Punjab

The secondary sector (consists of mining, manufacturing, electricity) of Punjab economy contributes 23 per cent to the state income. The manufacturing sector contributes 13.81 per cent to the state income (GoP, 2021) and its rate of growth has been decelerating in the recent years and was merely 1.1 per cent in 2018–2019. During Covid-19 pandemic lockdown, the manufacturing sector of Punjab was adversely affected just like the Indian industrial sector. Hence, it is significant to examine the implications of lockdown and identify the policy measures to revive this sector and transform it into a more dynamic and resilient sector. Three chapters included in this section provide a comprehensive view of the manufacturing sector in Punjab and offer public policy measures for making it more dynamic and vibrant in future.

In Chapter 8 entitled 'Making Punjab's Urban Informal Sector More Resilient While Securing Livelihoods during Post-Covid-19 Times', Varinder Jain analysed small informal urban industrial sector of Punjab and suggested public policy measures to reduce challenges faced by it. He has argued that informal enterprises in urban Punjab operate either as Own Account Enterprises (OAEs) or the Establishments—the former operate with relatively limited scale of operation and suffer from low worker productivity. But the latter despite having relatively better scale of operation remain exposed to competition besides suffering from low productivity of labour and capital. A variety of growth constraints continue to retard the operational performance of these firms. Similarly, the informal firms in urban Punjab are found to be having relatively limited access to formal credit when compared with their counterparts in other major Indian states. All this indicates nothing but the fragile state of informal enterprises in urban Punjab which got worsened further due to onslaught of COVID-19 pandemic. It is thus suggested that there is urgent need to step-up business resilience of informal enterprises. In fact, the state should not merely be the tax collecting agency; rather it should act as a facilitator to promote these firms who are striving in a competitive environment. Besides, firms the informal workers to suffer from prevailing conditions of livelihood insecurity which need to be contained. Provisions should be made for workers' capability building and sector-specific skill training. Finally, a contributory social security system with state, employers and workers as contributors, should be instituted to safeguard informal workers against contingent insecurity.

Punjab industry has suffered unprecedented losses due to shutdown of production of manufactured goods. Swati Mehta, in Chapter 9 entitled 'Covid-19 and MSMEs in Punjab: Challenges Ahead', investigated the local and global value-chains and resultant losses from the lockdown. Punjab has about 2.3 per cent of the total MSMEs in India with large proportion of micro enterprises. Major industries of Punjab include the manufacturing of hosiery, readymade garments, automobile parts, bicycles, hand tools, machine tools, sports goods, etc. that contribute considerably in the local and global value-chains.

It is estimated that the minimum loss that the industrial sector of Punjab suffered due to complete lockdown was around Rs. 40,000 Cr. However, it was found that industries of Punjab face numerous problems mainly related to infrastructural bottlenecks, obsolete transport facilities and institutional hurdles. The author suggested that the process of *continuous learning* should be adopted with co-evolution of different actors, organizations and institutions for making the industry competitive and to meet the long-term objective of making India self-reliant with the recent call for 'Atamnirbhar Bharat'.

The government of India announced several policy measures to revive the MSME sector through releasing the credit constraints faced by the sector. Satish Verma, in Chapter 10 entitled 'Implementation of Emergency Credit Line Guarantee Scheme (ECLGS) in Punjab: An Assessment of Performance of Scheduled Commercial Banks', highlighted the benefits of scheme to MSMEs in Punjab. The author has stated that the impact of Covid-19 was devastating across all the sectors of the economy. Among all, the worst hit is the small businesses and MSMEs in the state. The public sector banks have been slow in disbursals whereas the private banks have been lukewarm in sanctioning the accounts. The banks need to expedite disbursal of loans especially in three major districts in the state, and should also prevail upon all the potential borrowers to avail benefits of it. The private banks in the state were mainly concentrated on big ticket loans, and were not providing working capital loans under ELC, which were permitted under the scheme. They may be directed to handle small ticket loans also, besides extending all the loan facilities available under other schemes.

To improve the credit off-take, particularly by small and financially distressed and strained borrowers, the author suggested that the RBI may permit restructuring of NPA loans in such a manner that the excluded units can become eligible for loans under it, restart and revive. In addition, one-time interest waiver for the lockdown period or interest subvention should be granted, and the installments be suitably restructured. This is important because the demand is very slow to revive, and these measures are mostly supply-side centric and exclude fresh spending, investment and job creation.

4 Covid-19 Pandemic and Its Impact on Labour

During the Covid-19 induced lockdown, all establishments, both public and private, shut their production and the workers engaged in these establishments were rendered unemployed without any option, movement and interaction of the population. It had an adverse impact on the marginalized sections of society whose livelihood depends on day to day earnings.

In this section we have included three chapters. Ashapurna Baruah and Indervir Singh, in their Chapter 11 entitled 'Employment Participation of Rural Women in Punjab: A Need for Policy Retrospect', have analyzed the working and living conditions of female workforce in Punjab. The authors argued that the prevailing public policy and gender norms restrict the mobility of female workforce and has confined to villages. Therefore, according the work availability in the rural areas, the females are facing high degree of unemployment in rural Punjab.

Baruah and Singh have provided empirical evidence based on primary survey regarding women's willingness to work if work is available in the villages. They have further investigated that during the Covid-19 pandemic times the women's employment was more severely hit as compared to their male counterparts. To alleviate such a situation, the authors suggested some practical policy measures such as establishing business enterprises and infrastructure projects that can employ female workforce in the rural Punjab.

Punjab among the major states of India has the highest proportion of scheduled castes among its population. It is very important to understand how Covid-19 pandemic has affected this class of workers. Deepak Kumar, in Chapter 12 entitled 'Covid-19 Pandemic and the Scheduled Caste Workers in Rural Punjab: A Need for Structural Transformation', attempted to understand the plight of SC workers in rural Punjab. With COVID-19 pandemic and its attendant problems, it is imperative to understand the kind of challenges posed to the most marginalized segment of workers in one of the most prosperous states of India. After examining the socio-economic status of Scheduled Caste Workers in rural Punjab, the author has tried to understand their predicament in the period of pandemic. Kumar finds that with larger population of workforce returning back to their villages in Punjab, the SC workers being historically landless have been exposed to greater risk than usual as they lack most basic of the resources to have a dignified life. With hardly any resources to fall back upon and devoid of basic economic and cultural capital they are poised to face more and more crises in the pandemic phase. The author identified ownership of land as one of the fundamental principles of Punjabi social structure and draws attention to the need for structural transformation in order to obviate deepening of existing inequalities and usher in an era of larger equality.

In Chapter 13 entitled 'Livelihood of Agricultural Labourers in Punjab: Emerging Policy Issues', Sukhpal Singh has provided empirical evidence regarding the livelihood issues faced by agricultural labour working in the countryside of Punjab. The author has argued that capitalist development model of Punjab agriculture has squeezed the employment opportunities which displaced human labour in farm sector. As a result, agricultural labourers are pushed towards unemployment, under-employment and low earnings. A field survey of 180 agricultural labour households of the state during 2017–2018 reveals that 80 per cent of these households were indebted. Their annual income from all sources was Rs 108,404 against the debt amount of Rs 81,470. It is suggested by the author that the compensation should be provided to all deceased labour families wherein suicide happened due to indebtedness or economic distress. The land related legal entitlements of these families should be ensured and the wage rates and actual working days should be enhanced. Moreover, the housing conditions, healthcare and education of the labour families must be improved. As agricultural labour households are undergoing a process of transformation wherein they are leaving the agricultural wage market due to crisis-led push factors, there is a need to develop rural industrialization with special emphasis on agro-based industries. For an enduring solution to their problems, the right to work and old age pension should be ensured for this working class.

5 Covid-19 Pandemic and Services Sector of Punjab

Service sector, which includes both economic and social services (the components are Transport, Storage and Communication; Trade, Hotels and Tourism; Banking and Insurance Services; Education; Health and Administration), of Punjab contributes 47.18 per cent of the GSVA in 2019–2020 (GoP, 2021). This sector of the economy has been growing at 7.02 per cent per annum in 2019–2020. The lockdown due to Covid-19 has severely affected the services sector of the economy but the empirical evidence shows somewhat differential impact. The trade, hotel and tourism have suffered the most. Public health services were heavily burdened with the patient load but the private sector almost shut down during the lockdown period. The education sector is struggling to come to the terms. Therefore, it is pertinent to include three chapters in this section examining health, education and services sector as a whole.

In Chapter 14 entitled 'Covid-19 and Health Care Services in Punjab: Consequences and Challenges', Varinder Sharma has traced the history of pandemic and compared it with the current one. He has also provided, in a comparative framework, the situation of health care services in Punjab. The author has argued that the epidemic has always remained a part of our history. In nineteenth and twentieth centuries, the frequent epidemics like malaria, small pox and plague occurred in Punjab. Presently, the pandemic covid-19 has not only hit the economy but also put at test the capabilities of health care services. The health infrastructure in the rural areas is not fully functional. The availability of health institutions (PHC, SHC, CHC) is in short supply. Along with this the availability of health manpower especially the specialist doctors are in acute shortage. The females are significantly contributing in nursing care. The critical care services in government hospitals are in shambles. The current expenditure on health as percentage share of GDP is just 1.58 per cent in India and in Punjab it is less than one per cent. For policy suggestions, the author emphasized that there arises a need to raise the share of GDP in health sector up to 2.5 per cent. The continuous casualization of services of health professionals must come to an end. The treatment of the patients especially of poor and middle class should be free at the time of epidemics and pandemics.

Kamlesh Narwana and Angrej Singh Gill, in Chapter 15 entitled 'Making Quality Education Accessible to All: Policy Perspective on School Education in Punjab', has examined the education which has suffered the most from the Covid-19 pandemic. The authors have argued that the school education system of Punjab is at the crossroads amid four important policy and context changes, viz. neo-liberal economic reforms, National Education Policy 2020, a decade of implementation of RTE Act and 'covid-19' shocks. The study highlights that the dismal learning outcomes, crumbling teacher education and questionable working conditions of teachers emerge as major challenges in the context of improving the quality. Also, the private schools, which have proliferated significantly during the neo-liberal reforms era with parental inclination, have led to reproduce social inequalities. Moreover, given that burden of the private school education in terms of household expenditure is very high which makes these schools increasingly unaffordable, it becomes imperative to regulate these schools with comprehensive policy and perspective by specifying stringent guidelines and regulations, particularly in terms of fee structure. It is suggested by the authors that there is an urgent need for adopting multi-pronged strategy for efficaciously improving the quality of education at government schools. The closing down of physical classrooms and its replacement with 'online education in distance mode' has further widened the prevailing social inequalities as students from underprivileged sections are suffering the most. To revive education in the current situation, it is suggested that the Covid-19 predicament can be visualized as an opportunity to construct an inclusive education system, inter-alia, by beholding the public trust in government schools.

Covid-19 pandemic hit the services sector of Punjab very hard. It is well known that trade, hotel and tourism suffered more heavily and their return to normal level is difficult to predict. In a similar vein, Manjit Sharma and Pushpak Sharma, in Chapter 16 entitled 'Covid-19 Pandemic and the Service Sector of Punjab: An Assessment of Impact and Policies for Revival', have examined the impact of lockdown due to Covid-19 on the services sector of Punjab economy. While pointing out the importance of the services sector of the Punjab economy, the authors have argued that Punjab's service sector contributes nearly one half of the state's gross value added and two-fifth of total employment. The empirical evidence suggests that there was an overall decline in the state's revenue and employment level in trade, hotel and tourism, transport and real estate services during the pandemic period. Informal labourers lost their livelihood opportunities and absence of social security pushed them to the brink. The authors recommended that the state must abdicate neo-liberal policies and increase public investment with demand driven objectives for the rejuvenation of the service sector of the Punjab economy.

6 Covid-19 Pandemic, Philanthropy, Migration and Diaspora

Punjab has a long and a rich tradition of philanthropy. Punjab attracts lot of migrants from various states of India especially from Uttar Pradesh and Bihar. The migrant labour comes to seek both rural and urban employment opportunities. However, the Punjabi population is very dynamic and working and living both in various parts of India and abroad. It is important to understand the community participation to look into basic needs of the poor amidst Covid-19 pandemic. In this vein, Baldev Singh Shergill, in Chapter 17 entitled 'Basic Human Needs and Non-State Actors in Punjab: Understanding the Lives of Poor Amidst the Covid-19 Pandemic', has examined the community participation to fulfill the basic needs of the poor and the vulnerable. The author asked two questions, that is, what are human needs of the poor and vulnerable and who are they. These two questions have emerged very prominently in the discussions and debates during Covid-19 pandemic in the context of Punjab. The author has focused on investigating the role of state and the role played by the non-state actors: socio-religious institutions, social organizations, individuals and society at large. It is emphasized by the author that what is the possibility to fulfill the basic human needs of the marginalized and vulnerable sections of society in the prevailing economic development processes. During the Covid-19 pandemic lockdown, the poor section of the society had faced huge suffering from food, shelter and clothing and public social services comprising safe drinking water, health and education. The author concluded from the empirical evidence that the efforts done by the social organizations and volunteer organization were appreciable but was inadequate. The author has suggested structural reforms both in the functioning of the state and the rural society to fulfill with dignity the basic human needs of the poor and the vulnerable.

Lakhwinder Singh, in Chapter 18 entitled 'Punjab's Migration Crisis under Lockdown and Beyond: Some Suggestions for Public Policy', highlighted the plight of the migrant workers based on empirical evidence. He argued that the migration and economic development are intimately linked. The process of economic transformation and dynamics of capitalist economic development triggers rural–urban migration. As economic theory underlines the factors that generate expectations of better life and higher level of welfare are the main factors that allow human beings to take decision to shift from rural to urban areas. However, there are other factors such as rural distress that force the workforce to shift to the urban location for survival. But the fact remains that there is a huge workforce that keeps on changing their location for earning the livelihood. When the workers migrate from one location to other location, they face several difficulties as well. Recently, the spread of COVID-19 pandemic has generated high degree of uncertainty of both survival and employment. The stringent lockdown and continuous spread of COVID-19 infection halted economic activities and resulted in unemployment. Due to non-payment of wages, the migrant workers came under immediate stress and in the absence of transport facilities walking back home. As government realized the situation and arranged the special trains, there were 10 lakh workers from Punjab registered to travel back to the native place. The author has examined on the basis of extensive field survey, the working and living conditions of the migrant workers who comes from rural to urban areas from within Punjab and other states. In addition to that the author has also examined the factors that determine the upward mobility. The author suggested that the state government has to follow new policy perspective to improve upon the working and living conditions that covers both normal and shock times.

The diaspora originating from Indian Punjab has spread globally. But its presence in United Kingdom and also in North America (USA and Canada) is distinctly marked. Shinder Thandi, in Chapter 19 entitled 'Diaspora Well-Being and the Covid-19 Pandemic: Some Reflections on Public Discourses on Impacts in the USA and UK', has examined the impact of Covid-19 lockdown and other measures on the diaspora. The author argued that despite living in 'rich countries' and carrying the label of a relatively wealthy diaspora, the Covid-19 pandemic, nevertheless, disproportionally impacted these communities and exposed some of the hyper myths surrounding relative prosperity of the Indian diaspora in different ways. However, the impacts on Indian communities in USA and UK are varied, with the latter being more exposed due to both socio-economic, demographic, locational factors and occupational structure. Further, the higher socio-economic status of the US Indian community, especially in the health and medical profession, has given the community greater public exposure in a positive way. Furthermore, a noteworthy observation regarding the Sikh community requires a mention. In every location in the diaspora but especially in the USA, UK and Canada, the community has used the opportunity offered by the lockdowns and the pandemic to publicly display their core value of selfless service (*seva*). As the pandemic led to lay-offs and high unemployment and with more people falling into income poverty and becoming reliant on food banks, many Gurdwaras (Sikh temples) stepped up to provide *langar* (food) to tens of thousands of people on a daily basis. This public relations activity undoubtedly had a positive impact on public perceptions about the Sikhs, especially in the USA where the community has struggled to escape the curse of mistaken identity. With the availability of vaccines, the focus of governments will now undoubtedly shift towards rebuilding economies and pursuing policies to help people in adapting and adjusting lifestyles to the new post-Covid-19 normal. The author hoped that in this post-Covid-19 period there will still be a political desire on the part of present administrations to help rebuild minority ethnic communities.

One of the more likely outcome of this pandemic may be that it leads to increase in positive discourses within the Indian diaspora communities around health education, diet and lifestyles which may leave the community better prepared and less exposed in case of recurrence. More optimistically, author expected that it may even generate greater collective action to mobilize and lobby for more health care facilities and health education in their neighbourhoods.

7 Covid-19 Pandemic and Governance of Punjab Economy

Punjab economy, for a considerable period, has been lagging behind compared to other dynamic states of India and its per capita income ranking has been sliding. In the recent years, the rate of growth has been decelerating even prior to the pandemic (GoP, 2021; Singh and Singh, 2016). The Covid-19 pandemic shock has devastated the Punjab economy. All the sectors of the economy have suffered loss of production, revenue and employment. However, the impact of the lockdown varied from severe to moderate across all the sectors of the economy. Therefore, the timely public policy actions are important for the revival and rejuvenation of the economy. Four chapters included into this section are promising in terms of providing public policy solutions for the rejuvenation of Punjab economy in the short, medium and long run.

Sucha Singh Gill, in Chapter 20 entitled 'Governance Structure and Punjab Economy Under and Post-Covid-19 Lockdown', has examined the state of Punjab economy, its governance structure, impact of lockdown on various sectors and offers public policy suggestions for revival of the economy. The author has argued that the governance structure of Punjab economy has largely moved from a state supported system during pre-1991 towards a neo-liberal policy regime giving greater role to market forces in the recent period. The government has significantly withdrawn from health and education providing more space to the private players. Even in agricultural marketing, the opening has been allowed to the private players. The policy issues are handled largely by politicians and bureaucrats more in consultation with corporate players. Except for few subsidies, all other affairs are governed by private players. The governance structure in the state is now dominated by three parties viz; Indian National Congress, Shrimoni Akali Dal and Aam Adami Party. At present all the three parties have formally similar agenda for governance and promises for the people. The author has identified gaps in the governance structure, revenue losses due to lockdown and other illegal economic activities that undermine the capacity and capability of the State. He has also enlisted the measures taken and efforts made by the state government to contain the virus, provide facilities such as arrangements of train and bus services to the migrants. The author, after making sector-specific estimated losses, has provided public policy relevant to that sector for its revival and rejuvenation.

In Chapter 21 entitled 'Punjab's Post-Covide-19 Economic Policy under Indian Federalism', Pritam Singh has examined the devastating impact of Covid-19 pandemic and public policy solutions in the context of Indian federal framework. The author has argued that any policy response that can be visualized in Punjab has to keep the global scenario of climate crisis and economic crisis in mind and the limitations that a state government has within India's federal capitalist economy. These limitations can be partially overcome by stretching the policy discourse that is usually associated with what a state government can do to include what other civil society institutions can do, and partially by utilizing the full potential of what a state government can do within federal limits. A political environment within India as a whole has to be created in which Punjab has a crucial role to play despite its small size and relatively low bargaining power in India's parliamentary politics to encourage state governments to be bold in their efforts to break the stranglehold of central/federal power. An institutionalized centralization has been increasing right from the framing of India's constitution but becoming so overwhelming more recently that not to confront the central powers has become normal. Due to this stifling normalization, it happens too often that the state governments stop too soon before stretching to the limit their capacity to take initiative and action in policy formulation and implementation. The author has suggested that a normalization of economic relations with Pakistan, where Punjab state should be allowed to play an important role even at the cost of amending the Indian constitution. The local efforts should be stepped up in terms of use of resources in a manner to reduce waste to further reduce the greenhouse gas emissions. The author emphasized that the revival of Punjab economy requires recasting Centre-State relations.

Revenue raising capacity determines the government capacity to take appropriate public policy measures. Jatinder S. Bedi and Gayatri Prabhakar, in Chapter 22 entitled 'Implications of Covid-19 on the Revenue of Punjab under GST Regime', examined the revenue losses and also suggested the public policy solution to handle such a reduction in revenue. The authors argued that Punjab has a wide gap between its expenditure and revenue receipts. COVID-19 has further worsened the situation with increasing need for public spending, while the revenue is contracting substantially. The introduction of GST though has resulted in loss of fiscal autonomy for the state of Punjab by 18.1 percentage points of its revenue resources. The co-operative federalism trust with which the GST concept was introduced has taken a major hit after the Centre has gone back on several of its commitments as the shortfall in SGST revenue collection is likely to cross Rs 3 lakh crore during financial year 2021. Some amicable solution, however, may now be found out with latest proposal of the Centre to borrow Rs 1.10 lakh crore, which it will pass on to the states as a back-to-back loan. With several such unexpected problems surfacing on the SGST front and depleting trust between the centre and states, the problem for Punjab has compounded as the revenue of the state from its own resources is also not growing. The authors have suggested that there is an urgent need for the state to look for viable alternative revenue options to remain prepared for medium to long-term scenario. The various state Governments' give several unnecessary doles in the form of SGST refund with the objective to attract the investment in the state, but this defeats the very purpose of one nation—one market. Not sure why the Centre is looking the other way in such cases and instead passing laws related to matter primarily classified as the state subject, for example, by passing agricultural 'mandi' tax.

Sukhpal Singh, Lakhwinder Singh and Kamal Vatta, in Chapter 23 entitled 'Public Policy and Governance Reforms for Post-Covi-19 Recovery and Sustainable Growth and Development in Punjab', have brought together various policy perspectives and suggestions on major sectors of the state economy i.e. agriculture, industry, services, health, education and governance of the state economy. It has weaved into the discussion the existing policy documents of the state such as draft agricultural policy, 2018, industrial and business policy, 2017 and the Ahluwalia Committee (2020) report recommendations as available and critically examine their goodness and weaknesses from the perspective of people centric livelihood based on growth and development policy framework. It has made sector specific as well as general growth and development inducing and promoting policy suggestions based on the findings of the chapters in the book as well as other sources of such insights. It has specifically dwell upon and recommend policy and stakeholder action on major burning policy issues like groundwater depletion, free power for irrigation, stubble burning, cropping pattern, land leasing issues, agricultural market reforms, agro-industrialisation strategy, innovations in various sectors and the pro-poor programmes like MGNREGS and small producer livelihood focused policy mechanisms.

8 Concluding Remarks

Punjab economy has been undergoing a multidimensional crisis. The Covid-19 pandemic shock has devastated the economy of Punjab further. The essays collected in this volume written by scholars engaged in development policy and more so in conducting research studies on Punjab economy have examined the various facets of the economy and come out with enduring policy suggestions. The essays organized in six themes vary from agricultural development to public policy issues relating to state, national and international domains. The multidimensionality of economic crisis needs multidimensional analysis and public policy suggestions, which is hoped that this volume provides. The Covid-19 pandemic has spread across the globe and continues to create formidable challenges for human survival and wellbeing despite the several measures of wearing face masks, sanitization, social distance, tracing, testing and lately vaccination. Therefore, the studies contained in this volume will remain relevant for conducting analysis and suggesting public policy solutions for other regions and countries alike. It is hoped that this volume will initiate debate on development policy and will attract the attention of academia, NGOs, public policy makers, political leadership and public policy implementing agencies. The book uses simple language, free from mathematical notations and complex econometrics estimates will be handy for the lay public. The public policy lessons that emerge from this volume will not only help to rejuvenate the Punjab economy but also will be helpful to similarly situated developing economies to recover from the Covid-19 pandemic shock and move on the path of self-sustained economic development.

References

Banerjee, A. V. (2005) Notes Towards a Theory of Industrialization in the Developing World. In N. Banerjee and S. Marjit (Eds.), *Development, Displacement and Disparity: Indian in the Last Quarter of the Twentieth Century*, New Delhi: Orient BlackSwan, pp. 139–159.

GoP. (2021) Economic Survey 2020–21, Chandigarh: Economic and Statistical Organisation, Government of Punjab.

Iqbal, N., and Misra, U. (2020) Ease of Doing Business-How States are Ranked and What's the Difference Now, *Indian Express*, September 17. New Delhi.

Jain, V., and Singh, L. (2020) Global Spread and Socio-Economic Determinants of Covid-19 Pandemic, *Seoul Journal of Economics*, 33(4): 561–600.

Lee, K. (2020) Varieties of Capitalism and Re-thinking the East Asian Model of Economic Growth after the Covid-19: Rebalancing Shareholder and Stakeholder Capitalism, *Seoul Journal of Economics*, 33(4): 487–504.

Singh, L., Bhangoo, K. S., and Sharma, R. (2020) *Agrarian Distress and Farmer Suicides in North India*, New Delhi: Routledge-Taylor and Francis Group.

Singh, L., and Singh, N. (2016) Economic Transformation and Development Experience of Indian Punjab-An Introduction. In L. Singh and N. Singh (Eds.), *Economic Transformation of a Developing Economy: The Experience of Punjab, India*, Singapore: Springer, pp. 1–25.

Singh, L., and Singh, S. (2002) Deceleration of Economic Growth in Punjab-Evidence, Explanation and a Way Out, *Economic and Political Weekly*, 37(6): 579–586.

Singh, S. (2021) Punjab Agriculture: Pinning Hopes on Private Sector for Revival, *Economic and Political Weekly*, 56(2): 10–12.

Agricultural Sustainability in Punjab: A Way Forward

Sukhwinder Singh

1 Introduction

Punjab's economy is predominantly agrarian (Singh and Singh, 2002). However, the share of agriculture to the Gross State Domestic Product (GSDP) has declined from 49% in 1980–1981 to 28% in 2019–2020 with about 26% workforce engaged into farming and its allied activities. The state GSDP grew at about 6% between 2015–2016 and 2019–2020 whereas the average growth rate for agriculture and allied sectors remained only 1.7% between 2012–2013 and 2016–2017 (GoP, 2020). Due to conducive agro-climatic conditions and a widespread application of green revolution technologies, Punjab could increase its cropping intensity up to 189% and produce 18 and 12% of India's wheat and rice, respectively. However, Punjab's current cropping patterns, which largely concentrate on wheat and rice production, are not sustainable, especially economically and environmentally. In the following sections, the current cropping patterns in Punjab are analyzed in the light of three pillars of agricultural sustainability, i.e. economic, environmental, and social.

S. Singh (✉)
Public Health Foundation of India, Gurgaon, India
e-mail: sukhrec@yahoo.com

S. Singh et al. (eds.), *Covid-19 Pandemic and Economic Development*,
https://doi.org/10.1007/978-981-16-4442-9_2

2 Economic Sustainability

Economic sustainability of a farm enterprise depends mainly on crop yield, cost of cultivation, and produce prices. The average per hectare yield of wheat, rice, basmati, and cotton was 4.0, 6.8, 4.8, and 2.4 t/ha, respectively. However, the cost of cultivation (A1) for cotton was the highest (Rs 68,604/ha) followed by basmati (Rs 62,071/ha), rice (Rs 53,362/ha), and wheat (Rs 39,060/ha). Basmati was the highest profit generating *kharif* crop followed by rice, wheat, and cotton (Singh, 2020c). A couple of other studies (Singh et al., 2017; Raju et al., 2015) also reported that basmati fetched the highest gross returns and net returns using market prices, economic prices, and natural resource valuation. However, basmati does not come under the Government of India's Minimum Support Price (MSP) umbrella. On the other hand, cotton generated the lowest per hectare net profit that could be attributed to its higher cost of cultivation. Additionally, cotton cultivation is known to be prone to the highest level of yield and marketing-related risks when compared to other *kharif* crops (Chand, 1999) which could dent its net profitability.

From an economic sustainability angle, a typical farmer spent Rs 84,374 and earned Rs 12,055 from each hectare annually. A typical farm enterprise of 4.8 hectares could generate an annual income of Rs 50,201 which does not include income from allied activities e.g. dairy, fishery (Singh, 2020c). As per a national sample survey (NSSO, 2014), income from other activities than crop production such as allied farming activities e.g., dairy, poultry etc., including wages in Punjab during 2012–2013 contributed up to 40% to total income of a farm household. Thus, adding this assumptive figure of estimated income from other allied farming activities to Rs 50,201, an average farmer household could have earned Rs 83,668 from all sources. Analyzing this figure in the context of farmer livelihoods in Punjab, an average monthly income of a farmer household comes to be Rs 6,972. That means an average farmer household of five members in Punjab is living on Rs 1,395 in a month. Considering the per-capita income, a member of a farming family of Punjab has Rs 46 ($0.93) to spend in a day. If those who live on $1.25 a day are poor as per IFAD (2011) estimation, an average farm household of "so-called" agriculturally advanced state like Punjab is in deep poverty. Even the Indian government's estimates on poverty line for 2011–2012 (Planning Commission, 2013) revealed that a person living in rural Punjab is to be considered below poverty line (BPL) if he or she earns less than Rs 1,054 ($21) per month. Therefore, Punjab's current cropping patterns are economically unsustainable and need a multidimensional investigation.

3 Environmental Sustainability

The environmental sustainability of Punjab's cropping systems can be investigated by examining the current status of its national resources, mainly soil and groundwater. Due to indiscriminate application of chemical fertilizers and pesticides in the recent past, soil health in Punjab has been a debatable issue mainly because of lack of pragmatic scientific inquiry. Singh and Benbi (2016) through a systematic and multifaceted study provided a deep understanding of the soil health issues in Punjab. Contrasting the main body of literature, they argued that Punjab soils had become healthier between 1980–1981 and 2010–2011, particularly with respect to Soil Organic Matter (SOM), Phosphorus (P), and Potassium (K). The pH exhibited a declining trend, whereas Electrical Conductivity (EC) stayed almost constant. While endorsing these results, Benbi and Brar (2009) reported that intensive agricultural practices by allowing a greater root biomass addition and decomposition in the surface soil because of increased crop productivity have improved the SOM by 38% and reduced the soil pH by 0.8 units between 1980–1981 and 2005–2006. While associating this with crop productivity, Shergill (2013) argued that the rice and wheat yields had increased from 2.7 t/ha in 1980 to 4 (rice) and 4.5 t/ha (wheat) in 2005. However, these crop yield increases could be associated with improved seeds varieties which resulted in greater nutrient removal, i.e. nutrient mining, from soils (Benbi et al., 2006).

Groundwater depletion in Punjab, in general, and in the central zone (rice belt covering 50% land area of Punjab), in particular, is a serious concern in relation to the environmental sustainability of farm enterprises in Punjab (Singh and Park, 2018). Between 2000 and 2010, the groundwater level on 92% of the farms in the central zone, had depleted by more than 0.60 m annually. Despite Punjab government's consistent but largely failed crop diversification policy and programs, the area under rice cultivation in Punjab has constantly been increasing since 1990 (GoP, 2019). Punjab government's latest crop diversification plan suggested that the area under rice should be reduced from 3 to 1.6 million hectares (PSFC,

2013). Additionally, Benbi (2018) argued that the environmental sustainability of rice has declined overtime as the greatest decline in energy use efficiency was observed in the cultivation of rice followed by wheat and maize. It is likely that if the existing policy framework for groundwater resources in the state, i.e. free electricity to farm sector particularly for rice cultivation, and MSP regime continues, Punjab might end up losing much of its groundwater resources. Since it is a complex problem with a range of policy, economic, attitudinal, social and political dimensions, a multidimensional approach might help overcome further over-extraction of groundwater resources in Punjab.

4 Social Sustainability

Although the expansion and intensification of farm machinery in Punjab played a crucial role in boosting the production as well as productivity of main crops thus achieving the national food security, it displaced much of rural farm labor, side-lined many rural artisans, and pushed smallholders out of business by making small farms economically unviable (Sidhu et al., 2011; Singh, 2012). Smallholders, despite constituting 30% of the total landholdings and operating 8% of Punjab's total land area, had inequitable access to various farm resources, e.g. landholding, irrigation sources, farm machinery and extension services, which are the key determinants of farm profitability (Singh, 2014). Although owning a tractor is uneconomical for a smallholder, only 50% of smallholders owned tractors compared to 72 and 83% of medium and large holders, respectively. Further, about 14% of the smallholders had no access to any source of irrigation and were dependent on rented irrigation from medium and large holders (Singh, 2014). Further, only 11 and 47% of the smallholders had Kisan Credit Cards and had access to credit facilities available with the Primary Agriculture Credit Society (PACS), respectively whereas 75% of the medium and large holders each had Kisan Credit Cards and were PACS account holders. Being not accommodated properly by the PACS, smallholders go to non-institutional sources, i.e. local commission agents, who charge exorbitantly higher interest rates and generally exploit them to the extent that they have to either sell off their land to them to pay off their debts or commit suicide (Singh, 2014).

With respect to agricultural extension provided by the Department of Agriculture (Punjab) and PAU Ludhiana, only 28 and 64% of the smallholders were connected to these networks, respectively, whereas the corresponding figures were 22 and 75% for medium holders and 42 and 92% for large holders (Singh, 2014). Smallholders, who are otherwise efficient in terms of per unit productivity and have been contributing significantly to food security (Chand et al., 2011; Dev, 2012) were largely marginalized in terms of limited access to farm machinery, irrigation sources, agricultural subsidies, institutional credit, and extension services. The culture of mono-cropping and subsequent mechanization of farm operations pushed farm labor, local artisans, and women out of farming in Punjab whereas in other Indian states, they are contributing to farm sector considerably (Singh, 2014).

5 Conclusions and Policy Recommendations

Punjab agriculture is currently passing through a very critical phase as a continued reliance on wheat and rice production and an overdependence on underground water resources have raised questions on the overall sustainability of agriculture in Punjab. However, the soils of Punjab are still healthy and can keep producing a variety of crops if the cycle of mono-cropping (wheat-rice–wheat) can be broken. Punjab's current cropping patterns are highly intensive with low diversity. A reduced crop diversity mainly in the *kharif* season with a focus on rice intensification and a regime of free-of-cost electricity supply to farm sector have had an adverse effect on groundwater resources while an overdose of fertilizers and pesticides and over-capitalized farm machinery have undermined the economic sustainability of farm enterprises. Since agricultural sustainability of Punjab's farming enterprises is a complex problem with a range of policy, economic, attitudinal, social and political dimensions, a multidimensional approach is required. The following policy measures could form the basis of such an approach:

1. Crop diversity and groundwater resources are significantly associated with each other (Singh and Park, 2018). As the past crop diversification endeavors by the Punjab government have largely failed (PSFC 2013); therefore, future policies and programs related to crop diversification need to be more practical and pragmatic bearing in mind the agro-climatic conditions and market potential of different crop combinations in all three agro-climatic regions of Punjab. Probably, Punjab government may learn from Haryana who has recently planned to make farmers diversify from paddy to

less water consuming crops like maize, cotton, bajra, pulses and fruits and vegetables on a land area of about one lakh hectares. Under "Mera Pani, Meri Virasat" program, Haryana government has come up with a crop diversification plan to discourage farmers from paddy cultivation in eight blocks where the groundwater levels have already gone beyond 35–40 m. Farmers are advised to sow paddy on 50% of total land area of their farm in these eight blocks and those not implementing the government orders would lose certain government incentives and privileges. Farmers, those who will replace paddy with suggested crops, will get an incentive of Rs 7,000–8000 per acre. Moreover, farmers will get 85% subsidy on installation of micro-irrigation system in the diversified crops area (Singh, 2020a). This endeavor will not only help save the groundwater resource but also reduce the number of incidents of rice crop stubble burning. Considering the current state of groundwater resources in the central zone of Punjab, which covers more than half the land area and contains 70% of total tube wells, has a majority of blocks under over-exploited (water withdrawal exceeds recharge) category with the highest rates of groundwater depletion across Punjab (Singh and Park, 2018). Punjab government can restrict paddy cultivation in these nine-districts of the central zone to save groundwater resources and reduce rice stubble burning. However, Punjab governments have to provide some financial incentives to diversifying farmers to sustain their economic losses. Additionally, the proposed crop diversification plan should address the productivity and marketing-related risks so that farmers feel convinced and can have enough confidence to experiment with alternative crops. This will need a close synchronization of policy, research and extension agencies so that whatever is planned by the policy makers and endorsed by the researchers, the same should be disseminated to farmers with no communication gap.

2. Punjab policy makers should be aware that wheat-rice makes the best crop combination in terms of lower productivity risks and higher economic returns compared with other suggested crop combinations; therefore, the future policies can also target technical diversification in terms of reducing water use in wheat-rice cultivation. As the adoption of water conservation technologies is low in Punjab, government could initiate more pragmatic programs to disseminate water-saving technologies, such as micro-irrigation, direct seeding of

rice providing additional incentives to farmers. However, researchers should evaluate the success rate and economic rate of return of all the technologies before prescribing them. Further, although PAU has made considerable efforts to provide the latest varieties of seeds to maintain yield rates of crops, these efforts so far have been restricted to wheat and rice. To reduce capital investment on farm machinery, more custom hiring centers should be opened at village level providing entire range of farm equipment to widen up the access of farm machinery to small and marginal farmers.

3. The current regime of free electricity to farm sector is not really benefitting a large portion of farmers who are either not using groundwater or not able to install big tube wells to pull water from deeper levels. Therefore, this regime should be rationalized by ending power subsidy to medium and large farmers cultivating more than 10 acres so that small and marginal farmers could be sustained.
4. Interestingly, cropping intensity had no negative impact on soil health (Singh and Benbi, 2016) and groundwater resources (Singh and Park, 2018); Punjab government can encourage farmers to sow a third (preferably non-irrigated) crop, i.e. a legume, during May–June. It will not only bring higher returns to farmers but also improve soil health by supplying additional nitrogen. However, it does not mean that farmers can sow a third crop along with cultivation of rice in the *kharif* season. They have to either stop rice cultivation or reduce the area under rice to spare water for the third crop. Additionally, scientists have to provide short-duration crop varieties to facilitate cultivation of three crops in a year and extensionists might need to update their knowledge on new crops and their cultivation methods as they have specialized around wheat-rice production systems for decades.
5. "The Punjab Preservation of Sub Soil Water Act, 2009" which currently forbids farmers to transplant rice before 15th June, needs reviewing as one-fifth of the farmers surveyed agreed to delay sowing of rice by another two weeks. Additionally, as monsoons reach Punjab by the first or second week of July, June 15th could be extended to June 30th as that would help save water used for rice cultivation without compromising the productivity levels. Actually, Punjab government should discourage paddy cultivation and find out alternative *kharif* crops which can be sown any time between May and July. As higher cropping intensity have no negative impact

on soil health and groundwater resources, farmers should be encouraged to sow three crops in a year because the agro-climatic and marketing conditions allow farmers to increase cropping intensity up to 300%. This will not only bring higher economic returns but also improve environmental and social sustainability of farm enterprises in Punjab.

6. Surpassing the state governments' domains, the Indian government passed an ordinance to amend three laws related to production, storage and marketing of farm produce. Two of them are relatively more relevant in the context of economic sustainability of farm enterprises in Punjab. First, Farmers' Produce Trade and Commerce (Promotion and Facilitation) Ordinance, 2020 (FPTC) which allows trading of farmer produce out of designated APMC markets and provides a facilitative framework for electronic trading within and across states. It allows farmer producer organizations (FPOs), which are generally into pre- and post-production aggregation, trading and value addition, to establish e-markets. However, the real concern here is how many FPOs can make use of this opportunity as they are not defined as "buyers" unlike cooperatives and co-operative societies (Singh, 2020b). Second, Farmers (Empowerment and Protection) Agreement on Price Assurance and Farm Services Ordinance, 2020 (FAPAFS) is nothing but "a badly designed contract farming law" which leaves out many aspects of modern contract farming practices, like contract cancellation clauses; delayed deliveries or purchases, and damage therein; and "tournaments" in contract farming (Singh, 2020b). Essentially, neither of them is in the interest of either farmers or consumers. Probably they aim to provide conducive environment to big companies and farm produce traders to restrict government procurement agencies from buying directly from farmers, and disallowing state governments to charge marketing fee which they use to develop and maintain rural infrastructure.
7. In the post-COVID-19 phase, Punjab government might consider promoting rural agribusiness, i.e. food processing (which is currently non-existent in Punjab), and fine-tuning the current agricultural marketing systems to improve the overall agricultural sustainability in Punjab.

References

Benbi, D. K. (2018) Carbon Footprint and Agricultural Sustainability Nexus in an Intensively Cultivated Region of Indo-Gangetic Plains, *Science of the Total Environment*, 644: 611–623.

Benbi, D. K., and Brar, J. S. (2009) A 25-year Record of Carbon Sequestration and Soil Properties in Intensive Agriculture, *Agronomic Sustain Developments*, 29: 257–265.

Benbi, D. K., Nayyar, V. K., and Brar, J. S. (2006) Green Revolution in Punjab: The Impact on Soil Health, *Indian Journal Fertility*, 2: 57–66.

Chand, R. (1999) Emerging Crisis in Punjab Agriculture, Severity and Options for Future, *Economic and Political Weekly*, 34(13): A2–A10.

Chand, R., Prasanna, P. A. L., and Singh, A. (2011) Farm Size and Productivity: Understanding the Strengths of Smallholders and Improving Their Livelihoods, *Economic and Political Weekly*, 46 (26–27): 5–11.

Dev, M. S. (2012) Small Farmers in India: Challenges and Opportunities [online]. Mumbai, India: Indira Gandhi Institute of Development Research. June. Available at: http://www.igidr.ac.in/pdf/publication/WP-2012-014.pdf [Accessed 15 October 2013].

GoP. (2019) Statistical Abstract of Punjab, Chandigarh: Economic Advisor to Government of Punjab, Government of Punjab.

GoP. (2020) Punjab Economic Survey 2019–20. Economic and Statistical Organisation, Department of Planning, Government of Punjab. Available at: https://www.esopb.gov.in/Static/PDF/EconomicSurvey-2019-20.pdf.

IFAD. (2011) Annual Report 2011, Rome, Italy: The International Fund for Agricultural Development. Available at: http://www.ifad.org/pub/ar/2011/e/full_report.pdf.

NSSO. (2014) Key Indicators of Situation of Agricultural Households in India: NSS 70th Round, National Sample Survey Office, Ministry of Statistics and Programme Implementation. Available at: http://mospi.nic.in/Mospi_New/upload/KI_70_33_19dec14.pdf.

Planning Commission. (2013) Press Note on Poverty Estimates 2011–12, New Delhi, India: Planning Commission, Government of India. Available at: http://planningcommission.nic.in/news/pre_pov2307.pdf.

PSFC. (2013) *Agriculture Policy for Punjab*, Chandigarh: Punjab State Farmers Commission.

Raju, S. S., Chand, R., Srivastava, S. K., Kaur, A. P., Singh, J., Jain, R., … Kaur, P. (2015) Comparing Performance of Various Crops in Punjab Based on Market and Economic Prices and Natural Resource Accounting, *Agricultural Economics Research Review*, 28(347–2016–17211): 189–198.

Shergill, H. S. (2013) Improvements in Soil Fertility in Punjab under Green Revolution: The Evidence and the Mechanisms, *Journal Agricultural Develop Policy*, 23(1): 18–30.

Sidhu, R. S., Singh, S., and Bhullar, A. S. (2011) Farmers' Suicides in Punjab: A Census Survey of the Two Most Affected Districts, *Economic and Political Weekly*: 131–137.

Singh, L., and Singh, S. (2002) Deceleration of Economic Growth in Punjab: Evidence, Explanation and a Ways-out, *Economic and Political Weekly*, 37(6): 579–586.

Singh, S. (2012) Institutional and Policy Aspects of Punjab Agriculture: A Smallholder Perspective, *Economic and Political Weekly*, XLVII(4): 51–57.

Singh, S. (2014) Determinants of Agricultural Sustainability in the Indian Punjab with a Special Reference to Extension Systems, PhD Thesis, University of Reading, UK.

Singh, S. (2020a) Haryana Pushes for Sustainable Farming. The Business Line, *The Hindu* (online) June 09. Available at: https://www.thehindubusinessline.com/opinion/haryana-pushes-for-sustainable-farming/article31780634.ece.

Singh, S. (2020b) Tale of Two Flawed Agri Ordinances. The Business Line, *The Hindu* (online) June 22. Available at: https://www.thehindubusinessline.com/opinion/tale-of-two-flawed-agri-ordinances/article31883449.ece.

Singh, S. (2020c) Economic Sustainability of Farm Enterprises in the Indian Punjab: A Case Study, *Journal of Agricultural and Crop Research*, 8(8): 147–158.

Singh, S., and Benbi, D. K. (2016) Punjab-soil Health and Green Revolution: A Quantitative Analysis of Major Soil Parameters, *Journal of Crop Improvement*, 30: 323–340. https://doi.org/10.1080/15427528.2016.1157540.

Singh, S., and Park, J. (2018) Drivers of Change in Groundwater Resources: A Case Study of the Indian Punjab, *Food Security*, 10(4): 965–979.

Singh, S., Kaur, P., Sachdeva, J., and Bhardwaj, S. (2017) Profitability Analysis of Major Crops in Punjab: Some Evidence from Cost of Cultivation Survey Data, *Indian Journal of Economics and Development*, 13(1): 71–78. DOI:https://doi.org/10.5958/2322-0430.2017.00010.5.

Impact of COVID-19 Lockdown on Punjab Agriculture

Kamal Vatta, Shruti Bhogal, Cameron A. Petrie, Adam S. Greens, and Sandeep Dixit

1 Introduction

Punjab agriculture has played an unparalleled role in the growth and development of India ever since the advent of Green Revolution in the mid-1960s. The success of green revolution led to the prosperity and development of rural masses as evident from the highest levels of average monthly income of a farming household in Punjab (GoI, 2017). Contribution of state agricultural sector towards ensuring food security, poverty alleviation, uplifting rural economy and generating employment is notable

K. Vatta (✉)
Department of Economics and Sociology, Punjab Agricultural University, Ludhiana, India

S. Bhogal · S. Dixit
Centers for International Projects Trusts (CIPT), New Delhi, India

C. A. Petrie
Department of Archaeology and McDonald Institute for Archaeological Research, University of Cambridge, Cambridge, UK

A. S. Greens
McDonald Institute for Archaeological Research, University of Cambridge, Cambridge, UK

S. Singh et al. (eds.), *Covid-19 Pandemic and Economic Development*,
https://doi.org/10.1007/978-981-16-4442-9_3

(Dhillon et al., 2010). With only 1.52% of the total geographical area, Punjab is the largest producer of wheat and paddy and significant contributor to the national pool of foodgrains. This is due to the highest levels of crop yields, cropping intensity of 190% and almost entire area under assured irrigation as compared to the rest of the country (GoP, 2020). A combination of innovative technology, agricultural infrastructure and supportive government policies has enabled the state to become the 'bread basket of India'.

Contributing over 28% of the Gross Value Added of the state in 2019–2020, agriculture and allied activities employs 26% of the labour force in the state. Despite large scale farm mechanization, mainly driven by the model of Green Revolution, labour continues to play a crucial role in state agriculture. Activities like paddy sowing and transplantation, cotton picking, animal husbandry, etc. are labour intensive. In addition to local labour, the state agriculture is heavily dependent on migrant labour, which usually arrives via cyclical migration every year during the peak agricultural season—sowing and harvesting (Kaur et al., 2011). With the aforementioned vitality of the state agriculture directly and indirectly supporting various sectors and individuals dependent on it, any disruption in this sector would mean a disruption in not only the state but national welfare as well.

2 Covid-19 and Punjab Agriculture

The unexpected pandemic COVID-19 and its relentless spread brought country-wide socio-economic disruptions, sparing none of the sectors of the economy. The pandemic arrived during a time when north-west India was approaching the harvesting time for Rabi crops, especially wheat; thus, impacting the agriculture sector in Punjab.

In order to inhibit the spread of COVID-19, the Punjab government effected a state curfew on March 22, 2020, which was later converted into a state-wide lockdown thereby, virtually shutting down almost all economic activities, except essential services, in the state. In this backdrop, the state agriculture was expected to be exposed to unprecedented challenges, with likely implications on marketing and production during the approaching rabi harvesting season in the month of April; followed by kharif sowing season that begins in mid-June. Since Punjab is one of the major wheat-growing states and almost all the marketed surplus is procured by the national procurement agency (Food Corporation of

India), restrictions in movement of people and goods carriers were likely to have adverse consequences on the smooth harvesting and sale of produce. The fact that the majority of the farmers are dependent on this network of sale, engendered apprehensions about the resultant adverse impact on farmers' revenue.

The immediate outcomes due to the extended pandemic lockdown were predicted to be a shortage of labour and the resultant hike of wages of the limited labour available. Due to sealing of state borders and restricted interstate movement, the necessary migrant labour was feared to be unavailable; hence, the likely labour shortage was almost inevitable. In addition, shortage of machinery and farm inputs were also expected to be an issue since their availability was also expected to be impacted by the lockdown. Further precipitation of this into increase in farm costs like wages of labour, machinery rentals and costs of farm inputs like seeds and fertilizers, and other farm inputs and services was plausible. The ramifications of such disruption were expected to be grave for resource-poor smaller farm households that form about one-third of the total farm households in the state.

The present study attempts to identify and assess the full impact of the pandemic induced economic slow-down on agricultural production and marketing, and understand perspectives and needs of farmers for undertaking smooth agricultural operations.

3 Sampling and Methodology

In this direction, a survey was developed, pre-tested and then data was collected from 120 farmers through telephonic interviews and personal visits (wherever possible). These farmers are a part of the ongoing FP4-TIGR2ESS project. The farmers were approached, briefed about purpose of the survey, and were surveyed after receiving their consent. Each telephonic conversation took about 20–25 min and each personal interview lasted between 40 and 50 min per person. The survey was conducted in May to get a fair picture of the impact of pandemic on rabi crop as the procurement of wheat in the state is generally over by this time. The details of the study sample are provided in Table 1.

Table 1 Details of the study sample

Category of farmers	*No. of farmers*	*Average area of landholding (Acre)*
Marginal (≤2.5 acres)	15 (12.5)	1.90
Small (≤5 acres)	24 (20.0)	4.09
Semi-medium (≤15 acres)	49 (40.8)	9.59
Medium (≤25 acres)	16 (13.3)	19.84
Large (> 25 acres)	16 (13.3)	36.03
Total	120 (100.0)	12.43

Note Figures in parenthesis are percentages of the total

4 Results of the Survey

4.1 Rabi Season

Analysis of the survey data revealed that wheat was grown on 85% area followed by potato and fodder on about 7% and 6% area, respectively. COVID-19 pandemic lockdown was expected to impact various facets of agriculture that are broadly classified as production and marketing factors. A detailed study of these factors is revealed as under:

Production/Harvesting
With the onset of harvesting season, free movement of labour, agricultural machinery and agricultural produce are of paramount importance in order to ensure smooth process of harvesting; however, due to the pandemic-lockdown these were likely to be impeded. The study revealed that, farmers were facing more than one constraint with regards to smooth harvesting process. About 52% of the farmers were facing shortage of labour and about 35% paid higher wages to arrange labour (Table 2). Marginal farmers being resource-poor faced more such problem than their larger counterparts. Among all the problems faced by marginal farmers in the process of harvesting, struggle to arrange labour and the subsequent high expenditure on wages were prime concerns. In some villages wages went up by almost 50%. On the other hand, availability of machinery did not appear as a major challenge as only about 9% of farmers complained

Table 2 Problems faced during harvesting of Rabi crops (multiple response) (%)

Category of farmers	*Scarcity of labour*	*High wage rate*	*Availability of Machine*	*High hiring charges of machine*	*Any other*
Marginal	71.43	28.57	-	-	-
Small	50.00	33.33	16.67	-	-
Semi-medium	48.65	35.14	10.81	-	5.41
Medium	54.55	27.27	-	9.09	9.09
Large	50.00	42.86	7.14	0.00	-
Total	51.85	34.57	8.64	1.23	3.70

of their poor or untimely availability and less than one per cent farmers had to pay higher rentals for the machinery.

The role of state government in strategic and timely arrangement of required machinery is appreciable as it ensured the movement of harvesters in Punjab from other states for their sufficient and timely availability. All the agricultural services were excluded from the purview of curfew to facilitate smooth harvesting activities.

Marketing

A widespread adverse impact of Covid-19 was expected on wheat procurement in Punjab but the state government planned and implemented an effective procurement strategy. The study revealed that only one-third of farmers faced issues of delayed and staggered procurement. The government followed extensive measures to ensure smooth and timely procurement of wheat through a token system, and promoted a staggered procurement system that would limit gathering of farmers in the *mandis*, avoid a sudden rush for transportation, etc. Very few farmers reported selling below the MSP. About 13% of the total farmers experienced delayed payments, mostly the ones sourced through middlemen. Another 18% of the total farmers experienced problems of transportation, especially for transporting the produce to the markets (Table 3). Overall, the problems faced during the wheat procurement were not widespread unlike as expected when the lockdown was initiated.

The aforementioned constraints were likely to impact the farmers with regards to management of their produce. However, about 73% of the total farmers sold their produce in the *mandis* immediately after harvesting

Table 3 %age of farmers facing problems in marketing of rabi crops (multiple response)

Problem	*% farmers*
Delayed procurement	30.0
Staggered procurement	31.4
Sold at price lower than MSP	2.9
Delayed payment	12.9
Transportation issues	18.6
Any other	2.9

Table 4 Pattern of management of rabi produce (%)

Management strategy	*% farmers*
Sold directly in the market	73.4
Stored before sale	5.8
Others/multiple	20.8

while only about 20% had to store wheat to follow the norms of staggered procurement (Table 4). It was found that both ways, all the produce of the state was managed well, and none was dumped.

Contrary to the apprehensions of widespread decline in yield of crops and credit, only 12% of the farmers complained about problems in accessing credit, primarily due to restrictions in movement; and only about one-third of farmers experienced decline in the yields due to reasons other than the lockdown.

5 Farmers' Initiatives

Despite facilitation of procurement by the state government by tweaking policies and guidelines of lockdown, farmers also resorted to some measures independently. While almost 28% of the farmers tried to address the labour shortages by hiring local labour, about 8% of the total farmers involved family labour to mitigate such shortages. Of the total farmers, about 6% eased the burden of higher expenditure on wages by adopting mechanization, though about 17% had to incur higher wages (Table 5 a and b).

About 4% of the total farmers were observed to have experienced delayed harvesting as they were waiting for their turn to hire the

Table 5 Measures to tackle labour issues (%)

(a) Scarcity of labour

Category of farmers		Arranging local labour	Family Labour
Marginal		33.3	0.0
Small		25.0	0.0
Semi-medium		32.7	4.1
Medium		18.8	18.8
Large		18.8	18.8
Total		27.5	7.5
(b) High wages			
Category of farmers	Adopted mechanization	Incurred higher wage	Negotiated for lower wages
Marginal	6.7	6.7	0.0
Small	4.2	12.5	0.0
Semi-medium	8.2	16.3	2.0
Medium	0.0	18.8	0.0
Large	6.3	31.3	0.0
Total	5.8	16.7	0.8

machinery; on the other hand another 2% of the total farmers also faced issues in arranging machinery due to sudden rush in demand for the same, though they were able to arrange the same in time (Table 6).

Transportation was the second most prominent problem, preceded by labour issues that were faced by farmers. In an attempt to deal with the issues pertaining to transportation insufficiency, about 9% of the total farmers ended up incurring higher cost for the same (Table 7). However, about 3% of the farmers preferred to store their produce to be moved and sold later, when the lockdown constraints were to subside.

Table 6 Measures to tackle machinery shortage (%)

Category of farmers	*Arranging machinery*	*Waiting*
Marginal	0.0	0.0
Small	0.0	8.3
Semi-medium	4.1	4.1
Medium	0.0	0.0
Large	0.0	6.3
Total	1.7	4.2

Table 7 Measures to deal with transportation issues (%)

Category of farmers	*Incurring higher cost*	*Pooling resources with fellow farmers*	*Storing and selling in mandi (part)*	*Completely stored*	*Sold locally*
Marginal	0.0	0.0	0.0	0.0	0.0
Small	12.5	4.2	4.2	8.3	4.2
Semi-medium	6.1	2.0	2.0	4.1	2.0
Medium	12.5	0.0	0.0	0.0	0.0
Large	18.8	0.0	0.0	0.0	0.0
Total	9.2	1.7	1.7	3.3	1.7

The pandemic fear and lockdown caused a sudden rush in demand for transport relative to its supply, thus creating constraints during harvesting and marketing. Nonetheless, all the farmers were seen to have had adopted various means to resolve these issues, though in some cases they ended up incurring a higher cost.

6 Kharif Season

The kharif season was to start with the sowing of cotton and maize and transplantation of paddy. The demand for labour was expected to grow more than 12 times than in the wheat harvesting period, and most of the labour was required for transplantation of paddy. Labour supply was hampered as many of the seasonal migrant workers, the primary agricultural workforce, could not reach the Punjab state due to restrictions in interstate travel, and many other migrant labourers that were residing in the state reverse migrated to the native states. A glaring mismatch between the demand and supply of labour and the consequent rise in wages was expected to ensure a considerable shift in the cropping pattern, increase in area under basmati rice, shift to direct seeding of rice and short-duration rice varieties and mechanical alternatives of transplantation. All these strategies could help in reducing labour demand or spreading the sowing over a longer period for better management.

The study revealed that the farmers had no intention to reduce area under paddy (compared to previous year) as it provided higher returns. However, the area under Basmati was expected to increase. No other major changes were expected in the cropping pattern in response to the covid-19 situation.

7 Problems Likely to Be Faced During Kharif Season

Farmers were apprehensive of future course of action with regards to farming in the presences and further spread of COVID-19. During kharif season, labour shortage was perceived as the most probable problem (72%); while upward of 20% farmers perceived facing problems in arranging inputs like seeds and fertilizers (Table 8). The proportion of farmers perceiving such problems increased with the increase in land size, which means that relatively large farmers perceived more problems than their smaller counterparts.

In order to deal with the anticipated problem of labour shortage and the subsequent higher costs, majority (31.7%) of the total farmers, expressed the plausibility of adopting mechanization for paddy sowing. Therefore, they are prioritizing arrangement of machinery, especially DSR machines that would promote labour saving (Table 9). Such approaches would also promote water saving. Another 19% of farmers are planning to arrange labour from their own and nearby villages to meet the required demand. A category wise analysis reveals that while more of the marginal farmers are keen to arrange labour, a larger proportion of the rest of the farmers are planning to undertake labour substitution with machinery.

In order to deal with the perceived problem of shortage of seeds, about 9% of the total farmers were expected to arrange the same from fellow farmers, while about 6% were planning to procure from Punjab Agricultural University well before time so as to avoid any delays during sowing

Table 8 Problems expected to be faced during Kharif season (%) (multiple responses)

Category of farmers	*Buying of improved seeds*	*Buying of fertilizers/agro-chemicals*	*Hiring of labour*	*Hiring of machinery*	*Prices of crops*	*Marketing of crops*	*Methods of cultivation*
Marginal	9.52	14.29	47.62	9.52	9.52	4.76	4.76
Small	16.67	20.83	70.83	8.33	4.17	0.00	12.50
Semi-medium	20.41	20.41	73.47	10.20	12.24	8.16	14.29
Medium	25.00	31.25	62.50	25.00	12.50	6.25	31.25
Large	31.25	18.75	81.25	18.75	12.50	6.25	31.25
Total	20.83	21.67	71.67	13.33	10.83	5.83	17.50

Table 9 Measures to deal with perceived shortage of labour

Category of farmers	*Arranging local labour*	*Arranging machinery*	*Arranging both local and machinery*	*Crop diversification*	*Fellow farmers*	*Hiring expensive*	*Waiting for labour*
Marginal	26.7	6.7	13.3	0.0	6.7	6.7	6.7
Small	20.8	29.2	4.2	8.3	0.0	0.0	8.3
Semi-medium	12.2	40.8	16.3	0.0	0.0	0.0	4.1
Medium	25.0	31.3	0.0	0.0	0.0	6.3	0.0
Large	25.0	31.3	12.5	0.0	0.0	12.5	0.0
Total	19.2	31.7	10.8	1.7	0.8	3.3	4.2

Table 10 Measures to deal with expected shortage of paddy seeds during Kharif season

Category of farmers	*Arrange from other farmers*	*Purchase from PAU*	*Seed purchased on high rate*	*Still waiting*
Marginal	0.0	6.7	0.0	6.7
Small	4.2	8.3	4.2	0.0
Semi-medium	12.2	2.0	2.0	4.1
Medium	12.5	12.5	0.0	0.0
Large	12.5	6.3	6.3	6.3
Total	9.2	5.8	3.3	3.3

(Table 10). In addition, only 3% of the total farmers were expecting to incur higher expenditure on seeds.

8 Information Dissemination

The government made extensive efforts to disseminate information to farmers to facilitate their day-to-day agricultural activities and decision making through various government departments and institutions. About 23% of the sampled farmers were getting the required information from government officials; shopkeepers, TV and online news-media and local farm societies were also performing a crucial role of information dissemination as 19, 18 and 10% respectively of the total farmers were receiving important information from these respective sources. Overall, the smaller

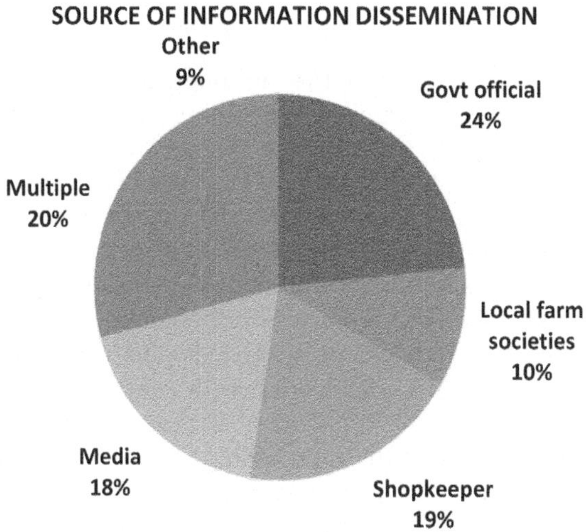

Fig. 1 Source of Information dissemination

farmers were seen to be dependent more on informal sources of information, like the shopkeepers, as compared to their larger counterparts that gained information largely from official sources like government, farm societies and media (Fig. 1).

9 Water Use

The majority of the farmers did not perceive any change with regards to use of water in the approaching Kharif season as compared to the last season. However, about 32.50% assumed that water use might increase; primarily due to a preponement date of sowing, which might tempt a larger use of water. However, about 5% believed that water use might decline due to adoption of different techniques of paddy cultivation, which were primarily labour-saving techniques. Nevertheless, only about 4% of farmers were very open to adopting new technologies, especially those that were less labour intensive and more water saving for paddy cultivation; while about 33% of the farmers were moderately open to experimenting with new techniques and technologies.

10 Conclusions and Implications

The present study brought out that although pandemic lockdown did impact various facets of Punjab agriculture, the state administrative machinery did manage to avert distress among the farming community, thereby, curtailing the feared impact. However, labour shortages and subsequent higher wages, and expensive and limited transportation were found to be the relatively common constraints for the farming community. However, these issues did not become widespread. Though a certain rise in farm and marketing costs were experienced, none of the Rabi produce of the state was lost or wasted due to the pandemic. Individual farmer initiatives in combination with state government support enabled management of the expected obstacles, and planning to tackle the likely constraints during the approaching kharif season was in process. The survey shows that the government needs to intervene to facilitate smooth agricultural operations and curtail the appreciation in farm costs. The government can incentivize workers who choose to work in agriculture. There might be some incentives for the migrant workers also to return to Punjab in the form of health insurance or food entitlements for some time.

The likely economic impact of COVID-19 pandemic-lockdown on agriculture in the forthcoming kharif season might be minimized if the crop diversification and less labour-intensive technique of paddy cultivation might be engendered in the future plans. Also, easy availability of paddy sowing machinery (DSR), by effecting sufficient availability of the required machinery with custom hiring centres and NGOs, would be very fruitful. These steps would not only minimize the feared immediate impact of COVID-19, but would also build strong grounds for growth of state agricultural sector and farmer prosperity in the long run.

In the long run, the following measures in the state may help to build resilience of the state to ward off adverse effects of such abrupt disruptions in the economy, farming sector and supply chains in particular.

1. Strengthening the role of agro-machinery service centres in the state in the public as well as in private sector to ensure timely, cost-effective and easy availability of farm machinery.
2. Strengthening of supply chains for quality seeds by active participation of various stakeholders such as Department of Agriculture and Farmers' Welfare (DAFW), farmers' cooperatives, FPOs, etc.

3. Strengthening of supply networks at the local level by involving village Panchayats, farmers' cooperatives and local traders. The focus should be on meeting the local demand effectively. The government may devise incentive mechanisms for strengthening such networks.

Annexure

See Tables 11, 12, 13, 14, 15 and 16.

Table 11 Measures to deal with delayed procurement

Category of farmers	*Transportation*	*No response*
Marginal	0.0	13.3
Small	0.0	4.2
Semi-medium	2.0	18.4
Medium	6.3	18.8
Large	0.0	25.0
Total	1.7	15.8

Table 12 Measures taken by farmers to deal with staggered procurement

Category of farmers	*Waiting*	*No response*
Marginal	0.0	0.0
Small	0.0	8.3
Semi-medium	2.0	22.4
Medium	6.3	18.8
Large	6.3	18.8
Total	1.7	16.7

Table 13 Measures taken by farmers to deal with delayed payments

Category of farmers	*Waiting*	*No response*
Marginal	0.0	13.3
Small	0.0	4.2
Semi-medium	2.0	2.0
Medium	0.0	18.8
Large	6.3	0.0
Total	1.7	5.8

Table 14 Measures to deal with perceived problem of machinery shortage

Category of farmers	*Arrange machinery*	*Wait*	*Arrange labour*
Marginal	6.7	0.0	6.7
Small	0.0	4.2	4.2
Semi-medium	4.1	4.1	2.0
Medium	12.5	0.0	12.5
Large	6.3	0.0	12.5
Total	5.0	2.5	5.8

Table 15 Readiness to adopt new technology for Kharif cultivation

Category of farmers	*Very open*	*Moderately open*	*neither*	*Moderately opposed*	*Very opposed*
Marginal	0.0	13.3	80.0	6.7	0.0
Small	0.0	41.7	45.8	8.3	4.2
Semi-medium	6.1	36.7	53.1	0.0	4.1
Medium	12.5	25.0	56.3	6.3	0.0
Large	0.0	31.3	62.5	6.3	0.0
Total	4.2	32.5	56.7	4.2	2.5

Table 16 Sources of dissemination of information to farmers (%)

Category of farmers	*Govt official*	*Local farm societies*	*Shopkeeper*	*Media*	*Multiple*	*Other*
Marginal	20.0	13.3	33.3	13.3	20.0	0.0
Small	16.7	8.3	33.3	8.3	16.7	16.7
Semi-medium	20.4	14.3	8.2	20.4	30.6	6.1
Medium	43.8	6.3	18.8	18.8	12.5	0.0
Large	25.0	0.0	18.8	31.3	12.5	12.5
Total	23.3	10.0	19.2	18.3	20.0	9.2

References

Dhillon, B. S., Kataria, P., and Dhillon, P. K. (2010) National Food Security vis-à-vis Sustainability of Agriculture in High Crop Productivity Regions, *Current Science*, 98: 33–36.

GoI. (2017) All Indian Rural Financial Inclusion Survey, NABARD, Government of India.

GoP. (2020) Economic Survey of Punjab, Economic and Statistical Organisation, Department of Planning, Government of Punjab.

Kaur, B., Singh, J.M., Garg, B. R., Singh, J., and Singh, S. (2011) Causes and Impact of Labour Migration: A Case Study of Punjab Agriculture, *Agricultural Economics Research Review*, 24: 459–466.

Need for Innovations in Crop Residue Management in Punjab: Lessons from the COVID-19 Pandemic

Rita Pandey, Shailly Kedia, and Anuja Malhotra

1 Introduction

During the COVID-19 pandemic, minimizing additional risks such as poor air quality is an important disease management strategy. Also, with COVID-19, existing health infrastructure is already under severe stress, and additional pollution related infections will only serve as a stress multiplier. In this policy brief, we focus on poor air quality (AQ) due to crop stubble burning in Punjab. What are the solutions to avoid this annual disaster in October–December 2020? The analysis in this piece brings to the fore some short-term practical measures and underlines that a medium to long term solution lies, among others, in making food production in

R. Pandey (✉) · A. Malhotra
National Institute of Public Finance and Policy, New Delhi, India
e-mail: rita.pandey@nipfp.org.in

A. Malhotra
e-mail: anuja.malhotra@nipfp.org.in

S. Kedia
The Energy and Resources Institute, New Delhi, India
e-mail: shailly.kedia@teri.res.in

S. Singh et al. (eds.), *Covid-19 Pandemic and Economic Development*,
https://doi.org/10.1007/978-981-16-4442-9_4

certain pockets of north India efficient in resource use and resilient to environmental and climate changes.

2 Annual Trends of Poor Air Quality Due to Paddy Stubble Burning

India has a huge imperative to address the annual trends of air quality during October–December 2020 in Delhi and other cities in north India when air quality levels reach up to twenty times higher than the safe threshold levels defined by the World Health Organization (PTI, 2019a). In Delhi, up to 50 per cent increase in air pollution on many winter days is attributed to agricultural fires. According to a recent source apportionment study, open burning emissions in Punjab, Haryana, and the northwest of Uttar Pradesh accounted for 15 per cent to 35 per cent of ambient PM 2.5 concentrations (GBD MAPS Working Group, 2018).

3 Why Do Farmers Burn Crop Stubble?

With the onset of winter, farm fires become rampant in northern part of India in the states of Punjab, Haryana, and western Uttar Pradesh. The problem of poor air quality is exacerbated for the already disadvantageous landlocked Delhi that has no rejuvenating ability like other coastal cities in India where pollutants are swept out towards the ocean. Over the years, parts of Northern states Punjab, Haryana, and Uttar Pradesh have moved to extremely specialized short duration varieties of rice–wheat cropping system. With the adoption of these varieties, a rice crop (June/July to October/November), followed by a wheat crop (November/December to March/April) rotation became popular in areas which earlier produced only wheat or rice in any one farming year. However, this cropping system perceived as 'efficient' has come at a huge environmental and ecological cost that includes environmental unsustainability and loss of resilience in the medium to long run.

The main reason for paddy (rice crop) stubble burning is the short time available between rice harvesting and sowing of wheat. A delay in sowing wheat adversely affects the wheat crop. The short window of time available between rice and wheat crops can also be attributed partly to the Punjab Preservation of Subsoil Act, 2009. Farmers get less than 20–25 days between two crops, and hence the quickest and easiest solution is to burn the crop residue (Jitendra et al., 2019). It is estimated that 20 million tonnes of rice stubble is produced every year in Punjab, out of which 80 per cent is burnt on the farm (DTE, 2019).

4 Crop Stubble Burning Creates On-Farm and Off-Farm Externality

Stubble burning creates externality in the form of emissions with implications for climate change and health costs to people in affected region, disruptions in economic activity (cancellation/delays in flights and trains, and slow road traffic and accidents). Stubble burning emits PM 2.5, which is the most adverse for human health, since the particles can get trapped inside the lungs and increases the risk of lung cancer by 36 per cent. Cost of air pollution due to stubble burning in India is estimated to be USD 30 billion annually (IFPRI, 2019). Burning 1 tonne of rice accounts for a loss of nitrogen (5.5 kg), phosphorous (2.3 kg), potassium (25 kg), and sulphur (1.2 kg) in the soil. Moreover, the heat from burning crop residue kills critical bacterial and fungal populations in the soil, apart from organic carbon (Hesammi et al., 2014).

Stubble burning emits PM2.5, which is the most adverse for human health, since the particles can get trapped inside the lungs and increase the risk of lung cancer by 36. According to (Kumar et al, 2015) people in rural Punjab spend more than Rs 7.6 crores every year on treatment for ailments caused by stubble burning. Cost of air pollution due to stubble burning in India is estimated to be USD 30 billion annually (International Food Policy Research Institute, 2019). Further, stubble burning reduces the availability of straw to livestock, which is already in short supply by more than 40 per cent (Kumar et al, 2015).

Since air quality is a public good, the role of central coordination/government becomes even more important. Which would imply that the government would need to either share the cost of compensation or the cost of abatement (reducing stubble burning), or both in different measures. Broadly, the application of incentive-based regulation can be a potential cost-effective way to control air pollution.

5 Recent Policy Interventions and Other Measures Taken

Various policy measures at the national and sub-national levels seek to resolve the problem of crop stubble burning in India. A National Policy for Management of Crop Residues is in place, along with a Crop Diversification Programme. According to the law, violators can be booked for disobedience of order duly promulgated by the government under (AirPrevention and Control of Pollution) Act. There are schemes to promote in-situ and ex-situ crop residue management through machines like happy seeder, rotavator, and baler. However, there are many gaps in terms of policy design, implementation, and awareness. The table below summarizes the key policy interventions. For a detailed discussion see Pandey et al. (2020) (Table 1).

6 Other Issues: Gaps in Policy Design, Implementation and Awareness

i. **Policy Issues**:

The national programme on crop diversification does not have clear provisions on outreach activities to sensitize the farmers about alternate crop options. Similarly, there is insufficient convergence with other programmes such as the National Rural Employment Guarantee Scheme, National Rural Livelihood Mission, and agro-enterprise related schemes which could help in management of paddy stubble or crop diversification.

ii. **Implementation Issues**:

- Unavailability of CRM machines has been a key issue in mitigating crop residue burning. In 2019, despite a sanction of 22,854 machines, only 14,625 were available for use (Nirmal, 2019).
- The in-situ management machines are still unaffordable to many farmers despite subsidy provisions. Happy Seeder costs INR 1.50 lakh and requires a 65-horsepower tractor. It is not affordable for small farmers to buy the machinery, even with the subsidy at current rates of 50 per cent (PTI, 2019b).
- Constraints in the supply-chain and rental markets are other issues impacting adoption of machines like happy seeder. Even

Table 1 Policy Interventions and other measures to address stubble burning

S. No	*Policy Intervention*	*Central/state government*	*Focus Area*
1	National Policy for Management of Crop Residues (2014)	Central government	• Promotion of technology for in-situ management of crop residue as well as uses of crop residues • Promotion of adaptive research
2	Crop Diversification Programme (CDP) under Rashtriya Krishi Vikas Yojana (RKVY), 2013–2014	Central government	• Demonstration and promotion of production of alternate crops for diversion of paddy cultivation and to restore the soil fertility However, the programme appears off-track as there was increase in area under Paddy cultivation in 2016 (Kedia, 2017)
3	NGTs Ban on Stubble Burning (2015)	Central government	• Ban on agriculture stubble burning in states of Rajasthan, Uttar Pradesh, Haryana, and Punjab under Sect. 188 of the IPC and under the Air and Pollution Control Act of 1981[1] However, following a ground level study, a government panel recommended to the NITI Aayog that a machinery-based solution may have greater potential (Vishnoi et al., 2017)

(continued)

Table 1 (continued)

S. No	*Policy Intervention*	*Central/state government*	*Focus Area*
4	Promotion of Agricultural Mechanization for In-Situ crop residue management (CRM)	Central government	• Financial assistance is provided to farmers for purchase of in-situ residue management machines • Establishing farm machinery banks • IEC for awareness on CRM
5	The Agriculture Policy for Punjab (2013)	State government	• The policy aims to make concerted efforts to reduce the area under paddy cultivation by 40 per cent from current levels in a span of 5–7 years
6	Field trials of technologies to decompose paddy (2019 onwards)	Central government	• The Indian Agricultural Research Institute (ICAR) has been expeditiously conducting field trials for such technologies
7	MoU between Punjab Government and CSIR-NEERI (2019)	State government	• MoU signed to extend technical support to the state for abatement of pollution, and waste management
8	Adoption of 100 villages by CII (2019)	Central government	• 100 villages adopted to guide zero crop residue burning by providing technical support through machineries and training, and a comprehensive awareness campaign
9	Paddy Straw Challenge (worldwide) Fund	State government	• Punjab's State Farmers and Farm Workers Commission have set up a fund of one million dollars to find an appropriate technology to address the issue (Sethi, 2018)

(continued)

Table 1 (continued)

S. No	*Policy Intervention*	*Central/state government*	*Focus Area*
10	Compensation to farmers for not burning paddy straw	State government	• In FY 2019–2020, the Punjab Government disbursed INR 19 Crore among 29,343 non-basmati cultivating small and marginal farmers, as compensation for not burning stubble @ INR 2500/acre (NewIndianXpress, 2019)[2]

though the CSS scheme provides 80% subsidy to cooperative societies to further rent out machines to farmers, most of the cooperative societies did not have funds to buy such machinery on even 80 per cent subsidy (Tribune, 2018).

iii. Lack of awareness, uncertainty about new technologies and misconceptions that Happy Seeder machine reduces yield are other issues impacting adoption of Happy Seeder.

7 International Experience

For years, crop burning was perceived as normal by several countries and open burning of crop residue was often overlooked to meet the growing demand for food as well as to maximize profits from cultivation. However, the problem was recognized as severe when the scale at which it is carried out became significant. In absolute terms, India, China are the biggest burners of crop residue in the world in terms of the kilos of biomass burned annually (Cassou, 2018). Steps taken by China, Australia and UK are as below:

- China banned burning crop residue in 1999 and imposed heavy fines on violators. CRM in China has "in-situ" focus which helps balance composition of nitrogen, phosphorous, and potassium in the soil (Sun et al., 2016).

- In Australia, comprehensive guidelines exist to deter for crop residue burning. There are certain exceptions where burning is allowed, such as clearing agriculture or regeneration of pastures.
- United Kingdom banned crop residue burning in 1993 due to environmental concerns. Farmers are pressing for return to licensed (limited and controlled) stubble burning which may be necessary in some cases to control Blackgrass (a weed) which is resistant to pesticides and herbicides. Burning of blackgrass is seen as the only solution to get rid of it (Tasker, 2012).

8 Way Forward

8.1 Need for Holistic Approaches

A holistic approach would be required to address the crop residue burning in a multi-disciplinary and multi-agency setting involving technical agencies, market-based economic tools, supporting agricultural and environmental policies, and awareness and capacity building of farmers is necessary. First and foremost, there needs to be a central coordinating mechanism for paddy stubble management and crop diversification with adequate resources clear assignment of responsibilities between national and sub-national agencies. The target should be putting a stop on crop residue burning in COVID-19 year at any cost.

8.2 Short-Term Measures

Addressing Practical Issues in Adoption and Availability of Happy Seeder

- Farmers' misconceptions regarding reduction in yield due to use of Happy Seeder and other CRM measures must be addressed through awareness campaigns and on-farm training.
- Current subsidies for CRM may be reviewed on a priority basis. A subsidy at Rs. 3000 per acre as compared to the current rate of subsidy of Rs. 2500 per acre may be more acceptable to farmers and might encourage removal of straw manually in cases where buying

happy seeders is unaffordable and the rental market for happy seeders is unable to meet the demand for machines in time.

- Even though the CSS scheme provides for establishing Farm Machinery Bank to provide hiring services to farmers, there are serious issues of timely availability of machines to farmers. This is another priority action that the concerned agencies need to deliver on.

8.3 Medium-Term Measures

i. Encouraging Crop Diversification/Rotation

While technological interventions may be useful in the short term, crop diversification as a policy intervention needs to be emphasized by the government. For instance, there is evidence that crop diversification (genetic variety, species, structural) can facilitate nutritional security and promote ecosystem services for pest and disease control and resilience to climate change variability and other extreme events (Lin, 2011). Resilient agriculture, in turn, contributes to productivity growth (Di Falco and Chavas, 2008).

It can be implemented in various ways such as crop rotation, poly-cultures, increased structural diversity, or agroforestry. A flexible policy environment will allow farmers to choose a strategy that increases resilience as well as provides economic benefits (Lin, 2011).

- Focus on crop diversification needs to be increased and the crop composition in the IGP region needs to be re-evaluated.
- A detailed study involving all stakeholders will be required to understand slow progress towards crop diversification in spite of regulatory policy nudges and fiscal policy incentives announced by both the central and state governments.
- Crop diversification package should be a mix of policy measures, encouragement of agro-business enterprises possibly under "Aatmanirbhar Bharat Abhiyan" scheme, awareness campaigns for farmers explaining the importance of the scheme for them and what it offers, economic incentives such as minimum support prices for alternative crops, along with infrastructure support like agricultural inputs for identified alternative crops.

ii. Other Issues

- More research is needed to understand the full implications of the Punjab Preservation of Subsoil Act, 2009 on crop stubble burning and the trade-offs therein. The short window of time available between rice and wheat crops can also be attributed partly to the Punjab Preservation of Subsoil Act, 2009. As per the Act, farmers are prohibited from sowing paddy seeds in nurseries before May 10 and transplanting the seedlings before June 10. The objective of the Act is to delay the sowing of paddy seeds so that the water used for harvesting these seeds can be reduced. There is evidence to show that the legislation did yield the desired results in terms of water conservation. However, by pushing the sowing of rice by a month may have contributed to stubble burning.
- Also, a deeper understanding of the issue of labour availability due to rice sowing and thus rice harvesting getting pushed to festive season (Deepawali and Chatth) and its impact on stubble burning and what could be the potential solutions to address it, is required.

Notes

1. The Punjab government took action against 2,923 farmers after receiving complaints against 20,729 cases of stubble burning in 2019. The enforcement teams had imposed environment compensation of Rs 41,62,000 in 1,585 cases, a red entry made in Khasra Girdawaris in 1,136 cases, and prosecution/FIR filed in 202 cases against the defaulting farmers (Sandhu, 2019). The State Government of Punjab during 2019–2020 imposed Environmental Compensation in 23,200 incidents of paddy straw burning as per the directions of NGT.
2. The farmer must meet three conditions to receive compensation: the total landholding should not exceed five acres; the farmer has not burnt paddy residue; the crop is non-basmati rice (Vasdev, 2019).

References

Cassou, E. (2018) Field Burning (English). Agricultural Pollution. Washington, DC: World Bank Group. Accessible at http://documents.worldbank.org/curated/en/ 989351521207797690/Field-Burning.

Di Falco, and Chavas, J.-P., (2008) Rainfall Shocks, Resilience and the Dynamic Effects of Crop Biodiversity on the Productivity of the Agro-ecosystem, *Land Economics*, 84(1): 83–96.

DTE. (2019) Stubble Burning: A Problem for the Environment, Agriculture and Humans. Retrieved from https://www.downtoearth.org.in/blog/agriculture/stubble-burning-a-problem-for-the-environment-agriculture-and-humans-64912.

GBD MAPS Working Group. (2018) Burden of Disease Attributable to Major Air Pollution Sources in India (Special Report 21), Boston, MA: Health Effects Institute.

Hesammi, E., Ali Benjavad, T., and Hesammi, A. (2014) A Review on the Burning of Crop Residue on the Soil Properties, *WALIA J*, 30: 192–194.

International Food Policy Research Institute. (2019, March 4) India's Stubble Burning Air Pollution Causes USD 30 Billion Economic Losses, Health Risks: Three-fold Risk Increase of Respiratory Diseases from Crop Residue Burning; Economic Loss Estimated to be Nearly USD 30 Billion Annually. *Science Daily*.

Jitendra, V., Shreeshan, I, Kukreti, K. P., Deepanwita, G. N., and Polash, M. (2019) India's Burning Issue of Crop Burning Takes a New Turn. Down to Earth, November 8. https://www.downtoearth.org.in/coverage/agriculture/river-of-fire-57924 [Accessed 22 May 2020].

Kedia, S. (2017) Paddy Stubble: The 'Burning' Conundrum. *Times of India Blog*, November 17. Available at: https://timesofindia.indiatimes.com/blogs/voices/paddy-stubble-the-burning-conundrum/.

Kumar, P., Kumar, S., and Joshi, L. (2015) *Socioeconomic and Environmental Implications of Agricultural Residue Burning: A Case Study of Punjab*, India. Springer Open.

Lin, Brenda B. (2011) Resilience in Agriculture Through Crop Diversification: Adaptive Management for Environmental Change, *BioScience*, 61(3): 183–193.

NewIndianXpress. (2019, November 15) 29,000 Punjab Farmers Who Did Not Burn Crop Residue Compensated. Retrieved from https://www.newindianexpress.com/nation/2019/nov/15/29000-punjab-farmers-who-did-not-burn-crop-residue-compensated-2062234.html.

Nirmal, R. (2019, November 17) Where Are the Happy Seeders that Punjab's Farmers Were Promised? Retrieved from https://www.thehindubusinessline.com/economy/agri-business/where-are-the-happy-seeders-that-punjabs-farmers-were-promised/article30000119.ece.

Pandey, R., Kedia, S., and Malhotra, A. (2020) Addressing Air Quality Spurts Due to Crop Stubble Burning During COVID-19 Pandemic: A Case of Punjab, Working Paper No. 308, National Institute of Public Finance and

Policy, New Delhi. https://www.nipfp.org.in/media/medialibrary/2020/06/WP_308_2020.pdf.
Press Trust of India. (2019, October 20) CII Adopts 100 Villages in Punjab, Haryana to Curb Pollution Through Stubble Burning. Retrieved from https://www.thehindubusinessline.com/news/national/cii-adopts-100-villages-in-punjab-haryana-to-curb-pollution-through-stubble-burning/article29752138.ece.
Press Trust of India. (2019, August 8) Happy Seeder Machines Help Reduce Air Pollution, more Profitable for Farmers: Research—Times of India. Retrieved from https://timesofindia.indiatimes.com/business/india-business/happy-seeder-machines-help-reduce-air-pollution-more-profitable-for-farmers-research/articleshow/70590861.cms?utm_source=contentofinterest&utm_medium=text&utm_campaign=cppst.
Sandhu, K. K. (2019, November 3) Stubble Burning: Punjab Government Takes Action Against 3,000 Farmers. *India Today*.
Sethi, C. K. (2018, September 22) Punjab Offers Million-dollar Reward to Anyone Who Can Solve Stubble-burning Problem. Retrieved from https://theprint.in/india/governance/punjab-offers-million-dollar-reward-to-anyone-who-can-solve-stubble-burning-problem/122554/ .
Sun, J., Haiyun, P., Jianmin, C., Xinming, W., Min, W., Weijun, L., Lingxiao, Y., Qingzhu, Z., Wenxing, W., and Abdelwahid, M. (2016) An Estimation of CO_2 Emission via Agricultural Crop Residue Open Field Burning in China from 1996 to 2013, *Journal of Cleaner Production*, 112: 2625–2631.
Tasker, J. (2012, July 30) Farmers Step up Stubble Burning Campaign. Retrieved from https://www.fwi.co.uk/arable/farmers-step-up-stubble-burning-campaign.
Tribune News Service. (2018) Co-op Societies Sans Happy Seeders Despite 80% Subsidy. Retrieved from https://www.tribuneindia.com/news/archive/punjab/co-op-societies-sans-happy-seeders-despite-80-subsidy-669387 .
Vasdev, K. (2019) Explained: Why Punjab Suspended Disbursing Bonus to Farmers Who Didn't Set Paddy Stubble to Fire. *The Indian Express*, November 21.
Vishnoi, A., Gupta, S., and Shukla, S. (2017, December 1) MGNREGA Won't Put out Crop Stubble Burning, Says Govt Panel. Retrieved from https://theprint.in/report/mgnrega-wont-put-out-crop-stubble-burning-says-govt-panel/19746/.

Household Gardens: A Promising Approach to Enhance Food Security and Sustainability

Amarjit Bhullar

1 Introduction

Household gardening is a prehistoric and widespread practice all over the world. Worldwide, household gardens have been recognized as, *"an important supplementary source enhancing the food and nutritional security"* (Galhena et al., 2013) along with ensuring the food sovereignty of the masses. *"Food production on small plots adjacent to human settlements is the oldest and most enduring form of cultivation"* (Niñez, 1984). In the history of agriculture, household gardens have been classified *"as mixed, kitchen, backyard, farmyard, compound or homestead garden"* (Terra, 1958; Rowe, 2009).

Ninez (1984) defined the household garden as, *"The household garden is a small-scale production system supplying plant and animal consumption and utilitarian items either not obtainable, affordable, or readily available through retail markets, field cultivation, hunting, gathering, fishing, and wage earning."* The household gardens, *"occupy land marginal to field production and labor marginal to major household economic activities. Featuring ecologically adapted and complementary species, household*

A. Bhullar (✉)
University of Northern British Columbia, Prince George, BC, Canada
e-mail: amarjit.bhullar@unbc.ca

S. Singh et al. (eds.), *Covid-19 Pandemic and Economic Development*,
https://doi.org/10.1007/978-981-16-4442-9_5

gardens are marked by low capital input and simple technology" (Galhena et al., 2013).

The technology lead growth of agriculture and commercialization and specialization of production undermined the importance of household gardens. The history of agricultural growth tells us that the world has, so far, witnessed two Green Revolutions. The first green revolution started in the 1930s in Europe and North America. It brought quick yield increases in maize and other temperate-climate crops with increased, intensified, and effective use of fertilizers, pesticides, crop species, machinery, and farm management. The second green revolution, which was there in some of the Indian provinces too, took place in the 1960s and 1970s and it passed almost the same technologies to the developing world and crops grown in the tropics. But the negative impact of chemical-based food is being felt both in developed as well as in developing world. The third potential green revolution is said to come from the Genetically Modified (GM) technology. GM products especially the seeds produced by using the genetic engineering in agriculture appeared in the 1970s and was commercialized in the 1990s mainly in North America. The advocates of this technology acclaim that it will result in another enormous increase in agronomic productivity and provide qualitative improvements in the food supply. The big differences between the first two green revolutions and the potential third one is that the latter has not been received with conclusive inquisitiveness as the GM organisms are perceived as unsafe to the human, animal, and plant health in the long run. The household gardens are free from the negativities associated with all the green revolutions. That is why the household gardens survived or even remerged. In Greater Vancouver Canada, Institute of Sustainable Food Systems, Kwantlen Polytechnic University in collaboration with city councils has come up with program to popularize the household gardens. Under this program the city councils give a small piece of vacant land to the residents to grow vegetables and the Institute of Sustainable Food Systems provides the know how. So even in the developed countries household gardens are being popularized now.

Mitchell and Hanstad (2004) listed five intrinsic characteristics of home gardens as: "*1) are located near the residence; 2) contain a high diversity of plants; 3) production is supplemental rather than a main source of family consumption and income; 4) occupy a small area; and 5) are a production system that the poor can easily enter at some level.*" The sixth characteristic of household garden is that the production is largely organic or produced with minimal use of chemicals.

The lockdowns, shutdowns, and imposition of curfews, necessitated to check the spread of COVID-19, have disturbed the food supply chains resulting in food shortages and price volatilities. So, covid-19 is an opportunity to think and revive the system of producing food items that can possibly be produced at local level as a safety net to meet supply shocks and price volatilities.

2 Rationale to Promote Household Gardens in Punjab

Punjab has moved in a different direction during the green revolution period. Punjab farmers were accustomed to produce not only a variety of food grains but also the vegetables, fruits, eggs, meat and milk for domestic use in the pre-green revolution era. But now with the exception to wheat, rice, and milk, most of the farming families are dependent on the market for the supply of other food items required for nutritional adequacy such as vegetables, fruits, eggs, meat, and other food grains. The result is nutritional inadequacy, higher expenditure, and lack of access to fresh and quality food. Farmers have enjoyed the economies of scale by producing wheat and rice but have forgone the economies of scope.

"The stagnant productivity, increasing costs, dwindling profits, receding water availability, declining soil productivity etc. *coupled with future uncertainties have brought about an economic, environmental and social distress in the agricultural sector of Punjab"* (Bhullar, 2018). Economic, environmental, and social tribulations are reinforcing each other, and the crisis is deepening persistently. The green revolution has completed a full cycle comprising high growth period, stagnation and now a period of crises. So, to come out of the prevailing impasse, there is an urgent need not only to revive but also to alter the Green Revolution into a new form that expands the scope of livelihood of the farmers beyond rice and wheat rotation. Since 1985, the stated policy and research agenda, in a broader sense, is for diversification of the cropping pattern, especially reducing the area under rice, to ease the strain on resources. Some farmers responded and struggled to grow alternative crops but after some time returned to the wheat and rice rotation due to the lack of marketing support. The household gardens can be a starting point of diversification as the farmers

will attain experience to grow unconventional crops at the small scale and then they can scale up to commercial production.

Nutritional security is a big concern especially in case of marginal and small farming families. A study found that the marginal and small farmers' families were consuming fruits, vegetables, pulses, and fats less than what is required in a balanced diet (Bhullar et al., 2010). Therefore, to ensure nutritional sufficiency of marginal and small farmers, an effort needs to be made to promote dairy farming and these farmers must be incentivized to produce fruits, vegetables, and pulses at their own farm in order to have access to the balanced food.

The adoption of household gardens faces a host of constraints in the developing countries (Hoogerbrugge and Fresco, 1993; Mitchell and Hanstad, 2004). These constraints include access to suitable and enough land to establish a home garden along with lack of ownership and usage rights, access to water, seeds and planting materials, weak extension and advisory services, access to labor, etc. Punjab farmers are almost free from all these constraints and the prevailing institutional support system is capable to provide the required back up for adoption and sustenance.

3 Institutional Support for Household Gardens in Punjab

Punjab Agricultural University (PAU) has developed field plans for farm gardens with potential to produce vegetables round the year. PAU has also developed a kitchen garden without soil (called vegetable nutrition garden model) in which all-season vegetables can be grown. This is a vegetable nutrition garden model and anyone who have some space in their house can use this model to grow vegetables regardless of the season. There is no use of pesticides, so it is healthy. The problem is that the soilless model requires space in the house and significant initial investment i.e. around Rs. 35,000 at 2018 prices.

Horticulture Department Punjab has developed low-priced special vegetable seeds kits containing the seeds of all vegetables grown in winter and summer. The kits contain seeds of vegetables like carrot, radish, turnip, peas, spinach, fenugreek, coriander, broccoli, beetroot, lettuce, sarson, etc., all of which can be easily grown on a small piece of land and provide fresh vegetables for a family of seven. With the help of these kits, residents can get vegetables almost round the year. The kits have been prepared by the horticulture department under Mission

Tandrust Punjab of the state government. Along with the seeds, the kit also includes a pamphlet containing the package and practices for growing vegetables.

However, PAU and Horticulture department need to extend it and include fruits plants and pulses in these gardens suitable for growing in the different agroclimatic zones and specify the land requirements for that.

4 The Policy Initiative

Considering the numerous advantages, the farmers must be supported and incentivized with a comprehensive policy to go far household gardens. The comprehensive policy should include:

- Free provision of seed kits and fruit plants to all the farmers of Punjab every year (distributed through stakeholder departments).
- Free provision of relevant literature with a mobile app.
- State of the art demonstration plots at PAU and Horticulture Department farms and extending these further to progressive farmers' fields.
- Short training for planning and caring the household gardens.
- Educating the women about the balanced food as well as training them to grow the vegetables and fruits.
- A roadmap to further move to integrated farming system.

5 Budgetary Requirement

The policy can be implemented using the existing research and extension networks that include PAU, Department of Agriculture, Department of Horticulture, Krishi Vigyan Kendras, Progressive Farmers' Associations. So, the implementation costs will be negligible. The cost of supply of seed kits assumed to be Rs. 200 per year including Rs. 100 for each seed kit for Rabi and Kharif seasons. There are about 11 lakh farms households in Punjab and thus the yearly cost of seed kits will be Rs. 22 crores. The cost of supplying 5 fruit plants to every farmer free of cost will be Rs. 11 crores considering Rs. 20 as cost per nursery plant. The logistical support will require another Rs. 2 crores. So, the total cost per year works out to be Rs, 35 crores. The policy support for promotion of household gardens must continue at least for 5 years.

6 Gender Roles

The household gardens can be taken care by the women and it will provide not only the employment to them but also can be a source of income.

7 Likely Concerns About the Policy

The most likely concern about the policy will be the perceived difficulty to revert back to the traditional farming system. No, it will not be a reversal. It will be a marginal change. The land requirement per farmer will be just half to one kanal and the rest of the production can be carried out "business as usual." The total land requirement for the state, if everyfarmer adopt this, will be 27,500 to 55,000 hectares. So, there will insignificant impact on the usual agricultural production.

8 Intended Benefits

- Since the production will be for household consumption, price and marketing concerns will not be there.
- Food diversity and a step to provide safe, healthy, nutritious, and balanced food in the rural areas.
- Organic food production is possible.
- Improving the food security in the rural areas.
- Environmental benefits from recycling the wastes.
- Training of the farmers to grow fruits and vegetables at a small scale.
- A small step toward diversification of agriculture.

References

Bhullar, A. S. (2018) Agricultural Crisis of Punjab: Costly Mistakes, *Economic and Political Weekly*, VIII(11): 27–30.

Bhullar, A. S., Mandeep, S., and Inderpreet, K. (2010) Income and Consumption Pattern of Marginal and Small Farmers in Punjab: An Analysis from Livelihood Security Perspective, *Advance Research Journal of Social Science*, 1(2): 77–82.

Galhena, D. H., Freed, R., and Maredia, K. M. (2013) Home Gardens: A Promising Approach to Enhance Household Food Security and Well-being. *Agriculture & Food* Security, 2(8). https://doi.org/10.1186/2048-7010-2-8.

Hoogerbrugge, I., and Fresco, L. O. (1993) *Homegarden Systems: Agricultural Characteristics and Challenges*, Gatekeeper Series No. 39, London, UK: International Institute for Environment and Development.

Mitchell, R., and Hanstad, T. (2004) *Small Homegarden Plots and Sustainable Livelihoods for the Poor*, Rome, Italy: LSP Working Paper 11.

Niñez, V. K. (1984) *Household Gardens: Theoretical Considerations on an Old Survival Strategy*, Peru, LI: International Potato Center.

Rowe, W. C. (2009) "Kitchen Gardens" in Tajikistan: The Economic and Cultural Importance of Small-scale Private Property in a Post-soviet Society, *Human Ecology*, 37(6): 691–703. https://doi.org/10.1007/s10745-009-9278-6.

Terra, G. J. A. (1958) Farm Systems in southeast Asia, *Netherlands Journal of Agricultural Science*, 6: 157–182.

Reforming Agricultural Markets in Punjab in the Federal Context for Post-COVID-19 Recovery

Sukhpal Singh

1 Introduction

Agricultural markets are central to agrarian transformation in Punjab but they are not being reformed as needed. Though Punjab was a pioneer in the 1990s allowing new channels like contract farming when other states were not even thinking of it yet, has fallen back on the reform front quite a bit. Now when the Union government has been persuading the states for reforms since early 2000s, Punjab has either lagged behind or taken adverse steps which were not in tune with the Indian trend. For example, it did not amend the APMC Act substantially until recently (2017 with rules notified in 2020, with the exception of providing for private markets in 2006; PMB, 2006) and enacted a separate contract farming Act in 2013 which was not needed and was never operationalized (Singh, 2013). Now, when the Union government has passed and enforced two Acts on two major state domains i.e. agricultural trade outside the APMC market yards/sub-yards and on contract farming, Punjab again needs to take a

S. Singh (✉)
Centre for Management in Agriculture, Indian Institute of Management Ahmedabad, Ahmedabad, Gujarat, India
e-mail: sukhpal@iima.ac.in

S. Singh et al. (eds.), *Covid-19 Pandemic and Economic Development*,
https://doi.org/10.1007/978-981-16-4442-9_6

call on its agricultural marketing legislation to make it consistent with the Central Acts. In this context, this article reviews the state of agricultural markets and agricultural market policy and regulatory reforms in Section 2 for their potential role in agricultural market development and reforms. It examines the Union Model APLM and CF&S Acts and amended Punjab APLM Act, 2017 for their implications for Punjab in Section 3. Finally, in Section 4, it suggests an agricultural market reform roadmap for Punjab and mechanisms for bringing about desired type and level of agro-market development in the state which is in tune with globalization as well as local needs and aspirations of the people of the state in the light of post-Covid-19 recovery of the state's agricultural economy.

2 Understanding Agri Commodity Markets of Punjab

Punjab's agricultural markets comprise of the wholesale grain and perishable produce markets known as Agricultural Produce Market Committee (APMC) markets and are supposed to be regulated, by and large. But, the most powerful stakeholder in these markets today is the Commission Agent (*Arthiya*) who is the product of the Green Revolution and the state led procurement of food grains and cotton by the Union government agencies like Food Corporation of India (FCI), and Cotton Corporation of India (CCI) from the state for decades now. The estimated number of Commission Agents (CAs) in the grain and cotton (APMC) markets in Punjab is 20232 and average number of farmers per CA is 52 (Singh and Bhogal, 2015). The interlocking of the credit, input, and output markets by the *Arthiyas* in the state has led to farmer indebtedness in the context of poor institutional credit reach which is both inadequate and costlier due to higher transaction costs despite its lower interest rate. The system of payment for the farmer produce through the CAs is the root cause of trouble for farmers as CAs who do unregistered and informal money lending at high rates of interest, and supply farm inputs and groceries to farmers on seasonal credit, besides the commission they get from public and private agencies for facilitating sale of farmer produce to them, recover their loans through this system of payment though the farmer produce is mostly bought by state agencies i.e. FCI and CCI or those authorized by them (Singh and Bhogal, 2015). It is in this context that the issue of direct payment to farmers for their produce has been hanging fire for so many years by now and remains unresolved despite the Union government push for the same.

That CAs have become well entrenched in the agricultural marketing and credit systems of the state accounting for 36% of total agricultural credit in the state, is well known. Further, the profile of CAs has also changed after the Green Revolution as now a large proportion of them are from the *Jat* (farming) caste, unlike the earlier CA profile when most of them were *banias* (trading caste). It is suggested that the new CAs with Jat background are stricter with their dealings with farmers for repayment and mechanisms to ensure repayment of loans, and also politically more connected and powerful (Singh and Bhogal, 2015).

However, this fact provides no logic for the relevance of CAs in the agricultural marketing system, but reflects the failure of another system i.e. credit. Rather, there could be a case for abolition of CAs in the state's grain and fibre markets where a large proportion of the produce (in all major crops of wheat, paddy, and cotton) is bought by the state agencies. The existence of CAs is undesirable for both farm produce markets as well as credit markets as interlocking practiced by CAs makes these markets non-competitive and exploitative. The abolition of the very institution of CAs is needed and states like Madhya Pradesh (MP) had taken such steps during the 1980s itself (Krishnamurthy, 2014; Singh, 2016). This should be much more feasible now as there can be more alternate agencies like Producer Companies (PCs), Primary Agricultural Co-operative Societies (PACS), warehouse receipt system, or electronic marketing platforms at APMC level which can take up the role of facilitating farmer produce handling in *mandis* or outside and obviate the need for informal sector credit as there would be prompt payment for produce or loans against produce through the warehouse receipt system.

Infact, PACS already buy from farmers at their doorsteps in many states like Bihar and MP and payments are directly made into farmers' bank accounts (Krishnamurthy, 2014). Unfortunately, the recent draft farmers' policy of the state does not deal with the reform of existing markets in the state—neither in terms of examining the model Agricultural produce and livestock markets (promotion and facilitation Act [APLM(PF)A], 2017) and the model Agricultural Produce and Livestock Contract Farming and Services (promotion and facilitation Act [APLCFS (PF)A], 2018) nor in terms of improving the regulation and governance of existing markets or their restructuring, especially perishable produce markets as they would be needed for new high value crops under diversified agricultural scenario. It fails to visualize any new market mechanisms to encourage new crops

(PSFFWC, 2018; Singh, 2018a) unlike Haryana's recent crop diversification policy for specific water stressed districts/blocks where incentive and support is provided to farmers to switch away from paddy to other crops which are less water consuming, and have procurement at Minimum Support Price (MSP) by state agencies or other market support promised by the state government (Singh, 2020d).

2.1 The Agricultural Market Reform in Punjab

Punjab is among a few states in India which had not amended the APMC Act until 2017 and had enacted a completely unnecessary separate Contract Farming Act (CFA) in 2013. The state, a pioneer in undertaking various measures to promote contract farming during the 1990s, was stuck on the APMC Act amendment due to the political economy involved in the policy reform and the role of various vested interests involved in the *mandi* system. It is yet another matter that the state has still not operationalised the Contract Farming Commission and its machinery even seven years after the enactment of the CFA though the Union government has designed the new Agricultural Produce and Livestock Contract Farming and Services Act (APLCF&SA), 2018 on the lines of its CFA, 2013 and now a central Acts on contract farming. Infact, contract farming did not need a separate legislation as many other states, including neighboring Haryana have legalized contract farming by amending the APMC Act. Therefore, it is important to understand why Punjab took the route of a separate legislation on this aspect instead of doing all the required reforms in the APMC Act (Singh, 2013).

The major reason for Punjab going for a separate Act on contract farming can be found in the political economy of the state's agribusiness sector wherein the farming and the trading interests are at loggerheads in protecting their (vested) interests. The direct purchase (when permitted with the APMC Act amendment) will reduce volumes in APMC *mandi*s and, therefore, *arthiyas*' hold on farmer produce, and the private wholesale markets (again under the APMC Act amendment) will create competition for these *arthiyas*/traders operating from APMC *mandi*s and the State agricultural marketing (*Mandi*) Board and its APMCs. This is the reason that instead of amending the APMC Act, which would upset the applecart of the *arthiyas* and the *Mandi* Board itself, the separate Act route was taken for contract farming. But, the state needs to recognize the primary stakeholder of the state's agricultural marketing system and the agricultural sector and then propose solutions, and not take the existing power play as given, if long term and sustainable solutions are to be sought. The best bet for making the CAs irrelevant would be to diversify the farm sector of the state as, when wheat, paddy, and cotton reduce in importance, the CAs as well as the state and its vested interest agencies would tend to wither away on their own. Further, the formal credit system would need to have better reach and more simplified procedures besides being bribe free to make a dent in the farm sector especially for small and marginal farmers who are excluded from the formal sector credit. The design of more innovative financing products for farm and allied sectors is what is needed for making institutional credit deliver.

This political economy of the state' s agricultural markets is also reflected in the report of the Vidhan Sabha Committee (PVSS, 2018) to examine the farmer and farm worker suicides in the state and recommend solutions to deal with it. Instead of pointing out that commission agent system in the state's agricultural market is one of the major reasons for farmer indebtedness due to the interlocking of product, input, and credit markets and therefore, recommending the abolition of the very system itself on the lines of Madhya Pradesh, the Committee emphasizes the 'strong undoable relationship'(nauh- maas ka rishta) between farmers and commission agents despite pointing out many cases of cheating and interlocking of credit and produce markets. Rather, it recommends that the informal money lending activity of the commission agents be brought under legal provisions. It even goes on to suggest that if in a case of a farmer suicide, there is a First Information Report (FIR) against the commission agent, then, a Superintendent of Police (SP) level official should examine the reasons for suicide before registering the FIR. Infact, the Committee did not even think it necessary to mention the issue of direct payment to farmers by the buying agencies for the sale of their produce which has been hanging fire for the last two decades. Even the draft farmers' policy 2018 only recommended a 20% cess on commission of CAs for creating a research and price stabilization fund for milk and non-MSP crops which would only burden the buyers as it would be passed on to them by the CAs (PSFFWC, 2018).

3 Union Level Reforms and Punjab

The conflict of interest has been cited as the main reason for taking out contract farming from the purview of the model APLM Act by the Union

Ministry of Agriculture and Farmer Welfare (MoAFW), ignoring the fact that there is even bigger conflict of interest in the case of provision of private wholesale markets which are still under the APLM(PF)A, 2017 (Singh, 2018b). Not only that, more recently, the Union government has enacted and notified two Acts which provide for separate channels of contract farming and direct purchase and limit the role of the APMC only to the market yard. So far as The Farmers' Produce Trade and Commerce (Promotion and Facilitation) Act, 2020 is concerned, it shifts the domain from the state to the Centre. Therefore, the relevance of the Model Acts is lost. However, the union Model Acts focus mostly on facilitation and promotion of agricultural markets and new channels like contract farming rather than regulation as the titles of the two Acts suggest (Singh, 2018b). Therefore, the logical questions that ought to be asked are: Do we need more *mandis* or more deregulation? Would only more *mandis* do or do we need more functional and effective *mandis*? Even if one agrees that APMCs are inefficient and ridden with corruption and malpractices, is moving away from them the solution? Should we throw the baby out with the bathwater or should we actually reform the APMCs as they are the last resort for millions of marginal and small farmers who would never be attractive to corporate buyers, individually or perhaps even collectively, through Farmer Producer Organisations? (Singh, 2020a).

The Farmers (Empowerment and Protection) Agreement on Price Assurance and Farm Services Act, 2020 is nothing but a badly designed contract farming Act. The use of the term 'farming agreement' itself is unusual as it can confuse with other arrangements like sharecropping or leasing agreements.' It also leaves out many sophisticated aspects of modern contract farming practice like contract cancellation clauses, delayed deliveries or purchase, and damages therein, and 'tournaments' in contract farming where farmers are made to compete with each other and paid as per relative performance which is banned in many countries. It is rather unfortunate that the Act links bonus or premium payment over and above the contract price with APMC *mandi* price or electronic market price which is anti-contract farming in nature. The price like many other basic aspects of contract should be left to the parties to negotiate and can't be tied to any other channel especially APMC price as the very rationale for bringing this law was to provide alternative channels to farmers and create competition for APMC markets as they were seen as not discovering the prices efficiently. Now, going back to the same *mandi* does not speak very well of the Act (Singh, 2020c).

Unlike The Farmers' Produce Trade and Commerce Act, this Act does not specify any penalties for any violations of the contract provisions which is surprising, to say the least. The Act is more about facilitation and promotion of the contract farming mechanism rather than its regulation! That the Act goes all the way to facilitate contract farming is clear from the fact that it mentions that the stock limits law (ESA ordinance) would not apply to contract farmed produce. Why should this provision of another Act be specifically mentioned in another law which has nothing to do with this law directly or indirectly? The aspects of farmer empowerment and protection mentioned in the title of the Act have been given a go by in its contents. The proof of any law is in its implementation but so far as farmer interest protection is concerned, these two Acts leave much to be desired in their design itself. (Singh, 2020c).

3.1 Punjab's APLM Amendments

The State of Punjab has amended the APMC Act recently (2017) keeping contract farming within the APLM Act, 2020 despite the MoAFW advising its exclusion and a separate legislation on it through its model Acts. The Punjab Agricultural Produce Markets (General) (Amendment) Rules, 2020 provide for special market yard, private market yard, producer market yard (Kisan *Mandi*) and producer consumer market yard (PCMY). The most important reform is the permission to establish private wholesale market as it would create direct competition for APMCs.

So far as the setting up of private wholesale market yard, which gives for the first time a choice of a public and a private *mandi* for the farmer seller, is concerned, the Act states 'The owner of private market yard shall develop the yard in an area not less than ten acres, by providing infrastructure facilities and amenities—and shall have a clear title with possession or lease hold rights by an agreement for a period of not less than thirty years. In any notified market area where the Government and the private markets shall co-exist: ....Provided that the above yard can be established only for the business relating to fruits, vegetables, livestock and its products, woods, flowers and cannot be established within a radius of five kms. from the existing notified principal or sub-market yards'(p. 4). This restriction applies to the other two markets i.e. PCMY and *Kisan Mandi* as well (p. 5). This provision shows that Punjab has protected its arthiyas and traders (kuccha and pucca arthiyas respectively) in the existing APMC *mandis* as most of them deal in foodgrains and cotton and, that too, for

FCI and CCI. By excluding these crops from new market arrangements, this vested interest has been largely left untouched by the new law.

As per the new Act, the private market operator is to ensure the payment of sale proceeds and issuing of Form-J to farmer or seller before lifting of agricultural produce, on the day of sale which is much needed. The other good aspect of the amended Act is that not only individuals but also groups, Farmer Producer Organisations and Farmer Producer Companies can also set up such markets as has happened in Maharashtra more recently. The license fee for private market year, PCMY, E-trading platform, and Kisan *mandi* would be Rs. 5 lakh, 2 lakh, 5 lakh and Rs. 2 lakh, respectively. Further, there is a bank guarantee of Rs. 25 lakh, 5 lakh, and 10 lakh for private market year, e-trading platform and *kisan mandi* respectively with the same being 50% or above if the player is a government agency or a co-operative institution.

The direct purchase provision (another important channel permitted since 2003 by model APMC Act) is extended to the existing licensees to facilitate direct purchase from producers with permission from the Chairperson of the Board (SAMB) at any place within the notified area of the APMC. Such licensees have to pay Rs. 10,000 fee to the Board. Even pre-harvest contracts which happen in fruit corps have been brought under this provision as it says 'Provided that if any licensee entered into a contract with a producer for standing crop of fruit and vegetable in the notified market area of the committee, such transaction shall be deemed sale and purchase of agricultural produce' (p. 20). An important question which arises is: when the model APLM Act, 2017 provides that the APMC would not regulate any transaction outside its market yard, how does this go with Model Act provision, the purpose of which was to curtail the powers of the APMCs. Further, now when the Union government has issued an Act on all buyers outside the APMC yard (new trade area), how does this Act comply with that by not regulating any transaction outside the market yard? Infact, the new trade area as the domain of the new central Act which is all places of transaction outside the APMC market yard/sub-yard would have serious implications for existing APMCs as there would be no levy of any market fee or cess on any purchase in new trade area by any buyer who would just need to have a Permanent Account Number (PAN) (Singh, 2020c). This would mean that it would become costlier to buy in APMC markets as the existing taxes would have to be paid to the APMC or the state agricultural marketing board. Soon, this tax differential would make all buyers and agents to shift to new trade area to lower their cost of procurement which would sound the death knell of the APMCs unless they fall in line to create a level playing field. The only hope for them for sometime is that the union and state government agencies may still keep buying through these APMC markets. Therefore, the new Act kill the APMC system by design! Most surprisingly, the Act still goes by state APMC notified produce when it defines scheduled farmer produce. Now, what is the relevance of APMC notified produce here when their domain is reduced only to the market yards? But, that would leave a part of the larger agricultural produce market completely unregulated despite two (union and state) Acts (Singh, 2020c).

So far as direct payment to farmer seller-a long pending and serious issue in Punjab, is concerned the Punjab APLM Act (2017) rules (2020) state: 'The Kaccha artiya or the buyer, as the case may be, shall make payment to the seller through electronic transfer after the weighment is over. If payment is not made by the *Kaccha Arhtiya* or buyer, as the case may be, in the manner, as stated above, then the same shall be recovered by the market committee concerned from him as an arrears of land revenue and the first lien shall be of seller's right and it shall be made to the seller concerned'. 'Provided further that the seller shall be at liberty to receive payment up to Rs. 10,000 in cash in a calendar month for the agricultural produce sold by him during that month... Delivery of agricultural produce after sale shall not be made or taken unless and until the *Kaccha Arhtiya* or, if the seller does not employ a *Kaccha Arhtiya*, the buyer has given to the seller a sale voucher in Form-J mentioning the payment mode and its authentication, the counterfoil of which shall be retained by the *Kaccha Arhtiya* or the buyer, as the case may be. Provided that a licensee entered into a contract with a producer under sub-rule (1-A), shall issue sale voucher in Form-J for the contract value of the agricultural produce' (pp. 20–21). This last provision shows that Punjab has retained direct purchase provision within the APMC domain despite the model Act of 2017 recommending its exclusion.

Punjab has made a new and unique provision in the amended APMC Act which states 'The Board shall levy price stabilization fund (PSF) on the sale of agricultural produce, which shall be collected by the market committee or the Board, as the case may be, from producer or seller, buyer, or *kaccha arhtiyas* in all the markets notified under Sections 7 to 7-F at the rates notified by the State Government from time to time. This fund shall not be utilized for the purpose other than the stabilization of prices of specified agricultural produce by the State government' (p. 23). Further, the owner of private market yard, PCMY and ***Kisan Mandi*** shall pay as contribution to the Board at the rate of 25% of the total collection of the user charges and shall deposit the same, into the 'Marketing Development Fund (MDF)' of the Board, during first week of next month. In case of e-trading platform, contribution to the MDF is @ 25% of total market fee collected on fruits and vegetables, @5% on livestock, and @60% on all other items of agricultural produce. Though one may question its levy on all market participants, but the provision of preventing its misuse is much needed given previous experience. Here too, the Union Act which creates a new trade area outside the APMC yard, bars the state governments from charging any levy or text from direct buyers or contract farming agencies. This has serious financial implications for the states as they would now find it difficult to maintain the APMC infrastructure and that would be another blow to the APMC leading to their premature death.

Also, surprisingly, the amended Act has no mention of livestock produce throughout and mentions it only in case of MDF. It is surprising that Punjab has not found it questionable to include livestock in APMC market domain when the nature and dynamics of the two markets are entirely different. More importantly, Punjab could have thought of abolishing the ***arthiya*** system on the lines of what MP did in 1985 but that is a tall order for Punjab to follow given the political economy of its agricultural markets (Singh, 2020a).

It remains to be seen what position Punjab takes and how long it would take to amend its APLM Act, 2020 to provide for the supremacy of Union legislation. It is also not a different matter that the new Union Acts are passed without much consultation with the states and other stakeholders despite the fact that they take away the right of the states, lack both in design and comprehensive protection of farmer interest in direct purchase as well as contract farming arrangement (Singh, 2020b) like the 2003 and the 2017 model APMC Acts and the 2018 model APLCFSA which failed to make contract farming inclusive by not providing for group contracts unlike the Thailand policy on contract farming which mandated and encouraged group contracts (Singh, 2005). In Thailand, the state which partnered with the private agribusiness contracting agencies for extension and low interest credit to contract farmers through its department of agricultural extension and the bank for agriculture and agricultural cooperatives (BAAC) made it mandatory to have contracts with groups of farmers to protect the farmer interest and even provided training and exposure to contract farmers (Singh, 2005). Groups contracts are where farmers sign contract with a contracting firm or agency as one group. This helps them bargain better as it involves larger volumes of produce and also deal with contracting agencies more effectively as compared with individual farmers dealing with contracting agencies.

Unfortunately, the union Model APLM Act 2017 and the Punjab APLM Act 2017 (Rules 2020) still define CA as someone who would collect payment and pay to the seller (MoAFW, 2017; Singh, 2020a). This is startling for an Act of 2017 to propose as it is not clear what logic there could be in not paying the seller directly for her produce. This is a very regressive step in the Act and perhaps reflects the political economy of agricultural markets in India where the CAs have acquired a political clout and the state governments are not able to work for the primary stakeholder of such markets i.e. farmers. Even the position of Punjab state *Mandi* board is highly contested between farmer interest groups and the *arthiya* interest groups represented by farmers' unions and *arthiya* association, respectively. Infact, an amendment to the APMC Act in 2016 provides for three positions of Chairman, Senior Vice-Chairman and Vice-Chairman of the Board to be nominated by the state government.

The central agencies like FCI have been eager to pay directly to farmers but it is the state government which does not want this to happen! This is so because there is serious interlocking of output and credit and output and input markets where the CAs also engage in money lending to farmers informally and illegally and want their repayment to be recovered through this mode of indirect payments (through the CAs where the cheque is also in the name of the CA) to farmers by buying agencies.

There has been a constant battle on direct payments to farmers for their produce by buying agencies between the two lobbies in the state. Whereas the farmer lobby would like to have direct payments, the arthiya lobby opposes it tooth and nail. This is so as direct payments hit the business of interlocking of credit, input, and output markets run by arthiyas where a parchi (slip) system prevails for lending in kind to farmers and recovery of payments at the time of sale of produce (Singh and Dhaliwal, 2011). Despite a Committee of the Punjab government recommending direct payments by procuring agencies besides lowering the number of CAs in APMC markets in 1998, there has been no movement forward on this issue (Singh and Bhogal, 2015).

4 Way Forward and Conclusions

Under the Industrial Policy of the state (2017), the fruit and vegetable produce is deregulated from the APMC Act (GoP, 2017). Even the model APLM Act, 2017 did not exclude fruits and vegetables from the domain of the APMCs, unlike the proposals made during the UPA rule (Singh, 2020b). It is said that the policy has blindly copied the provision of delisting of fruit and vegetable produce from the new model APMC Act. Rather, it should have used it as an incentive to those buyers who go to farmer to procure directly or through contract farming arrangement.

Presently, the state has market infrastructure only in the form of APMC market yards, warehouses (used for food grains), and cold storages (used mostly for table/processing potato and seed potato), many of the latter not being warehouse receipt eligible. Punjab needs to focus on developing perishable produce markets for demand driven agribusiness development of its agricultural sector.

More importantly, Punjab needs to focus on aggregating its farmers for dealing with modern markets by making use of the Producer Companies Act which is more business like legal form of organization and is being supported in a big way by the Union government (Singh and Singh, 2014). The new farm produce trade and commerce Act, 2020 provides for e-markets being established by Farmer Producer Organisations (FPOs) though there are issues with the way the FPO is defined (Singh, 2020c). Punjab has missed the bus already on this once. A study of 49 clusters across Indian states including two in Punjab found that one cluster in Punjab (Fazilka) did not have any FPO at all and the other (Ludhiana) had 9 out of which 7 were defunct/non-existent (Arya CWS and Tata Trusts, 2018). Earlier, a study had found all the six PCs promoted by a private joint venture project in perishables non-functional in Malerkotla area (Singh and Singh, 2014). Given this, Punjab should not miss the bus again. It is important to realize that individual farmer-based model of agro development would not work as the nature of market has changed with new economic policy globally and in India.

Further, Punjab should plan and execute planned production and marketing strategy to achieve crop and enterprise diversification and agro-industrial development for domestic and export markets as has been achieved by countries like Thailand and Taiwan. For this, marketing development and marketing infrastructure and institutions are extremely crucial. Then only can primary producers can hope to get a part of the surplus generated in the food and fibre value chains.

References

Arya CWS and Tata Trusts. (2018) *A Comprehensive Study for Identification for Vibrant FPO Clusters for Effective Marketing Integration*, by Arya collateral warehousing services Pvt. Ltd. for Tata Trusts, Mumbai.

GoP (Government of Punjab). (2017, October) *Industrial and Business Development Policy, 2017*, Department of Industries and Commerce, Government of Punjab, Chandigarh.

Krishnamurthy, M. (2014) The Political Economy of Agricultural Markets: Insights from Within and Across Regions, in IDFC Rural Development Network. *India Rural Development Report*, Orient Blackswan, New Delhi, pp. 59–79.

MoAFW. (2017, April) *Model Act (The--- State/UT Agricultural Produce and Livestock Marketing (Promotion and Facilitation) Act, 2017*, MoAFW, Department of Agriculture, Co-operation and Farmers' Welfare, Government of India.

MoAFW. (2018, February) *Model Act (The--- State/UT Agricultural Produce and Livestock Contract Farming and Services (Promotion and Facilitation) Act, 2018*, MoAFW, Department of Agriculture, Co-operation and Farmers' Welfare, Government of India.

PMB (Punjab *Mandi* Board). (2006) *Manual of The Punjab Agricultural Produce Markets Law- Acts, Rules and Bye-laws*, PMB, Chandigarh.

PSFFWC (Punjab State Farmers' and Farm Workers' Commission). (2018, June) *Punjab State Farmers' Policy*, Draft, PSFFWC, Mohali.

PVSS (Punjab Vidhan Sabha Secretariat). (2018, March) *Report of the House Committee to enquire into farmer suicides and economic distress of farm workers due to indebtedness in Punjab state and suggest ways out*, PVSS, Chandigarh.

Singh, S. (2005) Role of the State in Contract Farming in Thailand: Experience and Lessons, *ASEAN Economic Bulletin*, 22(2): 217–228.

Singh, S. (2013, July 9) Regulating Contract Farming- Punjab Way, *The Tribune*, Chandigarh.

Singh, S. (2016) Arthiyas in Punjab's APMC Mandis: Inadequate Analysis and Solutions, *EPW*, 51.

Singh, S. (2018a, June 25) Seeds of a New Policy, *The Tribune*, Chandigarh, In Focus, p. 9.

Singh, S. (2018b) Reforming Agricultural Markets in India: A Tale of Two Model Acts, *EPW*, 53(51): 44–49.

Singh, S. (2020a, February 17) Amending Agri Market Law but Half- heartedly, *The Tribune*, Chandigarh.

Singh, S (2020b, June 19) Reform by Stealth, *Frontline*, 92–95.

Singh, S. (2020c, June 21) Tale of Two Flawed Agri Ordinances, *The Hindu Bussines Line*.

Singh, S. (2020d, June 9) Haryana Pushes for Sustainable Farming, *The Hindu Business Line*.

Singh, S., and Bhogal, S. (2015) Commission Agent System: Significance in Contemporary Agricultural Economy of Punjab, *EPW*, 50(45): 56–62.

Singh, S., and Dhaliwal, T. K. (2011) *Taking more than a Commission- a Critique of the, Commission Agent System in Punjab Agriculture*, Delhi: Aakar Books.

Singh, S., and Singh, T. (2014) *Producer Companies in India: Organisation and Performance*, New Delhi: Allied.

Impact of COVID-19 Pandemic on Dairy Industry in Punjab: Major Concerns and Policy Options

Naresh Singla

1 Brief Background

The livestock sector continues to drive rural livelihoods and contribute significantly to the agricultural economy of Punjab. The livestock sector accounts for 36.93% share in agricultural GVA of the state and witnesses an average growth of 5.40% during the period of 2012–2013 to 2018–2019 as compared to only 0.8% in crop sector (GoP, 2020). About 28.5% of the agricultural workforce are engaged in the livestock sector (Subash and Kaur, 2017). Milk is the main product of the livestock sector, which accounts for about 80% of the total value of output of livestock (NDDB, 2014).

Punjab produces about 12,599 thousand tonnes of milk and accounts for 6.7% of the milk production in the national milk basket (NDDB, 2018–19a). On an average, about two-third of the milk produced is marketed, while one-third is retained for home consumption. The major share of milk in Punjab is handled by unorganized sector, largely dominated by private milk traders/vendors/milkmen, who buy milk directly

N. Singla (✉)
Department of Economic Studies, School of Social Sciences, Central University of Punjab, Bathinda, India

S. Singh et al. (eds.), *Covid-19 Pandemic and Economic Development*,
https://doi.org/10.1007/978-981-16-4442-9_7

from producers and supply milk either directly to the urban consumers, or to informal institutional buyers (restaurants, tea stalls, etc.) or wholesalers and local retailers such as halwai shops/creameries/city-based private dairy shops, etc. (Kumar et al., 2011; Kaur and Singh, 2020).

Punjab also has a well-established network of milk cooperative societies at village level, which started as early as in 1973 on the pattern of Amul model under apex body, Punjab State Cooperative Milk Producers' Federation Ltd. (popularly known as Milkfed Punjab). As a result, Punjab has developed a vast network of milk cooperatives with 8,018 village level dairy cooperative societies, with about 4.10 lakh milk producers as its members, affiliated to 11 district milk producers' unions with 10 milk processing plants, which on an average procure about 17.66 lakh litres of milk per day against a consolidated milk handling capacity of around 21.85 lakh litres per day (NDDB, 2018–19b). Besides, Nestle India Limited, which is one of the first private players in the organized dairy sector, is also involved in milk procurement in Punjab since 1961. In 2015, Nestle procured about 1.2 million litres of milk per day from about one lakh farmers (Punjabi, 2015). Recently, Punjab has also seen the entry of Baani Milk Producer Company (MPC) Ltd. in 2014, which was operationalized as a producer company under the guidance of NDDB Dairy Services (NDS), a wholly-owned subsidiary of NDDB. Baani MPC Ltd. has enrolled 51,590 milk producers, of whom about 25% are women and 35% small holders from 1218 villages in 9 districts of Punjab (NDDB, 2018–19a). Thus, dairy sector in Punjab has witnessed rapid growth and structural shifts in terms of establishment of dairy cooperatives, producer companies and private dairy companies, which are involved into procurement, processing and retailing of milk. These are seen as one of the several pathways to diversify and boost the rural income and livelihoods in crisis ridden agrarian state of Punjab (Kaur and Singla, 2018a; Kaur, 2019).

2 Dairy Industry and COVID-19

Since milk is a highly perishable agricultural commodity, demand and supply of milk were quite volatile even in the pre-covid-19 period. The demand for milk and milk products is ever rising, elastic and influenced by several factors such as rising urbanization, increase in dietary consciousness such as preference for low fat milk, rise in income level, etc., whereas, supply of milk is often constrained by the several factors such as type of bovine, quality and cost of feed, availability of credit and risk-cover, availability of health and breeding services, functioning of livestock markets, information asymmetry in the markets, etc. (Rajeshwaran et al., 2014). COVID-19 pandemic has spread all over the world. In order to reduce the mortality rates, the different countries have responded to the pandemic by imposing lockdown and stringent measures such as imposition of curfew as was done by Punjab. Covid-19 has disrupted all the economic activities. The covid-19 driven lockdown is unique as both demand and supply have fallen down. All the economic activities of the economy have responded differently to the covid-19 pandemic.

However, the disruptions in agriculture and allied sectors has posed a major challenge as the vast majority of the workforce is still engaged in agricultural and allied activities, which may have serious implications for food production and in ensuring food security. It is expected that the implications will be more severe in various sub-sectors of agriculture in the crisis ridden rural economy of Punjab, where the income from farming is continuously dwindling, costs of production are rising and farm indebtedness and suicides are rampant.

As outlined earlier, the dairy sector is one of the major economic activities within the agricultural sector, which has performed much better as compared to all other sub-sectors of agriculture in Punjab. However, the dairy sector in Punjab is also likely to face several problems and challenges in the ongoing period of covid-19 as are faced globally and nationally. For example, in Canada, the milk producers have resorted to dumping of milk as the processing facilities are closed due to Covid-19. However, the supply chain of milk was found to be more resilient to the impacts of COVID-19 than other sectors as milk producers are financially more stable, losses are pooled and production/marketing efforts are relatively well coordinated (Weersink et al., 2020). Similarly, in the US, the impact of covid-19 has led to a shift in demand due to unpredictable and dramatic societal changes, which have lowered the milk prices, disrupted the supply chain and left the dairy industry without any government support (Mulvey et al., 2020).

On the other hand, in India, it is argued that smallholder dairy sector has adjusted well during Covid-19 (Lele et al., 2020). However, an empirical study by Popat, Ashish, Kadam and Mane (2020) in Satara district of Maharashtra revealed that during the period of Covid-19, prices of milk paid to the milk producers and milk procurement by dairy cooperatives were lower and inconsistent than those during the pre-covid-19 period. The payment to milk producers was also irregular during Covid-19 period. Still, the evidences of the likely impacts of Covid-19 on the dairy industry in terms of milk sales, procurement, costs of production and logistics, animal services, etc. are largely missing in the case of India in general and Punjab in particular. In this context, it becomes imperative to explore how does the dairy sector in Punjab, particularly the milk producers, get affected due to the outbreak of Covid-19? How do the milk producers and the state government respond to Covid-19 pandemic to ensure a sustainable dairy production system in the post-Covid-19 period? The first section explores the impact of Covid-19 on milk sales and procurement by dairy cooperatives vis-à-vis vendor-driven markets, while the second section brings out impact on cost of milk production and logistics. The effects on animal and training services are discussed in sector three of the paper. Last section attempts to find out likely impacts on interlinked credit transactions in formal and informal credit markets.

2.1 Decline in Sale and Procurement of Milk

During Covid-19 curfew, there was a sudden drop in demand for milk. The sale of dairy products had gone down due to health concerns, there was reduction of income of the dairy households, migration of labour to home states happened and there was closure of sweet shops and eateries. The small milk producers, who mainly supply milk to unorganized milk vendors suffered more than those who sold to well organized cooperative system of Milkfed and various private diaries. Some of the milk producers, particularly those selling to traditional milk vendors had to dispose of their milk at a price lower than the cost of production. The Milkfed too faced difficulty during Covid-19 to handle the additional milk procurement due to a surge in fresh milk supply and a concurrent major drop in demand for milk and milk products. The daily milk procurement was 26.5 lakh litre per day as on April 1, 2020, which was around 32% cent higher than their installed capacity. Some private milk plants agreed to procure milk from the farmers on the condition of deferred payment, while others started to practice a weekly milk holiday i.e. no milk collection on that particular day (Kaur and Singh, 2020). The disruptions in supply chain in milk procurement by private players and unorganized diaries led to diversion of milk towards the milk cooperatives, resulting in subdued producer prices (Rath, 2020). The Milkfed had to reduce procurement rate by Rs. 3 per litre for cow milk and Rs. 4.50 per litre for buffalo milk during

Covid-19. However, Milkfed has performed reasonably well as compared to milk vendors and traditional local diaries. Milkfed converted additional milk into skimmed milk powder (SMP) and ghee. Milkfed has also started door to door delivery of milk and milk products in order to release the pressure of excess supply.

2.2 *Increase in Cost of Dairy Production and Logistics*

The cost of producing milk and milk products has gone up during Covid-19 period. The cost of producing milk has increased due to the increase in cost of feed, while transportation of green fodder and wheat husk (tudi) is also affected due to the lockdown. About Rs. 350 billion feed industry in India is also reeling under severe crises as additional costs of logistics and raw materials accrued due to lockdown can not be passed on to the end users vis-a-vis the farming community engaged in rearing of cattle and other subsidiary activities. Further, disruption of logistics is a much more severe problem in livestock sector than crop sector as shortage of feed will likely lead to starvation and death of the milch animals. The problem is also compounded on account of the fact that dairy animals have short production cycle and animals require feed on a day to day basis to complete their cycle (Kumar et al., 2020).

2.3 *Rise in Animal Health and Their Productivity Issues*

Animal health services, which are already limited, are affected at several places due to imposition of lockdown, which has restricted the movement of veterinary doctors and availability of veterinary medicines. Though the services of veterinary doctors come under essential services, they do not operate as they did in pre-Covid period for fear of Covid-19. Further, most of the resources are diverted for prevention, diagnostics and minimization of COVID-19 impacts (Kumar et al., 2020). This has raised serious concerns in terms of adverse impacts on the health and productivity level of the dairy animals. A study by Kaur and Singla (2018b) reveals that provision of veterinary service and technical services provided by Milkfed to milk producers turned out to be one of the major reasons for their association with Milkfed. Therefore, it is likely that effects of Covid-19 on animal health and their milk productivity will be relatively low among Milkfed farmers than those selling milk to other channels due to better access to veterinary and technical services.

2.4 *Impact on Interlinked Credit Transactions*

Milk production is largely carried out as complimentary activity along with crop production. The regular flow of cash income from dairying not only helps the milk producers to buy crop inputs and animal feed for their cattle, but it also helps them to resettle the credit transactions done in informal and formal credit markets. It can be corroborated with the study by Singh, Kaur and Kingra (2008), which revealed that higher the income from dairying, lesser is the extent of indebtedness among the farmers in Punjab. However, during Covid-19, due to lower price for milk, effect on milk productivity, lack of assured procurement, availability of animal feed and lack of veterinary services due to lockdown, there is not only reduction of income from dairying, but also in regularity of income, which has serious implications for the producers, particularly landless and small farmers. Therefore, the milk producers are unable to pay/clear off their dues.

3 Policy Suggestions

In view of the emergence of the COVID-19 crisis, the following policy suggestions can help to protect the dairy industry in general and milk producers in particular to deal with COVID-19 like situation in Punjab.

a. Since milk procurement through dairy cooperatives tends to be more resilient than vendor-driven milk markets and losses to the milk producers are more in vendor-driven markets during the COVID-19, there is a need to create local milk grids, and linking milk grids to vendors, organized dairies and processors in the state and across adjoining milk deficient regions of other states/UT such as Jammu and Kashmir and Rajasthan. This will help to clear off the excess supply of milk during situation like COVID-19 and therefore, help the milk producers in getting remunerative price rather than depressed price.
b. There is a need to strengthen and expand the capacity of Milkfed, private plants and producer companies through easy financing from the commercial banks, cooperative banks and other financial lending agencies to meet working capital requirements of dairy plants, which will help to increase their operational capacity and meet the challenges of COVID-19 like situation.

c. Also, revamping of functioning of village level dairy cooperatives is required in order to ensure uninterrupted supply of cattle feed, provision of veterinary and technical services at milk producer's door steps and other inputs to meet the challenge of COVID-19 pandemic and afterwards.
d. The milk producer companies can play a much greater role than cooperatives during the period of COVID-19 by ensuring fair prices for milk, transparent transactions, ensuring participation of landless and small land holders and women, dairy inputs and technical services, etc.
e. Last but not the least, the setting up of a milk price stabilization fund can pave the way for stabilizing the income of the dairy producers, which in turn can help to sustain the diary sector post-COVID.

References

Government of Punjab. (2020) Economic Survey of Punjab (2019–20). Economic and Statistical Organisation, Department of Planning.

Kaur, I., and Singh, P. (2020, April 27) COVID-19 Effect: Dairy Sector in the Doldrums, *The Tribune*, Chandigarh.

Kaur, M. (2019) An Economic Analysis of Production and Marketing of Milk through Formal and Informal Milk Markets in Punjab, Unpublished PhD. thesis submitted to Department of Economic Studies, Central University of Punjab, Bathinda.

Kaur, M., and Singla, N. (2018a) Growth and Structural Transformations in Dairy Sector of India, *Indian Journal of Dairy Science*, 71(4): 422–429.

Kaur, M., and Singla, N. (2018b) Farmer's Participation in Formal Milk Markets in Punjab: How Inclusive and How Effective? In S. Singh, T. Satyanaryana and V. Kumar (Eds.), *Agribusiness Potential of Punjab*, Hyderabad: Indian Society of Agricultural Marketing, pp: 60–70.

Kumar, A, Nuthalapati, C. S. R., and Saxena, R. (2020) *Coronavirus Pandemic: Death Knell for Livestock and Livelihoods*, New Delhi: IFPRI, South Asia.

Kumar, A., Staal, S. J., and Singh, D. K. (2011) Smallholder Dairy Farmers' Access to Modern Milk Marketing Chains in India, *Agricultural Economics Research Review*, 24: 243–254.

Lele, U., Bansal, S., and Meenakshi, J. V. (2020) Health and Nutrition of India's Labour Force and COVID-19 Challenges, *Economic and Political Weekly*, 55(21): 13–16.

Mulvey, C., Peters, R., and Rutkowski, N. (2020) Impacts of COVID-19 on the US Dairy Industry. A Project Submitted to Worcester Polytechnic Institute, in partial fulfilment of the requirements for the degree of Bachelor of Science, Worcester, MA.

NDDB. (2014) Dairying in Punjab: A Statistical Profile 2014, National Dairy Development Board, Anand, Gujarat.

NDDB. (2018–19a) Milk Production by States/UT, National Dairy Development Board, Anand, Gujarat. Accessed at https://www.nddb.coop/information/stats/milkprodstate.

NDDB. (2018–19b) Annual Report, 2018–19, National Dairy Development Board, Anand, Gujarat.

Popat, S, Ashish, J., Kadam, R. S., and Mane, S. P. (2020) Effects of COVID-19 on Dairy Farming (A Case Study of Sangavi Village in Phaltan Tehsil of Satara District, MH), *JuniKhyat*, 10(6): 16–30.

Punjabi, M. (2015) *Nestle India's Dairy Development Initiative in the Punjab Region*, Rome: FAO.

Rajeshwaran, S., Naik, G., andDhas, A. C. (2014) Rising Milk Price–A Cause for Concern on Food Security. Working paper: 472, Indian Institute of Management, Bangalore.

Rath, D. (2020, April 29) A New White Revolution: How COVID-19 Could Benefit the Dairy Industry. *Financial Express*, Delhi.

Singh, S., Kaur, M., and Kingra, H. S. (2008) Indebtedness Among Farmers in Punjab, *Economic and Political Weekly*, 43(26/27): 130–136.

Subash, S. P., and Kaur, P. (2017) Sustainability of Livestock Sector in Punjab, *Indian Journal of Economics and Development*, 13(2a): 413–420.

Weersink, A., Massow, M. V., and McDougall, B. (2020) Economic Thoughts on the Potential Implications of COVID-19 on the Canadian Dairy and Poultry Sectors, *Canadian Journal of Agricultural Economics* (Special Issue Article): 1–6, https://doi.org/10.1111/cjag.12240.

Making Punjab's Urban Informal Sector More Resilient While Securing Livelihoods During Post-COVID-19 Times

Varinder Jain

1 Introduction

Onslaught of COVID-19 pandemic has dampened economic growth prospects across the globe (IMF, 2020). Both lives and livelihoods have been lost at a pace never seen before (Jackson et al., 2020; Sumner et al., 2020). Spread of COVID-19 pandemic across the globe has been alarming (Jain and Singh, 2020). In India also, the incidence of infections is evident across all the states. Punjab, being no exception, has also felt the pangs of this pandemic. Here too, the lives and livelihoods are being lost. As far as the latter is concerned, it is feared that the urban informal sector might have experienced significant losses. One may base such apprehension on two considerations: first, the firms in urban informal sector on account of their limited scale of operation and a variety of technical, marketing, financial and other constraints remain economically fragile with almost no resilience to offset a shock of such mammoth magnitude that shook the world economies. Owing to such fragility, most of these enterprises lack the wherewithal to support their workforce with either full or partial remuneration during lockdowns which were observed

V. Jain (✉)
Institute of Deveploment Studies, Jaipur, India

S. Singh et al. (eds.), *Covid-19 Pandemic and Economic Development*,
https://doi.org/10.1007/978-981-16-4442-9_8

to avert spread of COVID-19 infections; second, the urban informal sector remains characterised by the pervasiveness of livelihood insecurity—here, the workers, both wageworkers and the self-employed, remain economically vulnerable and occupationally-insecure, but with degrees of vulnerability varying vis-à-vis their skill and migration status (Jain, 2010).

In such a situation, an effort to build preparedness against any such future threat should focus on devising ways by which the resilience of informal enterprises may be strengthened and at the same time, ways should be devised to generate decent work conditions in Punjab's urban informal sector. With this focus, this paper discusses the significance and sectoral diversity in Punjab's urban informal sector (in Section 2). Section 3 examines ways to strengthen business resilience and Section 4 focuses on the question of livelihood security. Section 5 concludes the policy brief.

2 Significance of Urban Informal Sector in Punjab's Economy

Formal sector being a relatively small part of Punjab's economy remains limited to organised manufacturing, banking, health, insurance and other similar sectors. Informal sector, on the other hand, comprises 14.64 lakh enterprises that generate gross value added (GVA) worth Rs. 30,962 crore besides engaging 24.79 lakh workers (NSSO, 2016).

Informal sector activity is found in both rural and urban areas of Punjab (Fig. 1) but its relatively large dominance is found in the latter where 8.49 lakh enterprises generate GVA worth Rs. 23,015 crore. These enterprises account for 57.98 per cent of total informal enterprises in

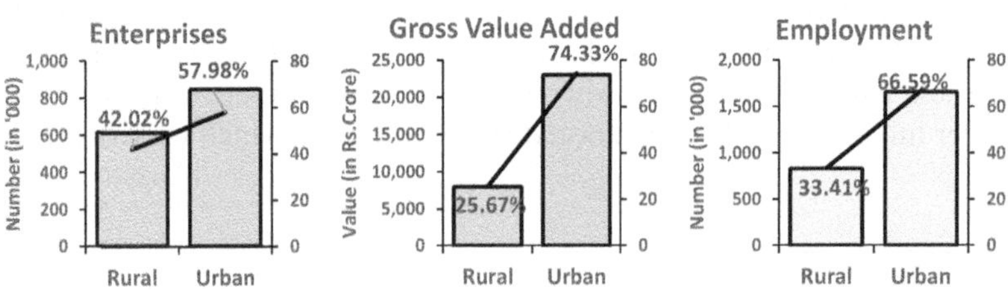

Fig. 1 Spatial distribution of informal sector in Punjab (*Source* Based on NSSO [2016])

Punjab. In fact, the GVA generated by these enterprises account for 74.33 per cent of the total GVA generated in the informal sector. These urban informal enterprises provide employment to 16.51 lakh workers which, in comparison to rural segment, remains almost double—share of urban segment in total informal sector employment is as high as 66.59 per cent.

2.1 *Sectoral Composition of Punjab's Urban Informal Sector*

Urban informal sector represents a heterogeneous set of activities which can be broadly classified into three key categories, viz. manufacturing, trade and other services. A glance at Fig. 2 indicates a significant presence of all these three categories in Punjab's urban informal sector. However, among the three, it is trade that accounts for a relatively large share in number of enterprises, gross value added and employment. Other services constitute the second major component of the Punjab's urban informal sector. The segment of manufacturing remains the third but a very important constituent of Punjab's urban informal sector. In fact, most of the small-scale industry in Punjab bears the characteristics of informal enterprises which per se are experiencing the challenges of survival in this era of competition (Singh and Jain, 2007; Jain, 2016).

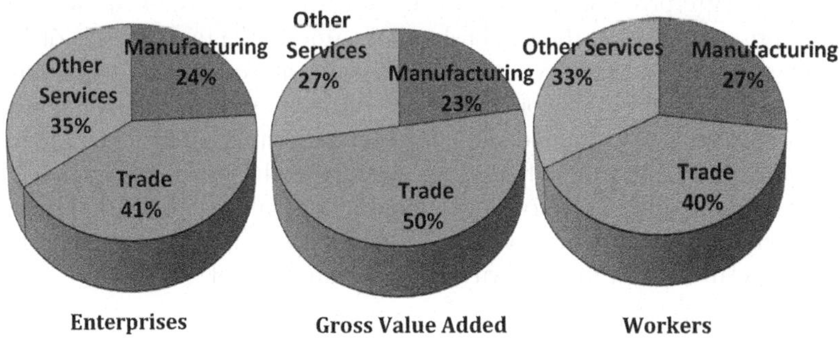

Fig. 2 Sectoral composition of Punjab's urban informal sector (*Source* Based on NSSO [2016])

Table 1 Key Ratios Depicting Firm Size in Punjab's Urban Informal Sector

Key Ratio	*Enterprise Type*	*Manufacturing*	*Trading*	*Other Services*	*All*
Fixed Assets per Enterprise*	OAE	1.41	1.98	1.62	1.72
	Establishment	6.16	7.86	9.75	7.86
	All	2.98	3.79	3.29	3.42
GVA per Enterprise*	OAE	1.17	1.73	1.10	1.36
	Establishment	5.25	6.88	6.17	6.23
	All	2.51	3.31	2.14	2.71
GVA Per Worker*	OAE	0.89	1.39	0.98	1.13
	Establishment	1.33	2.05	1.34	1.62
	All	1.15	1.75	1.16	1.40
Fixed Assets per Worker*	OAE	1.08	1.60	1.45	1.42
	Establishment	1.56	2.35	2.11	2.04
	All	1.37	2.00	1.79	1.76

Note *implies that the values are in Rs. Lakh
Source Based on NSSO [2016]

3 Business Resilience

3.1 Nature of Enterprises: Firm Size

Across the segments of manufacturing, trading and other services, the informal enterprises in urban Punjab operate either as Own Account Enterprises (OAEs) or the Establishments. Among the two, the size of the former in terms of fixed assets per enterprise or worker and gross value added per enterprise or worker remains relatively small (Table 1). These firms operating with limited capital, generate limited gross value added. Similarly, they also suffer from low worker productivity. The establishments, on the other hand, owing to their better scale of operation, remain relatively better. But, they too remain exposed to competition and suffer from a relatively low productivity of labour and capital.

3.2 Growth Constraints: Nature and Magnitude

Similar to other informal sector enterprises, the firms in Punjab's urban informal sector experience a variety of constraints ranging from erratic power supply, raw material shortages to marketing and financial constraints. Table 2 indicates the percentage of firms experiencing

Table 2 Distribution of Punjab's informal sector firms by category and growth constraints (% of all reporting)

Sector > Type of firm > Constraint	*Manufacturing*			*Trading*			*Other Services*		
	OAE	*ESTB*	*All*	*OAE*	*ESTB*	*All*	*OAE*	*ESTB*	*All*
I	11.85	13.99	12.59	0.59	3.52	1.44	13.53	5.84	11.97
II	2.43	3.22	2.70	0.16	2.77	0.92	0.39	0.34	0.38
III	64.09	38.29	55.13	56.36	33.93	49.81	48.38	45.16	47.72
IV	1.07	1.49	1.22	8.19	4.54	7.12	2.04	3.59	2.35
V	12.80	11.50	12.34	22.19	25.26	23.09	11.08	10.98	11.06
VI	0.42	14.35	5.26	0.12	14.32	4.27	0.00	12.96	2.63
VII	1.58	12.69	5.43	0.55	6.75	2.36	0.46	10.56	2.51
VIII	0.00	0.00	0.00	0.00	0.00	0.00	0.00	0.37	0.08
IX	5.77	4.46	5.32	11.84	8.91	10.98	24.13	10.19	21.30

Note I-Erratic power supply; II-Shortage of raw materials; III-Shinkage/fall of demand; IV-Non-availability/ high cost of credit; V-Non-recovery of financial dues; VI-Non-availability of labour as and when needed; VII-Non-availability of skilled labour as and when needed; VIII-Labour disputes and related problems; IX-Others
Source Based on NSSO [2016]

different constraints. A relatively high percentage of firms in manufacturing remain exposed to the constraints related to fall in demand, non-recovery of financial dues besides other issues related to erratic power supply and labour-related issues. Similar has been the case with trading and other services.

3.3 *Access to Institutional Finance*

The operational dynamism of informal enterprises remains conditioned by the financial constraints experienced by them. Most often, these firms suffer from the paucity of capital. In such a situation, it is the access to credit that facilitates the smoothening of their day-to-day business. One may assume that the enterprises in Punjab's urban informal sector might be having a better access to credit. But, an inquiry into the relative state of access to formal credit across major Indian states reveals the opposite (Fig. 3) where it is found that access to formal credit by Punjab's urban informal enterprises across manufacturing, trading and other services enterprises remains much lower than their counterparts in other Indian states. Such backwardness in access to formal credit impedes

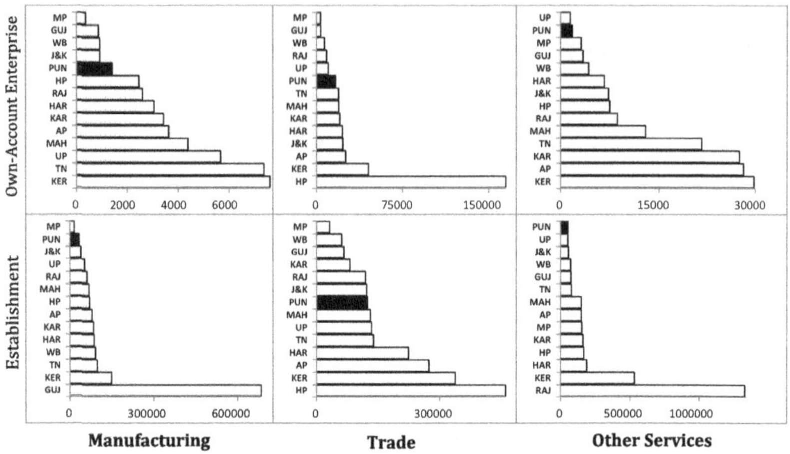

Fig. 3 Relative state of formal credit in Punjab's urban informal sector (*Source* Based on NSSO [2016])

growth and thereby calls for better access to finance as formal credit access is found to have a positive impact on the operational dynamism of informal enterprises (IFC, 2010).

3.4 *Stepping up Business Resilience: Key Considerations*

In this situation, it is pertinent to build business resilience of informal enterprises. In fact, the whole notion of business resilience centres upon seven pillars, viz. (1) resource adequacy, (2) technical edge, (3) market knowledge, (4) product uniqueness, (5) commercial prudence, (6) manpower planning and (7) networking (Table 3).

So, any effort to step-up business resilience should concentrate on strengthening capabilities across various sub-domains of these seven key pillars. Here, it needs to be mentioned that at present, the informal enterprises do not fare well across this resilience scale as Jain (2020) found Jalandhar's sports good manufacturing enterprises at a very low levels of business resilience which requires urgent corrective action.

Table 3 Key constituents of the business resilience

	Broad dimension		*Specific dimension*
A	Resource adequacy	A	Sufficiency of working capital
		B	Ability to raise funds when needed
		C	Easy access to required quality raw material without monopoly price
B	Technical edge	A	Knowledge & adoption of latest production techniques
		B	Worker adoption & adaptability to new techniques
		C	Ability to add efficiency and effectiveness in production process
C	Market knowledge	A	Knowledge of market size, customers, their tastes & demands
		B	Competitors' threat to potential business growth
D	Product uniqueness	A	Product design as per customers' tastes & preferences
		B	Ability to innovate in product design
E	Commercial prudence	A	Ability to produce at low cost while maintaining quality standard
		B	Ability to foresee future demand and arrange production accordingly
F	Manpower planning	A	Adequate access to skilled/trained workforce
		B	Possibility of outsourcing production process to external small units
G	Networking	A	Ability to develop sound networks in input & output markets
		B	Ability to enhance market coverage beyond national boundaries

Source Jain (2020)

3.5 *State as Facilitator*

Urban informal sector in Punjab in general and the manufacturing sector in particular has remained a victim of state's apathetic attitude. The state has not drawn any specific schemes for the upgradation of the informal enterprise in the manufacturing sector—same is the case with the trading sector. It could have been better if the state rather than being only a tax collection agency, might have played the role of a facilitator. If the state could have paid attention to the woes of informal enterprises, definitely some concrete solutions might have emerged. But, it is sad to learn that existing government apparatus could not provide a workable solution to the woes of informal sector enterprises.

Nonetheless, one should note that Punjab's small-scale industry possesses good potential. With a little state support, it may emerge again. For this, the state should evolve a serious strategy to rejuvenate informal manufacturing enterprises. At present, these enterprises are striving to sustain themselves in an era of competition. Sudden onslaught of COVID-19 pandemic has made them economically fragile.. In fact, there are several segments such as sports goods, machine tools, textiles, etc. which were known once across the world for their growth performance. With little support, they may emerge again.

4 Livelihood Security

An analysis of NSSO's 73rd round on informal enterprises reveals that among informal sector workers, the share of working owners is as high as 54.35 per cent. These working owners either operate 'own account enterprises' or head Establishments. Hired workers, helper/apprentice and other workers are the other categories. Among these, a major share is of the hired workers (35.83 percent), within which the share of informal hired workers is as high as 93.69 per cent (Table 4).

In fact, these are informal hired workers who suffer from pervasive livelihood insecurity in Punjab's urban informal sector. Jain (2010) defined wageworkers' livelihood insecurity across five domains, viz. job insecurity, economic insecurity, functional insecurity, agency insecurity and recognition insecurity. The informal hired workers suffer from all these five forms of insecurity. Owing to this, they never enjoy their work which has a bearing on their earnings and productivity. So, there is an utmost need to contain this livelihood insecurity by way of providing better work and job security.

4.1 Capability Building and Sector-Specific Skill Training

Jain (2008) found that acquisition of skill by wageworkers acts as a shield against their exposure to livelihood insecurity. Better skilled workers remain relatively less exposed to livelihood insecurity. So, given such evidence, it would be better to strengthen capacity building of the workforce. For this, specific institutions to impart training may be envisioned. Training in these institutions should be for short term along with some

Table 4 Workforce distribution by segment, gender and type of worker (%) in Punjab's urban informal sector

Segment	*Gender*	*Working Owner*	*Hired Workers*		*Helper/Apprentice*	*Other Workers*
			Formal	*Informal*		
Manufacturing	Male	43.73	0.34	47.49	1.16	7.28
	Female	68.75	0.09	7.92	2.22	21.03
	All	48.93	0.29	39.26	1.38	10.14
Trade	Male	57.51	0.23	32.29	1.34	8.62
	Female	58.42	0.59	17.53	5.10	18.37
	All	57.57	0.25	31.36	1.58	9.24
Services	Male	62.23	4.08	26.77	1.52	5.40
	Female	33.83	12.76	45.36	1.70	6.35
	All	54.93	6.31	31.55	1.57	5.65
All	Male	55.34	1.39	34.59	1.35	7.33
	Female	49.39	6.62	28.45	2.39	13.15
	All	54.35	2.26	33.57	1.52	8.30

Source Based on NSSO [2016]

provision for protection of earnings during training period—incentives may be given for recording better performance during the training period. As today is the age of sector-specific perfection, an effort should be made to devise institutions in such a way that they should impart sector-specific skills to the workers (Palmer, 2008). For this, skill requirements from specific industries may be inquired and at the same time, skill-gap studies and estimates derived by National Skill Development Mission (NSDM) on the sector-specific skill requirements should be considered by these institutions.

4.2 *Contributory Social Security System*

Informal workers do not have access to any form of social security system. In this regard, NCEUS (2006) proposed for instituting a social security system for informal workers. Along similar lines, it would be better to devise a contributory social security system for informal workers. In fact, the institution of this contributory social security system for informal sector would go a long way in not only providing economic security to the informal workers but also will contribute towards their life-fulfilment and protection against any contingency.

5 Summing-Up

Both enterprises and workers are integral to the functioning of Punjab's urban informal sector. If one segment remains insecure, so would be the second one. So, a better approach is to strengthen both so that each may become complimentary and supportive to the other. To attain this, business resilience of informal enterprises should be strengthened with adequate support from the state. At the same time, effort should be made to contain pervasive livelihood insecurity among working masses besides instituting a contributory social security system. On the whole, there is a need to adopt a visionary approach to contain the woes of informal enterprises and their workers.

References

IFC. (2010) *Scaling-up SME Access to Financial Services in the Developing World*, International Finance Corporation, World Bank Group. Available at: https://www.enterprise-development.org/wp-content/uploads/ScalingUp_SME_Access_to_Financial_Services.pdf [Accessed 31 June 2020].

IMF. (2020) *World Economic Outlook*, Geneva: International Monetary Fund.

Jackson, J. K. et al. (2020) *Global Economic Effects of COVID-19*, Washington, DC: Congressional Research Service.

Jain, V. (2008) Relative Advantage of Skill and Wageworkers' Exposure to Insecurity: How Debilitating is the Impact of Migration Status and Social Class, *The Indian Journal of Labour Economics,* 51(4): 927–938.

Jain, V. (2010) Dynamics of Insecurity in India's Urban Informal Sector: A Study of Manufacturing in Punjab, Unpublished Ph.D. Thesis, Jawaharlal Nehru University, New Delhi.

Jain, V. (2016) Manufacturing Sector in Punjab: Evolution, Growth Dynamism, Key Concerns and Rejuvenation Strategy, in L. Singh, and N. Singh (Eds.), *Economic Transformation of A Developing Economy: The Experience of Punjab*, Singapore: Springer, pp. 251–272.

Jain, V. (2020) Sports Equipment Manufacturing in India: A Firm-level Inquiry into Growth and Employment Dynamism, in R. Nagaraj (Ed.), *Industrialisation for Employment and Growth in India: Lessons from Small Firm Clusters and Beyond*, Cambridge University Press (forthcoming).

Jain, V., and Singh, L. (2020) Global Spread & Determinants of Initial Phase of COVID-19 Pandemic, Discussion Paper No. 18, Centre for Development Economics and Innovation Studies, Punjabi University, Patiala.

NCEUS. (2006) Social Security for Unorganised Workers, National Commission for Enterprises in the Unorganised Sector, Government of India, New Delhi.

NSSO. (2016) Economic Characteristics of Unincorporated Non-Agricultural Enterprises (Excluding Construction) in India, Report No. 582, NSS 73rd Round (July 2015 to June 2016), National Sample Survey Office, Ministry of Statistics and Programme Implementation, Government of India, New Delhi.

Palmer, R. (2008) Skills and Productivity in the Informal Economy, Working Paper No. 5, Skills and Productivity Department, International Labour Office, Geneva.

Singh, L. and Jain, V. (2007) Growth and Dynamics of Unorganised Industries in Punjab, *International Journal of Business and Globalisation*, 1(1): 60–87.

Sumner, A. et al. (2020) Estimates of the Impact of COVID-19 on Global Poverty, WIDER working paper no. 43, World Institute of Development Economics Research, United Nations University, Helsinki, Finland.

Covid-19 and MSMEs in Punjab: Challenges Ahead

Swati Mehta

1 Road to Revival: Focusing on Priorities?

Covid-19 brought numerous challenges for human lives and their livelihoods across nations. Nation states are struggling to save people from pandemic and hunger. Since the outbreak of coronavirus in November 2019, its spread is halting the economies across the globe, although at different times for different durations and different intensities. From Chinese province of Wuhan, the epicenter of the outbreak, the coronavirus spread its paws to South East Asia and Europe before entering South Asia. The affected economies remained closed, either fully or partially on an average for about three months disrupting the supply-chains and demand of different products across different nations. Apart from curbing the spread of coronavirus, the biggest challenge for the nation states is to frame and implement appropriate ***public policies*** to revive the stranded economies. Government of India (GOI) call for 'Atmanirbhar Bharat', a medium to long-term objective amidst immediate struggle to restart the economy with various non-fiscal, fiscal and monetary instruments, subsumed in the 'stimulus package' of Rs. 20 lakh crores. GOI focuses upon Micro, Small and Medium Enterprises (MSME)

S. Mehta (✉)
Punjab School of Economics, Guru Nanak Dev University, Amritsar, India

S. Singh et al. (eds.), *Covid-19 Pandemic and Economic Development*,
https://doi.org/10.1007/978-981-16-4442-9_9

in an attempt to join the broken supply-chains and to provide gainful employment opportunities to the people. The importance of MSMEs is manifested from the fact that its share in Gross Domestic Product (GDP) is about 28.9 per cent in 2016–2017 with about 633.88 lakh enterprises providing employment to about 11.10 crore people in India (MSME, 2018–19). Therefore, MSMEs can appropriately act as an important link to both demand and supply side of the economy across sectors. Combining this with the Kaldorian (1960) 'engine of growth theory' with industrialization[1]at the center,[2] it would be significant to examine the challenges and opportunities that MSMEs, especially from the manufacturing sector is facing in recent times. For the purpose, the focus of the paper is upon MSMEs in manufacturing sector of Indian Punjab in context of the recent policy announcements and expectation of changing 'world economic order'.

2 MSME in Punjab: Structure and Nature

Punjab is primarily an agricultural state with a considerable share of industries and services in State Gross Value Added (GSVA).[3] According to National Sample Survey Organization (NSSO) 73rd round, out of the total 633.88 lakh MSMEs in India, Punjab has about 14.65 lakh enterprises (2.3 per cent of the total MSMEs in India) providing about 24.80 lakh jobs (2.2 per cent of the total MSMEs in India) with a large proportion of micro enterprises (14.56 lakh enterprises) (MSME, 2018–19). Ministry of MSME adopted *Cluster Development Approach* for capacity building to enhance backward and forward linkages in the production chains. The importance of *clusters approach* or '*geographical concentration of interconnected companies*' (Porter, 2000) are increasingly acknowledged as a means of learning and technological accumulation for building competitiveness and value-upgradation (Giulani et al., 2005), although with the correct mix of internal and external organizations and institutions (Malerba, 2005). Punjab has in total 22 industrial[4] clusters with the maximum 14 clusters in Ludhiana district alone. Ludhiana has the clusters for the manufacturing of auto-parts, fasteners, machine tools, hand tools, wire drawing, sheet metal parts, bicycle and engineering parts, foundry and induction furnace, dyeing industries, printing and packaging, oil expeller & parts, tractor parts and knitted outwear. Punjab being an agricultural state also develops the agricultural implements clusters in Ferozepur and Mukatsar districts. However, an advanced machine cluster is also being developed at Mohali district of Punjab. Broadly, the important manufacturing exports from Punjab are largely from six industrial sectors (Fig. 1) textiles, bicycles & parts, auto-parts, Hand and Machine Tools, Electrical switchgears & accessories and engineering goods and sports goods. It is estimated that the minimum loss due to total lockdown to the manufacturing sector of Punjab state is around INR 40,000 Cr. with the man-days loss of 482 lakh persons employed.[5]

Ministry of (M/o) MSME has established 18 *Technology Centers* across India for providing stimulus to MSME sector. Of these two were established in Punjab namely, Central Tool Room (CTR) at Ludhiana and Central Institute of Hand Tools (CIHT) at Jalandhar (MSME, 2018–19). However, the development of MSMEs is the primary responsibility of the State government, which is undoubtedly supplemented by the policies and initiatives of the Government of India (GOI). As a revival strategy for the pandemic trodden economy, some measures were announced by Finance Minister, GOI on 13th May 2020 for the MSMEs, which would

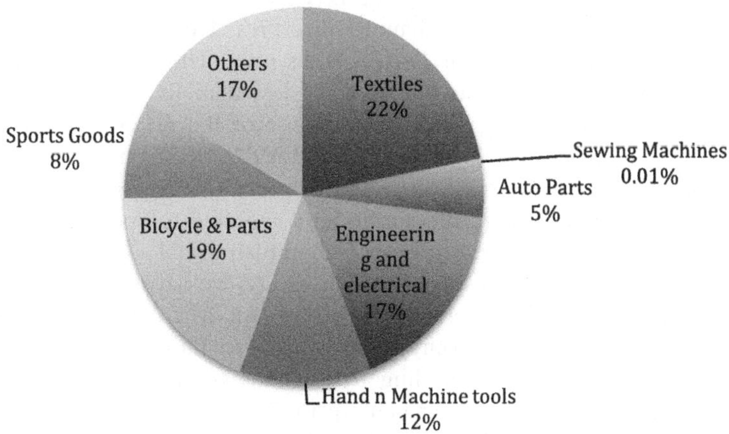

Fig. 1 Share of Exports from Industrial Sector in Punjab (*Source* Author's illustration from Statistical Abstract of Punjab (2018–19)
Notes 1. Total industrial exports are of INR 22,221.50 Crores (at current prices) for the year 2017–18. 2. Textiles are Hosiery and readymade garments; Auto-parts includes auto-spares and diesel engines; Electrical goods are switch gears and accessories; others include tanned & chrome leather and leather products, food products, handicrafts, drugs, carpets and other items)

be briefly outlined in next section with the discussion of its probable impact on Punjab manufacturing sector.

3 Roadmap for Revival: Focus on MSMEs

There are certain policies that were announced for the revival of the MSMEs in India with the expectation of providing initial inertia to the strangled economy. The revival of MSMEs would give a boost to the broken supply-chains from the supply side and would also be expected to push up the demand side by providing employment opportunities.

Redefining the Sector: The major change announced was concerning the amendment of the Micro, Small and Medium Enterprises Development (MSMED) Act 2006 for defining the sector. The *new* definition of the MSMEs is based upon both ***investment*** and ***turnover*** limits whereas the previous definition considered only the investment criterion. Second, earlier the defining criterion for manufacturing was different from services, which was done away with in the revised versions. Presently, Micro enterprise is one that has the investment limit of less than INR 1 crore and turnover of less than Rs. 5 crores. Earlier, it was the one with the investment limit of Rs. 25 lakhs only. The investment limits of Small enterprises are also revised from less than Rs. 5 crores to less than Rs. 10 crores along with the turnover of Rs. 50 crores. For the Medium enterprises, the investment limit was doubled from less than Rs. 10 crores to less than Rs. 50 crores and with turnover of less than Rs. 250 crores.[6] These revisions in the criterion are expected to boost the investment limits in the MSM enterprises which in turn would also have a direct impact on the turnover of these enterprises. As we have seen that more than 99 per cent of the enterprises in Punjab are 'Micro enterprises', the revised criterion would encourage investment in these enterprises. But some 'small enterprises' according to previous criterion would also be expected to fall under the 'micro enterprises' further swelling the section of MSMEs. Second, fulfilling both criterion of investment and turnover simultaneously would demand careful classification of enterprises to avail the relevant benefit.[7] Third, entrepreneurial fervor for the changed definition would be evident with the level of investment and henceforth turnover that may follow in due course of time, given the nature of credit facilities' apart from the overall strategy to revive demand[10] along with supply in the economy.

Easing Credit Facilities: GOI made announcements (https://msme.gov.in/) to boost investment in MSMEs including (i) guarantee free and collateral free loan of Rs. 3.00 lakh crores, (ii) payment of receivables to MSMEs within next 45 days and (iii) bar on domestic tendering up to Rs. 200 crores. These schemes can be understood under the umbrella of call for 'Made-in India' or 'Atmanirbhar Bharat Abhiyan'. The call for making India 'self-reliant' is not new in the history of her economic development. After Independence, the Second Five Year Plan has in its core the mission of making India 'self reliant' (Ahluwalia, 1991) that has its own empathizers and critiques over time. But the beginning of 1990s witnessed some reversal in policy framework in compliance with 'Washington consensus'. Again, the paradigm is shifting back to 'self-reliant' policies but with the broader aim for '***making India globally competitive***'.

About the specific policies for the revival of the MSMEs (https://msme.gov.in/) it was highlighted that under the 'guarantee free and collateral free loan' an amount of total Rs. 3.00 lakh crores is earmarked out of the Rs. 20 Lakh Crore package announced by GOI. The scheme has the moratorium of one year on payment of principal and is valid till 31st October 2020 or the time when the money allotted for the scheme is available. To reduce institutional bottlenecks, it was made mandatory for the department of GOI and the Central Public sector enterprises (CPSEs) to pay the receivables to MSMEs within next 45 days for easing the working capital conditions of MSMEs. Since this scheme is for both manufacturing and services sector across country, the extent of the benefits of the scheme depends upon the quantum of loan taken by Punjab-based entrepreneurs. Importantly, these schemes are largely to stimulate the supply-side bottlenecks, policies for demand revivals would encourage entrepreneurs much to take loans for future expansion. To boost demand, GOI however announced a scheme of putting bar on government procurements for the global tendering upto Rs. 200 crores[8] for providing boost to indigenous manufacturers and service providers under 'Aatmanirbhar Bharat' scheme. However, the quandary is that the government policies concerning MSMEs are largely supply encouraging, which is expected to bring momentum in the economy with probably enhanced investment which would boost employment to generate demand, however with some time lag[7].

4 MSMEs: Challenges for Learning and Competitiveness[9]

As discussed previously, Punjab is a manufacturer and exporter of varied industrial products. Each of these products possesses their respective 'learning' pattern, technological complexity, backward & forward linkages, relationship with suppliers, markets & competitors and institutional structures. This heterogeneity in attributes creates different opportunities and challenges for different enterprises producing different products. However, in the present section, an attempt is made to discuss some domestic and external challenges that the MSMEs in manufacturing sector in Punjab experience.

a. *Domestic Bottlenecks*

First, situated next to international border, Punjab is far from National capital (New Delhi), Trade capital (Mumbai) and knowledge hubs (Noida, Bangalore, Pune, Hyderabad). Although, the ***road-link*** is preferable option for imports and exports, the ***rationalization of rail-link cost*** is important (EXIM, 2019). Government of Punjab should speed up the process of bringing Ludhiana (*Times of India*, 2018) the manufacturing hub of Punjab on international air-map that would be beneficial not only for the local entrepreneur but also attract potential international investors in the state. Importantly, MSMEs in Punjab also have concerns regarding supply-chain ecosystem. Being an agricultural-based state, Punjab depends upon other states and countries[10] for most of the basic raw materials. A study done by Exim Bank (EXIM, 2019) found that pig-iron is imported in Punjab from Jharkhand and Odisha for auto-parts, hand-tools and machine-tools clusters; raw-rubber is imported from Kerala; and furnace oil is imported from Jamnagar. Subsequently, manufactured products are exported across the continents. Therefore, an effort should be made to provide ***advanced fast means of transportation*** at ***subsidize rates*** for the manufacturing clusters in Punjab.

Second, MSMEs in Punjab faces challenge concerning human capital. Migration to other countries from Punjab has increased over the years, thus creating a void in labour market. Labour working in MSMEs in Punjab is largely migrated from other states. MSMEs face difficulty in finding skilled labour and they usually resort to on-job training[7] to unskilled labour force. However, M/o MSMEs has established two Technology centres that not only provides technological supports to industries but also provides skilled manpower in tool engineering (MSME, 2018–19). However, to fill the abyss three points are suggested, one policy-makers should try to strengthen university-industry linkage for generating demand-based supply of manpower. Two, M/o MSME should establish specialized Technology Centres for ***automated manufacturing system*** to meet the future competitive requirements in Punjab. Labour Laws are another important aspects of concern not only to labour but also to domestic and international entrepreneurs. Flexibility in labour laws is largely being advocated by entrepreneurs[7] and some school of thoughts (Basu, 2009) which is largely rejected by labour unions due to contrary interests (Shyam Sundar, 2005). Therefore, the need is to find alternative policy framework for finding the middle competitive, skill-enhancing and evolutionary path. Third, industrialists in Punjab are also conserved about ***infrastructural bottlenecks*** in Punjab. To put in perspective, in the first month of 2020, industrialist demanded the reduced rate of power at par with adjoining states (*The Tribune*, 2020a).

b. *External Challenges*

There are certain challenges that MSMEs face from their counterparts from different countries. During the panel discussion concerning industries in Punjab, Ludhiana-based entrepreneur[7] found 'infrastructural' and 'institutional' bottlenecks as challenges that India and Punjab face in particular. As of 2020, World Bank compares Business Regulations in quantitative indicators in 190 economies and it covers 12 areas including the aspects related to '***starting a business, dealing with construction permits, getting electricity, registering property, getting credit, protecting minority investors, paying taxes, trading across borders, enforcing contracts, resolving insolvency, employing workers, and contracting with the government***'.[11] Whereas, these features are important for domestic entrepreneurs, they also act as an important means (or hindrance) for the foreign investment. According to the *Doing Business Report 2020*, out of 190 countries, India ranks 64, which is lower than that of China (rank 31), Singapore (rank 2), Hong Kong (rank 3), Malaysia (rank 12), Taiwan (rank 15) and Thailand (rank 21) amongst others. However, there are certain specific infrastructural backwardness that India and particularly Punjab is facing to attract the foreign investors. For example, '*rental factories*' or '*plug and play*' facilities are non-existent in Punjab that is attracting investment in countries like China, Vietnam and other Southeast Asian countries. In case of Textiles industry, the competition from countries like Bangladesh, Vietnam and Cambodia is increasing, for which Textile Parks (*The Tribune*, 2020b) could pave the way for gaining strength. Similarly, efforts should be made for '*product specific parks*' with state-of-art infrastructure and related organizations.[12]

Another challenge that MSMEs in Punjab in particular are struggling with is concerning un-coordinated nodes in the development of its '*knowledge ecosystem*'.[7] Efforts should be made for the evolution of '*learning*' '*systems*' (Edquist, 2005) by developing specific linkages between researchers, research institutes (within and outside Punjab) and entrepreneurs. 'Learning' within Clusters should be appreciated for the overall growth and sustainability of production and trade. At large, *dynamism* and *openness to change* is required amongst entrepreneurs to compete and upgrade their production systems. It was also found[7] that at times entrepreneurs have reservations in adopting '*compliances*' expected in regional/ global supply-chains. At the level of the state government also, the efforts towards promoting '*research*' is at backburner. It is pertinent to highlight that Punjab allocates only 0.02 per cent of state expenditure on General Research in 2014–2015 that was reduced further to 0.01 per cent of state expenditure of Rs. 78,153.72 crores (in revised estimates) for 2016–2017 (Statistical Abstract of Punjab, 2018). The resources devoted to research activities are thus very less as compared to National average of 0.7 per cent during the period (Department of Science and Technology, GOI, 2020).

5 Planning for Learning: A Right Strategy

Continuous learning is the appropriate strategy to survive, compete, sustain and leapfrog in the dynamic production processes with ever evolving technologies (Edquist, 2005). The world is moving fast in adopting the technologies of fourth industrial revolution (IR 4.0) like automation, artificial intelligence, block-chain technologies and alike. Moreover, Post-Covid' 19 world is also expected to redraw the 'rules of games' with changing world economic order. Therefore, to meet the future complexities of participation in regional/global production chains, Punjab should design coherent, dynamic policy for making 'learning' an evolutionary process for its industrial sector. Such an alternative policy framework, based upon 'systems approach' (Edquist, 2005) should focus upon the interaction amongst various actors (suppliers, producers, users), organizations (institutions, research institutions, universities) and institutions (rules of laws). Basically, efforts should be directed towards accumulating 'technological capabilities' through building 'absorptive capacity' (Cohen and Levinthal, 1989) with indigenous investment in research & development (R&D) and human capital so as to escape from the vicious cycle of 'low value-added trap'.[13]

6 Conclusion

Covid-19 has caused numerous challenges for lives and livelihoods across nations. Timely focused policy announcements would determine the pattern of growth for different sectors and economies in the post-lockdown times. To revive the economy, Government of India announced 'stimulus package' of Rs. 20 lakh Cr. including some policy and fiscal initiatives for Micro, Small and Medium enterprises (MSME) of different sectors. In this context, the paper focused upon MSMEs belonging to the manufacturing sector of Indian Punjab to bring forth the challenges that the sector faces in general and specifically due to Covid-19 lockdown. Punjab has about 2.3 per cent of the total MSMEs in India with large proportion of micro enterprises. Major industries of Punjab include the manufacturing of hosiery, readymade garments, automobile parts, bicycles, hand tools, machine tools, sports goods, etc. that contribute considerably in the local and global value-chains. It is estimated that the minimum loss that the industrial sector of Punjab suffered due to complete lockdown is around Rs. 40,000 Cr. However, it was found that industries of Punjab face numerous problems mainly related to infrastructural bottlenecks, obsolete transport facilities and institutional hurdles. It is important that the process of *continuous learning* is adopted with co-evolution of different actors, organizations and institutions for making the industry competitive and to meet the long-term objective of making India self-reliant with the recent call for 'Atamnirbhar Bharat'.

Notes

1. The growing share of services sector in India's growth is signaling to an alternative 'engine of growth' thesis. see: https://www.unido.org/api/opentext/documents/download/9928079/unido-file-9928079.
2. The empirical evidences in the history of economic growth found 'industrialization' as the 'engine of growth' from West to East. Whereas first industrial revolution ushered growth and development in Europe followed by the United States, the recent Asian miracles were also the result of the industrial catching-up with the incumbents.
3. The average share of agriculture and allied activities in Nominal GSVA for the years 2012–13 to 2016–17 is around 29.2 percent, industry is about 24.6 percent and services is at around 46.1 percent, respectively (Punjab Economic Survey, 2019–20) available at https://www.esopb.gov.in/Static/PDF/EconomicSurvey-2019-20.pdf.
4. Status of various clusters of Punjab available at: http://msmedildh.gov.in/STATUS%20OF%20VARIOUS%20CLUSTERS%20.pdf.
5. The estimation is based on the data extracted from Annual Survey of Industries.
6. The MSMED 2020 Notification dated 1st June 2020, effective from 1st July 2020, available at https://msme.gov.in/sites/default/files/MSME_gazette_of_india.pdf.
7. These points were discussed by the panelists during the 'Virtual Webinar-Decording 20 Lac Crore and Liquidity Solutions' held on 23rd May 2020 at 12:30 PM, Confederation of Indian Industry (CII) Ludhiana. The author is thankful to the Chairman CII, Ludhiana Zone for providing the access to the webinar.
8. 20 lakh crore stimulus package has announcements to stimulate agriculture and allied activities, MNREGA, ease of doing measures etc. with the expectation to provide boost to demand also. Details available at: https://www.thehindu.com/news/resources/economic-stimulus-package-details-of-20-lakh-crore-package-announced-by-union-finance-minister-nirmala-sitharaman-in-five-tranches/article31606806.ece.
9. The discussion in the section is based upon the Webinar available at: CNI Channel on 'Future Business after quarantine released on 27 April' 2020; 'Industry Post Corona with Chamber of Industrial and Commercial Undertakings (CICU) President, Punjab' released on 8 May, 2020; 'Industry Post Corona with Federation of Industrial and Commercial Organization (FICO) President, Punjab' released on 9 May, 2020; 'Industry Post Corona with Confederation of Indian Industry (CII) Chairman, Punjab' released on 15 May, 2020 available at: https://www.facebook.com/cnichannel/.

10. Punjab imports raw material from different countries. For example 'active pharmaceutical ingredients (API) for drug manufacturing is largely imported from China, Merino wool in woolen industry is imported from Australia.
11. http://documents.worldbank.org/curated/en/688761571934946384/pdf/Doing-Business-2020-Comparing-Business-Regulation-in-190-Economies.pdf.
12. Edquist (2005) define organizations as '*actors*' that are '*consciously created and have explicit purpose*'. For example, organizations like research and development labs, financial organizations, marketing facilities etc. can be develop.
13. In other words, it is challenging to maintain growth if firm/ industry remained confined to production of low-technological intensive products or remained confined in primitive production process, especially in the era of fourth industrial revolution (IR 4.0). Therefore, it becomes imperative for industry at large and MSMEs in particular to upgrade so as to contribute more in value-chains with gainful employment opportunities.

References

Ahluwalia, I. J. (1991) *Productivity and Growth in Indian Manufacturing*, New Delhi: Oxford University Press.

Basu, K. (2009) China and India: Idiosyncratic Paths to High Growth, *Economic and Political Weekly*, 44(38): 43–49.

Cohen, W. M., and Levinthal, D.A. (1989) Innovation and Learning: The two faces of R&D, *The Economic Journal*, 99(397): 569–596.

Department of Science and Technology (DST). (2020) Research & Development Statistics at a glance, 2019–20, Ministry of Science and technology, Government of India.

Edquist, C. (2005) Systems of Innovation: Perspectives and Challenges, in Fagerberg, J. D. C. Mowery and R. R. Nelson (Eds.), *The Oxford Handbook of Innovation*, New York: Oxford University Press, pp. 181–208.

EXIM (Export Exports-Import bank of India). (2019) Exports from Punjab: Trends, Opportunities and Policy Insights. Available at: https://www.eximbankindia.in/Assets/Dynamic/PDF/PublicationResources/ResearchPapers/112file.pdf.

Giulani, E., Pietrobelli, C., and Rabellotti, R. (2005) Upgrading in Global Value Chains: Lessons from Latin American Clusters, *World Development*, 33(4): 549–573.

Kaldor, N. (1960) *Causes of Growth and Stagnation in the in the World Economy*, New York: Cambridge University Press.

Malerba, F. (2005) Sectoral Systems: How and Why Innovation Differs Across Sectors, in Fagerberg, J. D. C. Mowery and R. R. Nelson (Eds.), *The Oxford Handbook of Innovation*, New York: Oxford University Press, pp. 380–406.

MSME (Ministry of Micro, Small and Medium Enterprises). (2018–19) Annual Report, GOI, downloaded from: https://msme.gov.in/.

Porter, M. (2000) Location, Competition, and Economic Development: Local Clusters in a Global Economy, *Economic Development Quarterly*, 14(1): 15–34.

Statistical Abstract of Punjab. (2018) Economic Advisor, Government of Punjab downloaded from https://www.esopb.gov.in/static/Publications.html.

Shyam Sundar, K. R. (2005) Labour Flexibility Debate in India: A Comprehensive Review and Some Suggestions, *Economic and Political Weekly*, 40 (22/23): 2274–2285.

Times of India. (2018, December 4) Punjab to Get Third International Airport Soon. Available at: https://timesofindia.indiatimes.com/city/ludhiana/punjab-to-get-third-international-airport-soon/articleshow/66931131.cms.

The Tribune. (2020a, January 25) Batala Industrialists Demand Reduction in Electricity Tariff.

The Tribune. (2020b, February 28) Industrialists Demand Mega Textile Park in Punjab. Available at: https://www.tribuneindia.com/news/business/industrialists-demand-mega-textile-park-in-punjab-48710.

Implementation of Emergency Credit Line Guarantee Scheme (ECLGS) in Punjab: An Assessment of Performance of Scheduled Commercial Banks

Satish Verma

1 Introduction

While expressing the concern that the economy is passing through "tough times due to closure of most of the economic activities", the SLBC (Punjab) has called upon the banks to play a major role in financing of "agriculture, MSMEs and other sectors to uplift the economy of the state" (SLBC, 152nd meeting, p. 2). Banking in Punjab has been slowing down since long and dipped sharply starting later half of March 2020 when the curfew/lockdown in the state was imposed (March 22nd). A perusal of banking trends in the state would indicate that the impact of the Covid starting from nearly mid-March 2020 in the state was so devastating that it overwhelmingly wiped out the gains, if any, achieved in the first two and half months of the quarter ending March 2020. The key sectors in the state like industry, trade, banking, hospitality, transport, tourism, etc., suffered slowdown/contraction in flow of credit reflecting the distressed state of the economy during the Covid. In this period,

S. Verma (✉)
Centre for Research in Rural and Industrial Development (CRRID), Chandigarh, India

S. Singh et al. (eds.), *Covid-19 Pandemic and Economic Development*,
https://doi.org/10.1007/978-981-16-4442-9_10

credit-deposit ratio declined across the board in the state; proportion of advances to weaker sections fell; number and amount of Kisan Credit Card (KCC) loans shrank; number of accounts and the loan amount to Micro, Small and Medium Enterprises (MSMEs) contracted, and the flow of loans to MSMEs, retail and other sectors under Covid-19 Emergency Line of Credit (ELC) scheme remained subdued.

To tide over the disruptions and revive the economy, the government announced a number of regulatory and liquidity measures to enable borrowers to overcome financial stresses due to Covid-19, maintain liquidity in the system, facilitate and incentivize bank credit flows and ensure normal functioning of the business, trade, manufacturing, etc. Of the over Rs. 20 lakh crore Covid stimulus package, the most significant is the Emergency Credit Line Guarantee Scheme (ECLGS) that provides for the fully guaranteed Rs 3 lakh crore collateral free additional working capital term loans facility to standard small businesses and MSME units as on February 29, 2019 that have combined outstanding loan of upto Rs 25 crore and turnover Rs 100 crore.[1] The additional working capital term loan facility, which is 20 percent of the outstanding as on ending February 2020, is a pre-approved sanctioned limit with a provision to opt-out. However, prior approval of the National Credit Guarantee Trustee Company (NCGTC) is necessary for the disbursal of loan. The scheme, announced on May 13, 2020, is operational from May 23 till end of October 2020. In this brief, an attempt has been made to evaluate the performance of scheduled commercial banks in implementing the Scheme in Punjab over June 22, 2020 and July 18, 2020.

2 Progress of Scheduled Commercial Banks in implementation of Emergency Credit Line Guarantee Scheme (ECLGS) in Punjab

Table 1 presents a comparative picture of the performance of public sector and private sector group of banks in implementing the scheme as on June 22 and July 18, 2020. The public sector banks until July 18 though had sanctioned loans to nearly two-fifth (39.24 percent) of their net eligible borrowers, but the accounts disbursed as proportion of the sanctioned declined to 50.55 percent. Besides, the amount disbursed as proportion of the sanctioned also declined at 49.08 percent (Table 1).In growth terms also, it was found that disbursals by public sector banks (accounts 51.70

Table 1 Bank category-wise performance of Scheduled Commercial Banks in implementing ECLGS in Punjab as on June 22, 2020, July 18, 2020 and August 31, 2020

Bank Category	*Number of accounts disbursed as % of net eligible borrowers*			*Number of accounts disbursed as % of the sanctioned*			*Amount disbursed as % of the sanctioned*		
	1			*2*			*3*		
	June 22, 2020	*July 18, 2020*	*August 31, 2020*	*June 22, 2020*	*July 18, 2020*	*August 31, 2020*	*June 22, 2020*	*July 18, 2020*	*August 31, 2020*
Public Sector Banks	27.32	39.24	66.25	54.74	50.55	69.27	56.83	49.08	65.98
Private and Small Finance Banks	12.25	11.86	17.33	92.83	82.69	78.14	96.23	84.55	90.99
Total	**24.93**	**33.43**	**53.99**	**56.55**	**52.08**	**69.90**	**69.74**	**60.14**	**74.87**

Note Regional Rural Banks have been permitted late, but have not reported any data till date. Cooperative banks have not been permitted to provide the loan facility

Source Office of the State Level Bankers' Committee, Punjab, Chandigarh. Author's calculations.

percent and amount 47.35 percent) were lagging behind the sanctioned (accounts 64.26 percent and the amount 70.63 percent) over this period.

On the other hand, the private banks' performance in relation to the accounts disbursed as proportion of the net eligible as on July 18 was poor (merely 11.86 percent). But the number of accounts, as well as the amount disbursed as proportion of the sanctioned, was very high (82.69 percent and 84.55 percent respectively). These proportions, however, are misleading as these involve a very small number of the accounts sanctioned. Thus, the private banks' performance at the first stage of implementing the scheme, i.e., sanctioning the account (11.86 percent), has been distressing. In incremental terms also, their disbursals were found to have grown at relatively a slower pace. Over June July 22 2018, the private banks' disbursal of accounts grew by 51.23 percent and loan amount by 43.71 percent, while the corresponding figures for public sector banks were higher at 70.63 percent and 47.35 percent respectively. Thus, in disbursals too, the public sector banks have recorded relatively a higher growth. Yet, a perusal of Table 1 indicates that the accounts as well as the loan amount disbursed as proportion of the sanctioned by the public sector banks on July 18 has been less than that almost a month ago (June 22). Overall speaking, whereas the public sector banks should ramp up their disbursals, the private banks' response, on the other hand, has been utterly lukewarm at the very first stage of implementing the scheme.

The data (not reported here to save space) reveals that, as on July 18, the share of private sector banks in accounts sanctioned in the state was less than 5 percent, while in loan amount sanctioned was 31 percent. Moreover, the loan amount sanctioned per account by private banks worked out to Rs 19.04 lakh and a mere Rs 2.09 lakh by public sector banks. It means that the private banks extended loans mainly to large borrowers. They shirk giving loans to small and financially stressed borrowers. The SLBC must proactively take up the matter with these banks.

If data tweeted by the Finance Minister, Nirmala Sitharaman, on July 17, 2020, is taken as the indicator, then it appears that Punjab has put up a better performance in regard to the accounts and amount sanctioned/disbursed under the scheme by the public sector banks in 71 industrial hub cities across the country. Following the data, Punjab ranks fifth in the number of accounts and amount sanctioned (after Gujarat, Maharashtra, Tamil Nadu and Uttar Pradesh) and fourth in the accounts and amount disbursed (excluding Uttar Pradesh among the above states) (Sitharaman, 2020). Moreover, whereas the accounts and the loan amount disbursed as proportion of the sanctioned by public sector banks across the country worked out to 57.14 percent and 65.44 percent, the corresponding proportions for Punjab were higher at 67.28 percent and 67.54 percent respectively. Thus, for the selected four industrial hub cities in Punjab,[2] the proportions were higher than all-India. However, the data is partial for only the selected industrial hub cities and excludes the private sector banks as well.

3 Spatial Performance of ECLGS in Punjab

With the number of eligible borrowers as well as the loan amount pegged under ECLGS to the status as on February 29, 2020, the proportions of the number of accounts sanctioned and disbursed, therefore, become the performance indicators. Columns 1 & 2 in Table 2 show the proportion of the accounts sanctioned out of net eligible, while Columns 3 & 4 depict accounts disbursed as proportion of the sanctioned as on June 22 and July 18, respectively.

The scheme seems progressing satisfactorily as nearly two-third (64.20 percent) of the eligible borrowers in the state had been sanctioned loan as on July 18, 2020 against 44 percent on June 22 (Table 2). Moreover, this proportion improved in all the districts over the period under consideration. District Mansa with over 95 percent tops the list, while the next best performers with nearly three-fourth proportions were Fazilka, Hoshiarpur, Jalandhar and Kapurthala. At the bottom are the two major industrial districts- Amritsar (55.04 percent) and Ludhiana (52.35 percent)- which is worrisome. Indeed, Ludhiana has consistently ranked at the bottom (22nd), whereas Amritsar's rank worsened from 17th to 21st over this period.

Disbursal of accounts by scheduled commercial banks in the state is the gray area, that as proportion of the sanctioned, dropped from 56.55 percent to 52.08 percent over the period (Table 2). Unfortunately, 16 districts (nearly three-fourth) reported a decline in the ratio- largest by Patiala, Barnala, SAS Nagar, Jalandhar and Ludhiana. Unfortunately, Jalandhar and Ludhiana districts stuck to their ranks-19th and about 14th respectively- on both the dates. Thus, the three major MSME and business hub districts in Punjab (Amritsar, Jalandhar and Ludhiana) have utterly lagged behind in one or the other indicator of implementation of the scheme. Ludhiana is the worst performer in respect of both. These

Table 2 District-wise performance of ECLGS in Punjab as on June 22, 2020, July 18, 2020 & August 31, 2020

District	*No. of Accounts Sanctioned as % of Net Eligible*			*No. of Accounts Disbursed as % of the Sanctioned*		
	22.6.2020	*18.7.2020*	*31.8.2020*	*22.6.2020*	*18.7.2020*	*31.8.2020*
	1	2	3	4	5	6
Amritsar	44.61	55.04	70.50	55.07	58.92	71.68
Barnala	39.97	66.64	72.43	60.96	41.29	60.10
Bathinda	51.54	64.92	67.95	66.15	63.17	82.10
Faridkot	53.71	68.42	75.46	62.76	62.96	69.23
Fatehgarh Sahib	55.93	65.58	73.25	51.50	62.31	80.32
Fazilka	56.68	76.41	81.11	46.49	46.38	64.77
Ferozepur	47.49	64.94	74.17	68.86	62.70	69.66
Gurdaspur	45.10	56.05	66.63	62.61	74.00	83.68
Hoshiarpur	57.56	72.04	76.94	51.12	53.60	78.34
Jalandhar	38.66	74.06	79.96	51.23	41.95	79.53
Kapurthala	44.86	73.92	80.54	54.19	48.07	83.17
Ludhiana	36.28	52.35	68.12	57.37	49.94	57.43
Mansa	58.03	95.42	96.56	60.27	55.30	69.37
Moga	48.74	62.64	69.29	69.64	63.58	77.85
Mukatsar	50.01	68.83	73.54	60.75	58.07	63.93
Pathankot	45.00	68.88	84.36	55.00	74.15	79.97
Patiala	43.77	65.59	73.97	62.23	40.42	57.52
Rupnagar	43.48	68.22	67.08	59.97	69.16	66.37
Sangrur	46.14	63.70	69.10	53.01	46.21	66.17
SAS Nagar	47.11	66.95	74.45	57.40	46.61	58.10
SBS Nagar	44.94	67.58	76.16	57.87	56.75	78.93
Tarn Taran	45.96	66.81	68.44	41.80	41.44	79.66
Punjab	**44.08**	**64.20**	**77.23**	**56.55**	**52.08**	**69.90**

Source Office of the State Level Bankers' Committee, Punjab, Chandigarh. Author's calculations

three districts together account for 42 percent of the eligible borrowers in the state. District Tarn Taran, however, has lowest proportion of the accounts disbursed in the state (ranked 22nd).

4 Evaluation and the Way Forward

The ECLGS forms part of the over Rs 20 lakh crores financial stimulus package and has been acknowledged as the most significant measure intended to help the strapped small enterprises. But, many of these will fail to crack the scheme and avail the benefits. For instance, the units which didn't have outstanding loan or were NPA as on February 29, 2020 fail to qualify for the scheme. Moreover, the loan limit is up to 20 percent of the outstanding as on February 29, 2020, the date on which most MSME units were in bad shape because of long drawn slowdown. Its retrospective implementation proved regressive for the units that had NPA loans as on February 29, 2019. Its benefits could have been optimized had the RBI announced restructuring of the NPA loans before announcing the cut-off date. Such a step would have made them eligible to avail the collateral free loan that would have offered them an opportunity to revive and make them viable. However, for such units, a separate 90 percent credit guarantee facility called the "Credit Guarantee Scheme for Subordinate Debt (CGSSD)" has been created that provides the promoter a personal loan of 15 percent of his stake or Rs 75 lakh, whichever is lower, for infusion as equity/quasi equity/sub debt in the business provided the unit was stressed (MSA 2 or NPA) as on 30.4 2020, was in regular operations during 2018–2019 and 2019–2020, was standard as on 31.3.2018 and is commercially viable.

Moratorium on payment of installments on existing term loans and the interest on working capital loans has been extended by another three months until the end of August 2020. Recovery of installments for this period has been shifted across the board and will become payable monthly from September 1, 2020, with the further provision that the banks may convert the accumulated interest for the deferment period into a funded interest loan which shall be payable by the end of March 2021. The installments thus will multiply in the subsequent year when loans raised under ECLGS would also become due. These measures will increase the debt burden of the units. Moreover, economic activities during most of the moratorium period (March 1–August 31, 2020) have remained either standstill due to curfew/lockdown or have been at their lowest ebb. With recovery not in sight, one-time interest waiver for the lock down period or interest subvention on these loans will provide the needed succor to the beleaguered units. In addition, payment of loan installments should be suitably restructured.

The stimulus package provides for interest subvention of 2 percent upto Rs 50,000/- Shishu loans, which are availed by the tiny units whose survival is under threat. It would be a great help if the Shishu loans sanctioned during the Covid period are charged at 4 percent rate as under the Differential Rate of Interest scheme. The loan of Rs 10,000/- to street vendors can also be brought under Shishu loans of Mudra scheme and be charged at 4 percent rate.

While welcoming the measures, businesses and industry cautioned that there is a challenge of delivery, i.e. the devil lies in details. Structural design of the scheme requires sharing of collateral on original loan with that under the scheme on pari passu basis (Purohit, 2020). Thus, collateral free loan does not mean the absence of collateral at all. Probably, this is the reason for a significant proportion of eligible borrowers opting out/ not responding (25 percent in Punjab). Similarly, banks are insisting on intensive documentation because they, as per the scheme, would know about the status of recovery of the loan not before the expiry of one year and three months since its disbursal. But, if it turns into NPA, the NCGTC will reimburse 75 percent of the guaranteed amount on submission of the claim and the rest on "conclusion of recovery proceedings or till the decree gets time barred whichever is earlier" (ibid.). That means, the banks also have to share default risk.

Despite clear directions, the banks are maintaining huge reverse repo deposits,[3] and being risk averse, avoid lending to MSMEs (Arunachalam, 2020). In Punjab, the SLBC has expressed concern that working capital loans are available under Emergency Line of Credit (ELC) to "farmers, self-help groups, MSMEs, individuals, pensioners and corporates", but the private banks are not providing working capital facility under the scheme (SLBC,152nd meeting, p. 7). Moreover, they are providing big ticket loans leaving the small loans to public sector banks. Their role in providing loans should be reviewed by the SLBC.

The businesses and industry faced tremendous disruptions and were not permitted activity during the lockdown period- the initial over one month overlapped with curfew in the state. The firms faced shortages of labor and raw materials, precipitous fall in domestic and external demand, finance problems and so on. Moreover, workers in large numbers migrated to their home states.[4] Therefore, the firms will take much longer to resume full-scale operations and achieve the break-even. Moreover, they are facing double whammy financial stress and slump in demand. Whereas the government has tried to ease liquidity for the firms, the measures are supply centric. Demand, on the other hand, remains highly subdued (Sharma, 2020). Indeed, these measures exclude fresh spending, investment and hence the job creation.

Finally, net eligible borrowers under the scheme in Punjab are merely 10 percent of the MSMEs. Despite being a 100 percent government credit guarantee scheme, almost 19 percent in the state have opted out. Response of another 6 percent is still awaited. Moreover, state's share in the Rs 3 lakh crore earmarked for the purpose comes to a miniscule 1.44 percent, and that too if the whole eligible amount is disbursed. That means the demand for credit by the small businesses and the MSMEs is very low, which is reflected in the state's declining credit-deposit ratio (currently at about 60 percent which is the minimum desirable).

5 Conclusions

Banking in Punjab has been slowing down since long; but it dipped sharply during the Covid period. Among all, the worst hits are the small businesses and MSMEs in the state. The public sector banks have been slow in disbursals whereas the private banks have been lukewarm in sanctioning the accounts. The banks need to expedite the disbursal of loans especially in three major districts in the state, and should also prevail upon all the potential borrowers to avail benefits of it. The private banks in the state are concentrating mostly on big ticket loans, and are not providing working capital loans under ELC, which are permitted under the scheme. They may be directed to handle small ticket loans also, besides extending all the loan facilities available under other schemes.

While several propositions have been made to improve the credit off-take, particularly by small and financially distressed and strained borrowers, the major suggestion is that the RBI should permit restructuring of NPA loans in such a manner that the units, which stand excluded because of the retrospective implementation of the scheme, could become eligible for loans under it, restart and revive. In addition, one-time interest waiver for the lockdown period or interest subvention should be granted, and the installments be suitably restructured. This is important because the demand is very slow to revive, and these measures are mostly supply-side centric and exclude fresh spending, investment and job creation.

Notes

1. Later, the eligibility for loans under the scheme was extended to "all Business Enterprises/ MSMEs/ individuals who have availed loan for business purposes with outstanding loans of up to Rs. 50 crore as on 29.02.2020,

and turnover of Rs. 250 crore in FY 2019–20... The term Business Enterprises/ MSMEs would also include loans covered under Pradhan Mantri Mudra Yojana (PMMY)" (Guidelines dated August 4, 2020).

2. The four industrial hub cities considered in Punjab are Barnala, Kaputhala, Jalandhar and Ludhiana.
3. According to one estimate, the banks' deposits in reverse rapo window stood at staggering Rs. 8 lakh crores in mid-May, 2020. (Major stimulus measures, May 14, 2020 by Insights editor).
4. As on May 3, 2020, over 6.52 lakh workers from Punjab had registered to return to their homes.

References

Arunachalam, R. (2020) Economic Stimulus Part I: Excellent Measures for MSMEs But Strong Need for Implementation Safeguards, Economy & Nation, May 13, 2020. Available at: https://www.moneylife.in/article/economic-stimulus-part-i-excellent-measures-for-msmes-but-strong-need-for-implementation-safeguards/60318.html [Accessed 7 July 2020].

Insight Editors. (2020) Major Stimulus Measures, May 14, 2020. Available at: https://www.insightsonindia.com/2020/05/14/major-stimulus-measures/ [Accessed 30 June 2020].

NDTV Profit. (2020) Nirmala Sitharaman Asks Public Sector Bank CEOs to Implement Economic Package, May 23, 2020. Available at: https://www.ndtv.com/business/implement-atma-nirbhar-bharat-package-nirmala-sitharaman-to-public-sector-bank-ceos-amid-covid-19-2233795.

Purohit, G. (2020) Emergency Credit Line Guarantee Scheme, June 13, 2020. Available at: https://www.mondaq.com/india/financing/952206/emergency-credit-line-guarantee-scheme [Accessed 22 July 2020].

Sharma, R. (2020, May 17) Letter to the Hon'ble Prime Minister, Govt. of India, New Delhi.

State Level Bankers' Committee. (2020, May 14) 152nd Meeting Agenda Papers, Chandigarh.

State Level Bankers' Committee. (2020, May 1) Minutes of Special SLBC Meeting to Review the Preparedness and Implementation of Packages, Relaxations Announced by Government of India/Reserve Bank of India in the Light of Covid-19 pandemic, Chandigarh.

Sitharaman, N. (2020) Available at: https://www.zeebiz.com/india/news-emergency-credit-line-guarantee-scheme-eclgs-over-rs-19k-crore-sanctioned-to-71-msmes-131545 [Accessed 23 July 2020].

Employment Participation of Rural Women in Punjab: A Need for Policy Retrospect

Ashapurna Baruah and Indervir Singh

1 Introduction

Neoclassical macroeconomic and growth models consider growth as an answer to all economic problems. The underlying assumption of these models is that benefits of growth created in urban formal sector will trickle down creating employment in urban and rural areas. The productivity and consequent wage differences in urban and rural areas will result in the movement of capital to underdeveloped areas and labour to urban and developed areas. This movement of capital and labour will result in higher growth and generate better job opportunities everywhere.

These models generally ignore the social and economic constraints faced by people. Even those models that incorporate market imperfections like search cost (Diamond, 1989) are not useful in understanding the implications of social institutions like gender norms. Governed by these models, the economic policies in India in the last three decades have led to an excessive focus on the expansion of economic activity (barring a few policies like the Mahatma Gandhi National Rural Employment Guarantee Scheme [MGNREGS] 2005). These policies have led to a lopsided development where growth figures do not match the employment data

A. Baruah (✉) · I. Singh
National Institute of Technology (NIT), Hamirpur, Hamirpur, India

S. Singh et al. (eds.), *Covid-19 Pandemic and Economic Development*,
https://doi.org/10.1007/978-981-16-4442-9_11

(Abraham, 2017). Employment of rural women is one of the biggest casualties of these growth policies (Fletcher et al. 2017). This is reflected in their low workforce participation and concentration in low paying occupations in rural areas (Baruah, 2016; Chowdhury, 2011; Mazumdar and Neetha, 2011).

Even high growth of the agricultural sector is unable to improve the female labour force participation in rural areas. Punjab, one of the most agriculturally developed states in India, has experienced a decline in employment opportunities for females over time (Baruah and Singh, 2020). Fall in demand for labour in rural areas coupled with gender norms forced them to stay unemployed or underemployed (this point will be discussed in the next section).

The ongoing COVID-19 (corona virus disease 2019) pandemic is likely to further worsen the employment prospects of women. The initial trends suggest that women's employment is more severely hit than their male counterparts (Deshpande, 2020). The governments are continuing with similar growth-centric policies to fight the economic fallout of the pandemic. The present paper re-examines these policies to assess their efficacy in generating employment for women in rural Punjab in times of pandemic. It is argued that such policies are unlikely to improve employment prospect of rural women and will only delay the overall recovery of the economy. It offers policy suggestion to improve employment prospect of rural women.

The paper is divided into four sections. The second section provides an overview of employment changes among women in rural Punjab since the Green Revolution. It discusses how the growth-centric policies have resulted in unemployment or underemployment among rural women in Punjab. The third section highlights the severity of employment problem in rural Punjab. The fourth section analyses the major policy measures taken by the central and the Punjab government and probes whether these policies can make any difference for rural women. Policy implications are discussed in the last section.

2 Agricultural Development and the Employment Change in Rural Punjab[1]

The employment opportunities in rural areas are intrinsically linked to agricultural development. Therefore, challenges and opportunities for employment among rural women need to be understood in the context of changes in the agricultural sector. The major changes in the agricultural sector in Punjab came in the mid-1960s. Punjab witnessed a rapid diffusion of the green revolution technology in mid-1960s resulting a spurt in its agricultural growth. The adoption of an intensive system of cultivation led to a significant productivity increase. Biochemical and mechanical technology played a major role in the intensification of cultivation. The adoption of biochemical technology, like high-yielding varieties (HYV), chemical fertilisers and pesticides, enhanced crop productivity. Mechanical technology initially came in the form of increased number of pump sets for irrigation, use of tractors for tilling and use of threshers. Over the years, Punjab saw increased use of machines in sowing and harvesting.

Punjab had just eight pump sets per one thousand hectares in 1962 which increased to 307 per thousand hectares in 2017 (Baruah and Singh, 2020). It led to a large expansion in irrigated area and surge in the use of groundwater for irrigation. By 2017–2018, nearly 71 per cent of the net irrigated area in Punjab was irrigated using pump sets (GoP, 2018). The gross cropped area under irrigation increased from 58 per cent in 1962–1965 (Bhalla et al., 1990) to 98.9 per cent in 2015–2018 (GoP, 2018).Similarly, the number of tractors increased from 2.4 per thousand hectares in 1961 to 79 per thousand hectares in 2018. Use of tractors brought larger area under cultivation and raised the cropping intensity. However, most of the increase in cropping intensity and the gross cropped area came in the first 25 years of the green revolution. Cropping intensity in Punjab went up from 129 per cent in 1962–1965 to 178 in 1990–1991 and to 189 per cent in 2015–2018 (Bhalla et al., 1990; GoP, 2018).The gross cropped area increased by 60 per cent from 1960–1961 to 1990–1991 (Bhalla et al., 1990; GoP, 2018). The increase was much smaller in the later years. During the 1991–1992 to 2017–2018 period, the gross cropped area had just 4 per cent increase (GoP, 2018). These trends suggest relatively minor change in cropping intensity and gross cropped area after 1990–1991.

Wheat and rice benefited the most in the initial years of the green revolution. The yield in wheat, which was growing at two per cent from 1952–1953 to 1964–1964, grew at 2.6 per cent from 1967–1968 to 1984–1985 (Bhalla et al., 1990). The improvement in yield of paddy was even higher. The growth of its yield increased from 1.7 per cent to 5.7 per cent in the same period. During the 1960–1961 to 1985–1986 period, the area under wheat and rice increased from 29.52 per cent and 4.8 per cent to 43.48 per cent and 26.86 per cent, respectively (Fig. 1). The

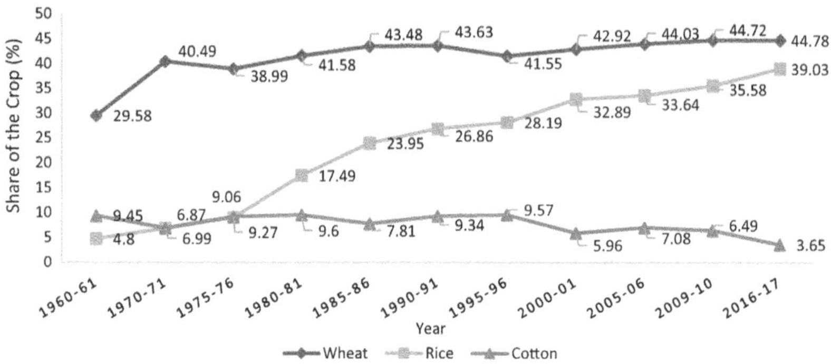

Fig. 1 Share of gross cropped area under wheat, rice and cotton in Punjab, 1960–61 to 2016–17 (in per cent) (*Source* Singh et al. [2014], Statistical Abstract of Punjab [2018])

productivity of other crops also increased over time. Between 1981–1982 and 2011–2012, the productivity of cotton, wheat and paddy and cotton increased by 434.8 per cent, 61 per cent and 98.1 per cent, respectively. Despite the high growth in per hectare yield of cotton, the frequent crop failures due to bollworm resulted in farmers shifting to paddy cultivation in the 1990s (Gill and Singh, 2006). By 2015–2016, about 84 per cent of the gross cropped area in Punjab was under two crops, wheat and rice (Fig. 1).

Based on the trend in labour use, the period of agricultural growth can be divided into two phases. The first phase, from the mid-1960s to mid-1980s, observed a rise in labour use. However, the trend was reversed in the second phase, the period after the mid-1980s. These trends were associated with the nature and extent of mechanisation in agriculture. While tractor use was associated with the decline in labour use in 1971–1972, tubewell irrigation had offset its negative impact (Agarwal, 1981). As a result, mechanisation had an effect of increasing labour use. Prihar and Sidhu (1984) found that full tartarised farms employed 10,411 person-hours of labour per farm in 1975–1976 compared to 8342 person-hours of partly tractor and partly bullock operated farms and 7177 person-hours of fully bullock operated farms. A large increase in the gross cropped area due to the use of tractors and ground water irrigation from 1962–1965 to 1990–1991 (as previously pointed out) was the main reason behind this trend.

Demand for female labour was relatively lower even before the green revolution. They were mostly engaged in sowing and harvesting activities. Both the activities remained largely unaffected during the first phase of mechanisation. An analysis of the wheat crop by Agarwal (1981) found harvesting and sowing to be mostly manual in 1971–1972. Women contributed nearly 19 per cent of the labour time in sowing and 19 per cent of the labour time in harvesting then. These findings suggest that female labour was mostly unaffected by the changes during this period.

The second phase saw a decline in labour use in agriculture. Mechanisation started replacing labour engaged in sowing and harvesting in this period. Labour use in agriculture declined from 1089 man-hours per hectare in 1985–1986 to 840 man-hours per hectare in 2006–2007 (Baruah and Singh, 2020; Devi et al., 2013). During the same period, tractor use rose from 14.01 hours to 31.83 hours per hectare and the use of combine harvester increased from 0.13 hours to 1.89 hours per hectare. As a result, labour use declined for all crops. During the 1981–1982 to 2016–2017 period, wheat and paddy cultivation had 66 per cent and 60 per cent decline in person-days per hectare, respectively (Fig. 2).While labour use remained high for cotton crop with a smaller decline (about 20 per cent from 1981–1981 to 2016–2017), a large shift in area under cotton to paddy cultivation in the mid-1990s (as discussed earlier) led to a much larger drop in demand for labour.

Increased use of machines in sowing and harvesting and a shift away from cotton crop significantly lowered the demand for labour in agriculture. The employment of women suffered the most due to this change. It led to most women becoming unemployed or underemployed. Baruah (2018), in a primary survey conducted in 2015, found that 49 per cent of the Dalit women in working age (age 15–59 years) and 26 per cent of the non-Dalit women were engaged in one or more agricultural activities in the district of Mansa (cotton is one of the main crops in the district). While Daljit women worked for 46 days in agriculture, the average was 36 for non-Dalit women. Only five per cent of the Dalit women got more than 100 days of work in agriculture with a maximum of 125 days in a year. None of the non-Dalit women, in the sample, reached 100 days of work in agriculture. Even cotton, which is a relatively labour-intensive crop, provided merely 35 days of work to Dalit and 22 days of work to non-Dalit women (Fig. 3).

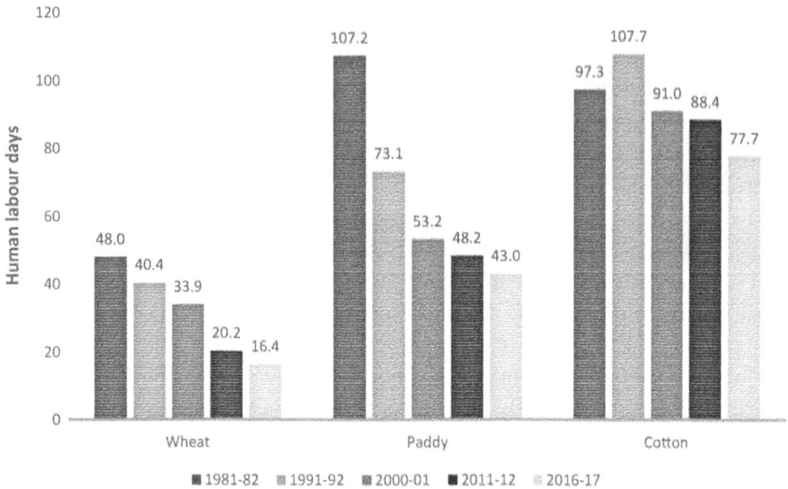

Fig. 2 Crop-wise use of human labour (days per hectare) in Punjab Agriculture (*Source* Toor et al. [2007]; The Commission for Agricultural Costs & Prices, various reports)

3 Female Labour Force Participation in Rural Punjab

The effect of reduced demand for labour can be seen in changes in the female labour force participation rate (FLFPR). The usual status shows rise in FLFPR from 34.7 per cent in 1993–1994 to 48.5 per cent in 2004–2005 (Table 1). However, it showed a worsening trend in the later years. FLFPR declined to 32.9 per cent in 2011–2012 which further fell to 15.4 per cent in 2017–2018. This is much smaller than male labour force participation rate which was more than 78 per cent for any year (Baruah and Singh, 2020; NSSO, 2019).

However, a deeper look at their status shows that the problem is much severe than observed in the usual status. The share of females in principle status lies between 5.4 per cent and 6.6 per cent. It means that during the 1993–94 to 2011–2012 period, the share of women, who were gainfully employed for the most of year, never crossed 6.6 per cent (the similar figure is not available for 2017–2018 due to non-availability of NSS unit-level data). The rest of the women were underemployed (had subsidiary

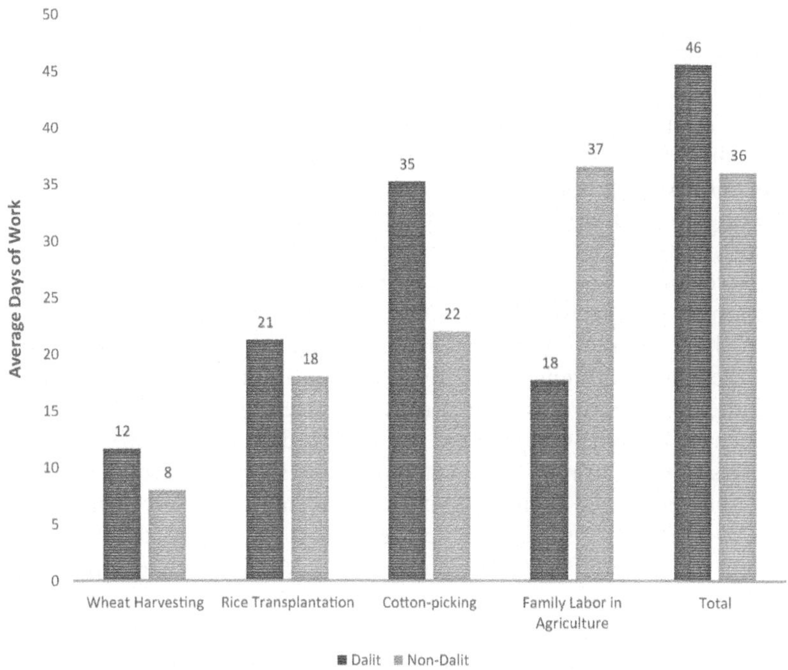

Fig. 3 Activity-wise Average days of work that Women have performed in agriculture during 2014–15 (*Note* The averages are based on data of women who were engaged in that particular activity
Source Baruah [2018])

Table 1 Female labour force participation rate by work status in Rural Punjab, age 15–59 years

Year	*Usual Status*#	*Principal Status*	*Subsidiary Status*
1993–94	34.7	5.4	29.3
1999–00	44.9	6.0	38.9
2004–05	48.5	6.1	42.4
2011–12	32.9	6.6	26.3
2017–18	15.4	-	-

Note # Usual status includes all those who have been workers under either principal status or subsidiary status. Usual status is also the labour force participation rate in this case
Source Computed from NSS unit-level data, various years and NSSO (2019)

status). Even in 2004–2005, when FLFPR reached 48.5 per cent, more than 86 per cent of the working women were underemployed.

Data on average hours worked per week during 2017–2018 also confirms the lack of employment opportunities for rural women. Both men and women in rural areas worked lesser hours throughout the year (Fig. 4). Working hours per week were the lowest for rural females. Rural working women worked 13 to 14 hours less per week than their male counterparts and 5 to 13 hours less than urban women. The gap between rural women and urban men was 18 hours or more per week.

Baruah (2018) found that total days of employment hardly ever crossed the six-month benchmark for female workers in total areas to call them gainfully employed. Even among Dalit women, who constitute the most deprived section, only 0.8 per cent was working more than 180 days. MGNREGS provided merely 22 days of work to Dalit and 14 days of work to non-Dalit women. A high share of these unemployed and underemployed women (about 66 percent) expressed their willingness to work. They stayed unemployed due to the unavailability of work within the village. These women, due to prevailing gender norms, are unable to travel to urban areas for work, unlike their male counterparts.

NSSO (2019) found that female workers in rural Punjab earned significantly less in 2017–2018. Self-employed and regular salaried females earn about 35 per cent and 70 per cent less than rural males in the respective

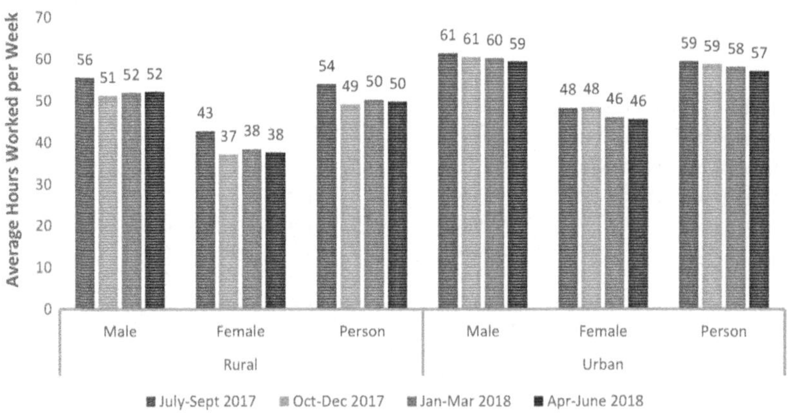

Fig. 4 Average hours worked per week during 2017–18 (*Source* NSSO [2019])

categories. Even urban women in these two categories earn 43 per cent and 95 per cent more than rural females. On an average, the wage rate for female casual workers (other than in public works) was 24 per cent less than rural males.

The prevailing situation is the outcome of the existing policy that ignores social institutions and expects growth in itself to take care of employment. Despite the failure of agricultural growth to generate employment, many experts still emphasise on agricultural growth and diversification to be the solution to employment problem in rural areas (Toor et al., 2007). It is often overlooked that the extent of mechanisation (which is increasing over time) has left little scope for such policies to be effective. Therefore, rural areas require policies that inherently consider women's employment indispensable.

4 Lacklustre and Inadequate Response to Pandemic

Fear of COVID-19 and the lockdown have led to a decline in economic activity and employment in India. IMF (2020) predicted 4.5 per cent contraction and a slower recovery of the Indian economy in 2020. The data from the Centre for Monitoring Indian Economy (CMIE) found an increase in unemployment to 25.5 per cent by 5 May 2020 from 7.4 per cent in the pre-lockdown period (Bertrand et al., 2020). The pandemic has hurt the employment prospects of women the hardest. Deshpande (2020), using the data collected by CMIE in April 2020, found that the loss of employment was 20 per cent higher among women compared to their male counterparts.

The situation in rural areas is likely to be worse. The rural workforce could get more work during the paddy transplanting season due to the non-availability of migrant labour(Gupta, 2020). However, it only provided work for a few days. The work was shared by male and female labour which meant that only a part of the work went to female labour. The male labour was finding it hard to get work due to lockdown and the fear of COVID-19. Also, the wage controls imposed by the panchayats limited their earnings (Gupta, 2020).

Notwithstanding the availability of work in paddy cultivation, the employment prospect of women is likely to have suffered serious damage because of the pandemic. Demand for non-essential goods and services dropped as the fear of COVID-19 has caused people to cut down their expenditure. Increased cost of travel (due to restrictions on public transport and higher fuel prices) and the fear of infection have made travelling to urban areas for work less attractive. These changes mean less work for female workers during the pandemic. COVID-19 outbreak has also triggered some long-term changes in the labour market. The current shortage of labour for paddy cultivation due to the pandemic has given a big push to mechanisation and is likely to permanently lower the demand for labour in agriculture (Kaur, 2020; *The Hindu*, 2020). Female workers, who have little scope to secure employment outside the agricultural sector, will be the most affected by this change.

The government policies, in the face of COVID-19 pandemic, have so far done little to ensure female employment in rural areas. Both the central and the Punjab government have introduced various policies to curtail the negative impact of the pandemic. Government of India has come up with a relief package which includes transfers of Rs. 1500 (over three months) in the Pradhan Mantri Jan Dhan Yojana (PMJDY) accounts of 200 million women, Rs. 1.7 lakh crore for free ration, Rs. 5.94 lakh crore of collateral-free credit to micro, small and medium scale enterprises (MSME), Rs. 2 lakh crore of concessional credit to farmers, an investment of Rs. one lakh crore in agricultural infrastructure, and Rs. 40,000 crores of additional allocation to MGNREGS(Balu, 2020).

The government of Punjab, in addition to the distribution of free ration to households, has transferred Rs. 3000 each to the accounts of 3.2 lakhs registered construction workers (Singh and Kumar, 2020) and announced a relief package for the real estate sector (GoP, 2020). To revive economic activity and boost investment, the government of Punjab has rolled back the hike in the minimum wage and increased the working time from 8 to 12 hours (Singh et al., 2020).To attract investment, the government of Punjab has also redefined the classification of a 'large factory' by changing the labour requirement for it from 'more than 500 workers' to 'more than 1000 workers' (PTI, 2020).

The above-mentioned policies of the central and the state government are focussed on the creation of growth, especially in the urban formal sector. These policies pay little attention to female employment or even overall employment and working conditions and terms. Some of the policies, such as increase in working hours, are likely to hurt female employment instead of facilitating it (see Bardhan, 2020).

Among all relief package and policies, additional funds for MGNREGS are the only measure that is directed to rural employment. While it is a welcome step, it has limited capacity to create employment. For example, MGNREGS, in the financial year 2019–2020, provided 48.4 days of work per household for the expenditure of Rs. 68,020 crores (GoI, 2020). Based on these figures, the additional allocation may only provide an additional 28 days of work per household in India. The benefits of these additional funds are likely to be smaller for Punjab. In 2019–2020, about 1.1 per cent of the total funds were allocated to Punjab (nearly 2.1 per cent of the rural population of India resides in Punjab). It provided 31.2 days of work per household. The days of work per household in Punjab were 36 per cent less than all India figure. Assuming a similar allocation of funds, 100 per cent utilisation and no additional households seeking work, the additional funds will just add 18 days of work per household in Punjab. This figure is also an optimistic estimate as it assumes that no new household will seek work under MGNREGS which is highly unlikely due to the present state of the economy. With a large increase in the number of households seeking work under MGNREGS, the days of work may even decline. Moreover, the additional funds for MGNREGS are a temporary measure with no effect on sustaining employment and earning of women.

5 Policy Implications

The discussion in previous sections shows that the existing policies are grossly inadequate to promote female employment in rural Punjab. These policies mainly focus on increasing agricultural growth. Even if the policies could achieve high growth in agricultural sector, it will be accompanied by higher mechanisation and is unlikely to generate employment in rural areas throughout the year. Policies which focus on agricultural growth, such as investment in agricultural infrastructure, may not be a solution to employment problem in rural Punjab. Employment programmes like MGNREGS also cannot address this issue. Households in Punjab are getting just 31 days of employment under MGNREGS. Even if the government could achieve the target 100 days of work in a year, it would constitute merely one-third of the year.

The dearth of employment opportunities in the rural area is clear for the fact that even rural males are working for lesser hours (Fig. 4). Migration and the daily commute to urban areas cannot solve this problem either. Baruah (2018) found that women often find it difficult to commute to urban areas for work in Punjab due to economic and social constraints. Higher dependence on urban areas to create growth and employment leads to urban–rural inequalities and exclusion of those who cannot travel to cities for work.

Hence, the rural economy needs a sustainable solution to combat unemployment. The economic policy in Punjab must centre on creating infrastructure and businesses in rural areas that can provide gainful employment. Punjab needs policies which facilitate the establishment of MSMEs in the rural areas by easing the norms for their establishment and ensuring faster clearance of the project. The preference should be given to those industries which employ women workers. Businesses, which can employ unskilled and semi-skilled labour after a short training, may prefer to invest in rural area if the government of Punjab commit itself to providing required infrastructure in rural areas and offer them incentives. A policy, which creates better employment opportunities in rural areas, will also lead to higher growth and faster recovery.

Note

1. The structure of the argument in this section is based on Baruah and Singh (2020).

References

Abraham, V. (2017) Stagnant Employment Growth : Last Three Years May Have Been the Worst, *Economic and Political Weekly*, 52(38): 13–17.

Agarwal, B. (1981) Agricultural Mechanisation and Labour Use: A Disaggregated Approach, *International Labour Review* 120(1): 115–127.

Balu, M. (2020) Covid-19: India Uses Crisis to Bring-in Economic Reforms as Package, *The Peninsula Foundation*. Retrieved July 23, 2020, https://www.thepeninsula.org.in/2020/05/25/covid-19-india-uses-crisis-to-bring-in-economic-reforms-as-package/.

Bardhan, P. (2020, May 10) Labour Law Suspension: Hit the Workers When They Are Down, Bloomberg Quint.

Baruah, A. (2016) Occupational Pattern and Workforce Participation of Women in Indian Rural Punjab: A Caste Perspective, *Millennial Asia*, 7(2): 153–183.

Baruah, A. (2018) *Changing Pattern of Dalit Women's Work in Contemporary Rural Punjab: Causes and Consequences*, New Delhi: Jawaharlal Nehru University.

Baruah, A., and Indervir, S. (2020) Employment of Women in Rural Punjab : Deconstructing Agricultural Growth Policy, *Economic and Political Weekly*, 55(26 & 27): 29–35.

Bertrand, M., Kaushik, K., and Heather, S. (2020) How Are Indian Households Coping under the COVID-19 Lockdown? 8 Key Findings. Retrieved May 24, 2020, https://www.chicagobooth.edu/research/rustandy/blog/2020/how-are-indian-households-coping-under-the-covid19-lockdown.

Bhalla, G. S., Chadha, G. K., Kashyap, S. P., and Sharma, R. K. (1990) *Agricultural Growth and Structural Changes in the Punjab Economy: An Input-Output Analysis*, Washington, DC.

Chowdhury, S. (2011) Employment in India: What Does the Latest Data Show? *Economic and Political Weekly*, 46(32): 23–26.

Deshpande, A. (2020) The Covid-19 Pandemic and Lockdown: First Effects on Gender Gaps in Employment and Domestic Work in India. Discussion Paper No. 30. Ashoka University, Department of Economics.

Devi, Y. Latika, Jasdev, S., Kamal, V., and Sanjay, K. (2013) Dynamics of Labour Demand and Its Determinants in Punjab Agriculture, *Agricultural Economics Research Review*, 26(2): 267–273.

Diamond, P. (1989) Search Theory, in J. Eatwell, M. Milgate, and P. Newman (Eds.), *Allocation, Information and Markets*, London: The New Palgrave.

Fletcher, Erin K., Rohini, P., and Charity Troyer, M. (2017) Women and Work in India: Descriptive Evidence and a Review of Potential Policies. Working Paper No. RWP18–004.

Gill, A., and Lakhwinder, S. (2006) Farmers' Suicides and Response of Public Policy: Evidence, Diagnosis and Alternatives from Punjab, *Economic and Political Weekly*, 41(26): 2762–2768.

GoI. (2020) MGNREGA Dashboard. Ministry of Rural Development, Government of India. Retrieved July 27, 2020, http://mnregaweb4.nic.in/netnrega/all_lvl_details_ dashboard_new.aspx.

GoP. (2018) Statistical Abstract of Punjab, 2018. Publication No. 958. Economic and Statistical Organisation, The Government of Punjab.

GoP. (2020) The Government of Punjab: Press Release. Directorate of Information and Public Relations, Punjab, India. Retrieved July 23, 2020, http://www.diprpunjab.gov.in/?q=content/major-relief-real-estate-sector-capt-amarinder-announces-stimulus-package-cope-covid-impact.

Gupta, V. (2020) Punjab: Labour Shortage in Lockdown Reveals Fissures in Farm Economy Ahead of Paddy Sowing Season, *The Wire*. Retrieved July 23, 2020, https://thewire.in/agriculture/punjab-paddy-farmers-labourers.

IMF. (2020, June) World Economic Outlook Update, International Monetary Fund.

Kaur, D. (2020, June 10) Labour Crisis, Mechanised Sowing Picks up in Punjab, *The Tribune*.

Mazumdar, I., and Neetha, N. (2011) Gender Dimensions: Employment Trends in India, 1993-94 to 2009-10, *Economic and Political Weekly*, 46(43): 118–126.

NSSO. (2019) Periodic Labour Force Survey (PLFS), 2017–18. National Statistical Office, Ministry of Statistics and Programme Implementation, The Government of India.

Prihar, R. S., and Sidhu, D. S. (1984) Impact of Mechanization on Labor Employment in Punjab Agriculture, *Indian Journal of Industrial Relations*, 19(3): 379–387.

PTI. (2020) Punjab Govt Amends Law to Facilitate Large Industrial Units, Create Job Opportunities, News18. Retrieved July 22, 2020, https://www.news18.com/news/india/punjab-govt-amends-law-to-facilitate-large-industrial-units-create-job-opportunities-2682457.html.

Singh, I. Sukhwinder, S., and Lakhwinder, S. (2014) *Punjab's Economic Development in the Era of Globalisation*, Delhi: LG Publishers.

Singh, I., and Naresh, K. (2020) Punjab's Fight Against COVID-19: Hopes, Fears and the Balancing Act, University Practice Connect, Azim Premji University. Retrieved May 27, 2020, https://practiceconnect.azimpremjiuniversity.edu.in/punjabs-fight-against-covid-19-hopes-fears-and-the-balancing-act/.

Singh, R., Shrusti, J. Maharathy, and Pathik, C. (2020) India: State-Wise Relaxation of Labour Legislations Amidst COVID-19, Mondaq. Retrieved July 22, 2020, https://www.mondaq.com/india/employment-and-workforce-wellbeing/946064/state-wise-relaxation-of-labour-legislations-amidst-covid-19.

The Hindu. (2020, June 7) Farmers in Punjab to Plant Around 25% Paddy with DSR Technology.

Toor, M. S., Bhullar, A. S., and Inderpreet, K. (2007) Agriculture-Led Diversification and Labor Use in Punjab: Potentials and Constraints, *Indian Journal of Labor Economics*, 50(4): 737–746.

COVID-19 Pandemic and the Scheduled Caste Workers in Rural Punjab: A Need for Structural Transformation

Deepak Kumar

1 Introduction

The first case of COVID-19 infection in India was reported on 30 Jan 2020. In little less than two months, as infected cases rose to 536, India imposed an unprecedented nationwide lockdown on 24th March 2020 to contain the spread of COVID-19 pandemic. With an approximate population of 1.3 billion people with many settled in densely populated pockets, the Indian government perceived a major health crisis. Though initial reaction of many countries was inclined towards lockdown, Indian case has been in news for being one of the most stringent and comprehensive lockdowns in the world imposed with less than four hours' notice to its citizens. Despite the stringent measures like a complete ban on public and private transportation by the government coupled with punitive action by police against erring citizens to curb the movement of people, panic and uncertainty caused by the sudden lockdown led to mass exodus of migrants from various parts of India. The haunting images of migrant labourers walking with their children and family for hundreds of miles without food and shelter exposed the highly unequal structure of Indian

D. Kumar (✉)
Punjabi University, Patiala, India

S. Singh et al. (eds.), *Covid-19 Pandemic and Economic Development*,
https://doi.org/10.1007/978-981-16-4442-9_12

society. The phenomenon also underscored the marginalized status of workers in the country as a whole. The threat of corona virus and its implications for the marginalized needs serious exploration.

This paper seeks to understand the impact of COVID-19 pandemic on the most marginalized workers in Punjab, one of the most developed states of India. It tries to look at the challenges posed by this pandemic to the Scheduled Caste workers in the state who predominantly reside in rural areas of Punjab.

1.1 Scheduled Castes in India

Indian society is peculiar owing to its caste-based social stratification. Primarily a product of Hindu social organization, caste system has gradually become part and parcel of daily existence of Indian society and gradually spread to non-Hindu communities as well. The recalcitrant nature of the institution of caste continues to haunt Indian society even after centuries of change. The most abhorrent feature of caste system has been the practice of untouchability which deprived certain members of society the most basic of their rights for a dignified existence. After independence, untouchability was declared unconstitutional and a punishable offence. However, due to their long history of stigmatized social existence, the untouchable communities were deprived socially, culturally, economically and politically. All these communities, hence, lacked the basic economic and cultural capital to begin with. Independent India recognized this historical injustice in society and made special provisions in the form of reservations in government jobs to ensure mainstreaming of these communities. The caste groups which suffered discrimination on the grounds of untouchability were identified, listed and referred to as the Scheduled Castes.

The metaphor of 'social distancing' strongly resonates with the idea of untouchability in India. The term 'social distancing' described the initial strategy recommended by WHO to contain the pandemic. The term was later rechristened as 'physical distancing' once WHO realized how its previously used term deepened socially discriminating policies against the vulnerable sections of society in various parts of the world. The case of Indian society in particular becomes significant as the caste-based social organization historically segregated a large chunk of population through social practices of untouchability leading to their segregation, isolation and marginalization.

1.2 *Untouchability in Contemporary India*

While untouchability prevailed over the centuries, it was constantly challenged over the ages by various forces. From the ancient times till the present, the most formidable opposition came from Budhism, Islam, Sikhism, Bhakti movement, Sufi tradition accompanied by various social reform movements. The onset of British Raj in India followed by India's independence movement brought new consciousness against the practice. In contemporary times, Westernization, secular education, democratic polity and most of all the Indian Constitution have posed a serious challenge to untouchability.

However, with its deep association with the traditional religious system of Hinduism, the practice of untouchability remains an extant reality. It continues to manifest itself in newer forms and different shades in many places. In their study Shah et al. found untouchability to be a 'pan-Indian phenomenon' whose 'specific forms and intensity vary considerably across regions and socio-historical contexts' (Shah et al., 2006). That untouchability is still practised in contemporary Indian society has been sufficiently reported by various studies (Mendelsohn and Vicziany, 2000; Louis, 2003; Kumar, 2001; O'Neill, 2003; Shah et al., 2006; Sarukkai, 2009). A recent study indicates changing attitudes towards this regressive practice but still finds more likelihood of it being practised in rural areas, more among Brahmins than others, among people with lower levels of education and poor community networks, and also more among cultivators than other occupational categories. (Thorat and Omkar, 2020). The case of Punjab becomes enigmatic as it is primarily an agricultural state dominated by non-Hindu social organization, Westernized to a great extent but with limited urbanization.

2 Scheduled Castes in Punjab

The status of Scheduled Castes (SCs) in Punjab is supposed to be somewhat different owing to the predominance of Sikhism and various religious and political reforms that have actively played their role in diluting the effects of caste system thus weakening the hold of caste-based Hindu social organization. Even the Hindu population in Punjab experienced certain reforms through Arya Samaj movement in the late nineteenth century. Another significant development during this phase was preferential recruitment of Sikhs in the British army thus constituting almost 20% of the British Indian Army by 1912 (Rajivlochan, 2018). Punjabi society, especially Sikhs, were thus favourably exposed to Westernization. Early twentieth century in Punjab also witnessed Ad-Dharmi movement inspired by Dr. Ambedkar instilling caste consciousness and political awareness among the Scheduled Castes (Juergensmeyer, 1988).

Despite the above-mentioned favourable factors the institution of caste still prevails in Punjab. The government of Punjab has made several attempts to ameliorate the conditions of SCs in the state and over the years made some notable progress in bringing these communities into the mainstream. However, the status of SCs is still far from satisfactory and therefore the efforts of the state need to be recalibrated.

2.1 Socio-Economic Status of Scheduled Castes in Punjab

Among all the states of India, Punjab has the distinction of having the highest percentage of Scheduled Caste population. As per the census of India, with a population of 88,60,179, percentage of SCs in Punjab is 31.94. In case of Punjab there are 39 sub-categories which have been enumerated in the Census of India. Of these 39 categories, the four sub-castes form the major chunk of the population. These are Mazhabis, Ravisadisas/ Chamars et al., Ad-Dharmis and Balmikis et al. Together these four groups constitute around 74% of the SC population in the state. In case we add the fifth largest category of Rai Sikhs, this segment crosses the 80% mark. The remaining 20% of the population is composed of the other sub-castes enumerated within the SC population (Census of India, 2011). Despite various sub-categories within SCs there are historically shared socio-economic and political conditions among these groups which make them into a single group.

The literacy rate among SCs in Punjab is 64.81% which is below the overall state average of 75.84% and the national average of SCs at 66.07% (Census of India, 2011). The sex ratio among SCs in Punjab is 910 while the national average of SCs is 945. The urban population among SCs in Punjab is 27% which is below the state average of 37.84%. It has been observed that with a higher degree of urbanization among SCs, the sex ratio in the community has improved. Higher percentage of SCs in rural areas also indicates their social deprivation as more than 85% of SCs in Punjab do not own agricultural land. 'In 2015–16, Dalits in Punjab owned just 6% of all operational holdings' (Bansal, 2020). Hence, most of the working rural population among Scheduled Castes is employed as landless agricultural labour. Their fate is closely linked to the fate of ailing cultivators of the state but without any land resource, their condition is more precarious. According to the Census of India (2011) only 1,25,544 Scheduled Castes were working as cultivators while 8,04,573 were working as agricultural labourers. The very few who owned agricultural land were small or marginal farmers surviving on poor quality land with meagre resources (Vatta, 2014). Among the total workers in the state, the SC workers constituted 32.13% which is close to their overall population in the state. However, the percentage of SC cultivators in the state is abysmally low at 6.97% (Table 1). The corresponding figure of Non-SC cultivators is as high as 93% of the total cultivators in the state. Their disproportionately low presence among the cultivators is matched only with their similarly disproportionate high presence among agricultural labourers with 68.89% of the total agricultural labourers. This indicates a high level of agrarian disparities in the workforce of SCs and Non-SCs in the state.

Table 1 Cultivators and agricultural labourers among SC & non-SC workers in Punjab- 2011

Category	*SCs*	*Non-SC*	*Total*
Total Population	88,60,179 (31.94%)	1,88,83,159 (68.06%)	2,77,43,338 (100)
Total Workers	31,79,438 (32.13%)	67,17,924 (67.87%)	98,97,362 (100)
Main Workers	25,18,169 (29.79%)	59,31,760 (70.21%)	84,48,413 (100)
Cultivators	1,25,544 (06.96%)	16,78,316 (93.04%)	18,03,860 (100)
Agricultural Labourers	8,04,573 (68.89%)	3,63,448 (31.11%)	11,68,021 (100)
Marginal Workers	6,61,269 (45.72%)	7,85,157 (54.28%)	14,46,426 (100)

Source Census of India 2011

Table: B-1 Main workers, Marginal workers, Non-workers and those marginal workers, non-workers seeking/available for work classified by age and sex

Table: B-1 SC: Main workers, Marginal workers, Non-workers and those marginal workers, non-workers seeking/available for work classified by age and sex for scheduled castes

2.2 *Inequality in Agrarian Structure of Rural Punjab*

The existing inequality in agrarian structure of Punjab along the caste lines can be traced back to the institution of caste itself which devoid a segment of population to own any means of production at all and hence survive by merely serving the non-dalits. In case of Punjab, despite the religious reform movements since the advent of Sikhism which had diluted the hold of Hindu social organization, the Land Alienation Act of 1900 enacted during the British period proved highly detrimental to Dalits. Though targeted at discouraging Hindu moneylenders from usurping agricultural land from the farmers, the legislation hinged upon a simplistic solution whereby only 'agricultural castes' were permitted to own agricultural land (Juergensmeyer, 1988). While the Jat Sikhs were identified by the Britishers as an agricultural caste, Dalits did not fit into such a crude category hence making them ineligible to own any piece of agricultural land. Even after independence, this anomaly in land-distribution was not addressed leaving most of the SC households devoid of access to agricultural land. Till date ownership of land therefore remains an important source of social and political status of a person in Punjab (Neale, 1979). Pangs of India's partition on the eve of Independence left a deep scar on the state and Sikh identity politics dominated almost all other narratives in the state for a long period. With the advent of Green Revolution in Punjab in 1960s, the capitalist mode of agriculture was experimented with helping India become self sufficient in food grains. Immediate success of this intervention brought glory to the agricultural community of the state and the traditionally land owning Jat Sikh peasantry reaped the benefits of the development. While the hard working farmers were duly recognized and eulogized for their efforts, the hard working agricultural labourers remained largely unrecognized, thus, the fruits of development were not shared equally in the state. The studies indicate that capitalist agrarian intervention exacerbated social and economic inequalities further (Sukhpal and Shruti, 2020; Bansal, 2020; Kumar, 1999). 'In 2002–03, Punjab had the highest inequality in rural land ownership' in the country (Bansal, 2020). Incidence of 'reverse tenancy' helps in analyzing agrarian structure of Punjab and makes visible the land inequality even more severe in the case of operational land holdings (Sugimoto, 2014; Bansal, 2020). The small and marginal farmers in Punjab 'operate only 10% of the cultivated area in Punjab; compared to the all-India average of 50%" (Bansal, 2020). With big land owners primarily being from Jat Sikh community and the landless and manual workers primarily from the Scheduled castes, the fissures along caste lines are becoming increasingly more perceptible (Vatta, 2014; Sugimoto, 2014; Bansal, 2020; Tylor et al., 2015). The effort to retain ownership of land by the landlords is manifested in various cultural practices too which can be seen prevalent among Jat Sikhs in their institutions of marriage, kinship and family (Kumar, 1999; Tylor et al., 2015). Land is thus not merely an economic asset for income or profit but also a source of political and cultural dominance in the state. Even among Punjabi diaspora, during various NRI *sammelans* held in the state during the last few years, land-related issue and feuds formed the most recurring theme in their deliberations. The remittances received from Diaspora are often used to enhance the social standing of the family by expanding size of their land ownership (Sandhu, 2019; Tylor et al., 2015). Hence, the historical structural inequality in agrarian structure gets reinforced through widening economic difference between the Jat Sikh landlords and the landless Dalit agricultural labourers.

3 Pandemic and Scheduled Caste Workers in Rural Punjab

As discussed above, the Scheduled Caste Workers in rural Punjab are primarily engaged in agricultural activity as agricultural labourers. Their landlessness in agrarian economy is one of their defining characteristics. Given this skewed nature of access to land as a resource, the bargaining power of Dalit agricultural labourers has been extremely weak. To make matters worse for these labourers, the big farmers preferred to hire cheaper migrant labour from Bihar and UP to maintain their profit from the land.

3.1 Return of Migrants

With the onset of COVID-19 pandemic, by the beginning of May 2020 around 10 Lakh workers registered to leave Punjab for their native places. Most of them hailed from UP and Bihar (The Statesman, 6 May, 2020). By the time government arranged Shramik Trains, almost 35% chose to stay back (News18.com, 24 May, 2020). As on 20 July 2020, more than 5,43,343 migrant workers had been facilitated by the Punjab government to return to their home state. (Punjab COVID-19 Response). While these are official figures, there are many unreported cases which indicate a much larger exodus of migrant workers from the state. On the other hand lot of Punjabi migrants returned from Maharashtra, Madhya Pradesh and other places. By the beginning of May 2020 around 4200 persons returned from Nanded out of which around 969 were found COVID positive. More peculiar to Punjab was the return of NRIs. An estimated 97,000 NRIs returned to Punjab between January and March 2020. Another 20,000 more were expected to arrive in India by mid-July. Unfortunately the returning NRIs faced social stigmatization in the beginning where they were initially treated as disease carriers and therefore were largely unwelcome (Nagpal, 2020). With a large chunk of NRIs returning from US, UK, Spain and Italy, Punjab was over cautious with a possible pandemic outbreak in the state. Most of these NRI migrants who returned hailed from Doaba and were mainly from the landless Dalit community (Rohini et al., 2020).

3.2 *Diminishing Returns from Agriculture*

After initial growth in demand in 1980s for agricultural labour despite mechanization of various farm processes, 1990s onward the demand for agricultural labour dwindled with spiralling costs of agriculture and further mechanization. Agricultural labour gradually shifted towards non-farm activities to supplement its income (Vatta, 2014). Moreover, wherever there was proximity to urban centres, labourers sold their services as informal casual labour. Even some of the marginal and small farmers found it increasingly unviable to sustain agriculture with rising costs involved in agricultural practices eventually pushing some of them to abandon farming and join labour market as unskilled labourers. There is also evidence that Non-SC workers end up in better paid jobs in non-farm sector compared to their SC counterparts (Sugimoto, 2014). With diminishing returns, agriculture remains insufficient to absorb the surge in available labour.

3.3 *Loss of Wages*

With the extension of lockdown the SC workers from urban centres have also joined the ranks of rural agricultural labour. Most of the studies indicate that occupational shift to non-farm activities has a pattern in which the landless SC workers often end up working for less remunerative jobs owing to their limited economic and cultural base. Earlier working in urban centres the migrant SC workers used to add to the family income back home through remittances. Ever since lockdown besides the loss of employment in urban centres, many have become a liability on the family resources.

3.4 *Rise in Indebtedness*

The indebtedness among agricultural labourers in Punjab is no less worrisome than that of the farmers. In fact, unlike landowning farmers, the landless agricultural SC workers are more susceptible to the vicious cycle of indebtedness as they end up borrowing credit from non-institutional sources. Non-availability of collaterals makes their credit worthiness even worse. Given the fact that most of the labourers are already under some debt, it becomes double whammy for the landless labourers with loss of wages on one hand and steeper interest rates on their credit on the other. The more the extension of lockdown the more they will get embroiled in debt.

3.5 *Potential Caste-Based Conflicts*

Social and political consciousness among SC workers supported by an egalitarian religion of Sikhism prompted them to assert their dignity and refuse to work under the local landlord. However, the recent economic crisis has pushed these SC workers back into the ambit of village politics where the lines of economic engagement are often determined by traditional caste hierarchy. The resulting situation in rural Punjab becomes a potential source of caste- based tensions. There have been instances where in the absence of migrant labour from UP and Bihar, the local labour is now more demanding. Similarly, the landowning Jat Sikh employers have also joined hands and have become more repressive towards the labour (Khanna, 2020). The last few years have also witnessed rising demand among SCs for their share in common village land for their subsistence. The Jat Sikh on their part have been reported to resist such endeavours through rigging of auction bids, violence and repression against Dalits, imposing restrictions on the use of common land in the village by Dalits and other such measures (Bansal, 2020).

The marginalization of Dalits become more obvious when one finds convenient acceptance of separate Gurudwaras and cremation grounds for

Dalits in almost all villages (Jodhka, 2002). Proliferation of over 9,000 *deras* in Punjab and constant shift towards these *deras* among Dalits in Punjab indicates at the simmering caste tensions in the state (Ram, 2007). Out-migration from the state over the past few decades had obviated to a large extent the possibilities of direct confrontation over limited resources. However, with extended lockdown the situation remains volatile till the tensions are resolved.

3.6 *Marginalization of Female SC Workers*

The feudal social set up of patriarchal Punjabi society leaves little scope for women female workers to look forward to. During the initial years of Green Revolution, the female workers used to contribute substantially to the family income by participating in farm activity. However, with the increase in farm income many farmers started opting for hired labour rather than family labour. Gradually the distinction between prosperous and poor families once again became coterminous with caste inequality. The SC female workers had an initial phase of better opportunities till 1990s when increase in mechanization of agriculture was accompanied by increase in farm incomes and demand for unskilled labour. However, after 1990s there was a decline in corresponding rise in employment opportunity in agriculture especially with large scale failure of cotton crops for many consecutive years (Baruah and Indervir, 2020). It has been found that agricultural labour remains less remunerative for female agricultural labourers but shift to non-farm activities is availed better by the Non-SC female workers as they are better placed in terms of social and cultural capital to make use of such opportunities.

There are certain groups within female SC workers who have been working as maids in other households. The social distancing norms of pandemic situation have made these maids redundant to a greater extent. Coupled with caste based bias of purity and pollution that militates against SC female workers it becomes difficult for them to find non-farm occupations in the current scenario.

3.7 *Diminished Accessibility to Health and Education*

The education and health are two significant sectors of economy that determine the long-term well being of a society. Ever since move for greater privatization of essential services of health and education in the state since mid-1990s, the state has conveniently withdrawn from its social obligation towards the poorest of the poor. Better health services and quality higher education have become increasingly cost intensive for most of the people in the state. The resultant pressure on limited resources makes SC households more vulnerable to further marginalization leading to diminished access to these basic facilities.

4 Conclusion

Post pandemic situation in Punjab remains precarious for its Scheduled Caste rural workers due to inherent social strains in its socio-economic structure. Unequal access to agricultural resources makes their condition more miserable as a class. State's focus on increasing productivity of land has overshadowed the question of land redistribution in the state. As long as the growth in agricultural productivity accompanied growth in income for everybody involved in agricultural activity the economic and social relations remained affable. However, with a shrinking share in agricultural profits and rising aspirations for a just and fair society, the demand for an equitable share in agricultural resources is likely to aggravate with time. Despite all the challenges faced in agriculture, the studies indicate that access to land still remains one of the most dependable means of livelihood and also the biggest source of income for rural households (Sugimoto, 2014). The accompanying *izzat* with land ownership remains a constant attraction for the people of Punjab. With increasing growth in infrastructure development by the state, acquisition of land is going to be a regular feature in the times to come. The experience in land acquisition has merely replicated the existing inequalities in the state. While the landowners get reasonably compensated for their land, the poor agricultural farmers are merely squeezed out of the equation and left to fend for themselves on their own (Kaur et al., 2020). Besides creating more equitable access to land in rural Punjab through cooperative farming etc., the state has to ensure crop diversification and pay special attention on agro-industry to absorb the teeming workers. As long as the primary source of inequality is not addressed all the subsequent developments will invariably keep adding layers to the existing structural inequality and deepen the existing divide further.

References

Ambedkar, B. R. (1990) [1948] The Untouchables, in V. Moon (Ed.), *Dr Babasaheb Ambedkar: Writings and Speeches, Vol. 7*, Bombay: Education Department, Government of Maharashtra.

Bansal, G. (2020) Land Struggle in the Time of Pandemic, *Frontline*, 37(15): 55–59.

Baruah, A., and Indervir, S. (2020, June 27) Employment of Women in Rural Punjab: Deconstructing Agricultural Growth Policy, *Economic and Political Weekly*, LV(26 & 27): 29–35.

Bhat, J. N. (1954) Untouchability in India, *Civilisations*, 4(4): 565–570. Available at: http://www.jstor.org/stable/41377660.

Census of India (2011).

Dahiwale, S. M. (Ed.) (2006) *Understanding Indian Society: The Non-Brahmanic Perspective*, Jaipur: Rawat Publications.

Deshpande, A. (2012) *The Grammar of Caste: Economic Discrimination in Contemporary India*, New Delhi: Oxford University Press.

Gupta, D. (1999) From Varna to Jati, in K. L. Sharma (Ed.), *Social Inequality in India: Profiles of Caste, Class and Social Mobility*, Jaipur: Rawat Publications.

Guru, G. (2009) Archaeology of Untouchability, *Economic and Political Weekly*, 44(37): 49–56.

Jodhka, S. S (2002, May 11–17) Caste and Untouchability in Rural Punjab, *Economic and Political Weekly*, 37(19): 1813–1823.

Jodhka, S. S. (2004) Sikhism and the Caste Question: Dalits and their Politics in Contemporary Punjab, *Contributions to Indian Sociology*, 38(1 & 2): 165–192.

Juergensmeyer, M. (1988) *Religious Rebels in the Punjab: The Social Vision of Untouchables*, Delhi: Ajanta Publications.

Kaur, Sandeep et al. (2020, April 25) Land Acquisition in Punjab: Jeopardizing Livelihoods Through Inefficient Implementation, *Economic and Political Weekly*, LV(17): 57–63.

Khanna, R. (2020, May 20) COVID-19: Reverse Migration Sparks Concern for Punjab's Paddy Season, *Down to Earth*, Accessed on https://www.downtoearth.org.in/news/water/covid-19-reverse-migration-sparks-concern-for-punjab-s-paddy-season-71254.

Kumar, D. (1999) *Land Reforms in Rural Punjab*, unpublished MPhil dissertation, Centre for the Study of Social Systems, Jawaharlal Nehru University.

Kumar, V. (2001) Untouchability in Uttaranchal, *Economic and Political Weekly*, 36(49): 4536–4537.

Louis, P. (2003) *Political Sociology of Dalit Assertion*, New Delhi: Gyan Publishing House.

Mendelsohn, O., and Vicziany, M. (2000) *The Untouchables: Subordination, Poverty and the State in Modern India*, New Delhi: Cambridge University Press.

Nagpal, S. (2020, March 29) The Fall of NRI: How Covid-19 Has Altered the Image of Punjab's Darling Community, The Print, Available at: https://theprint.in/opinion/the-fall-of-nri-how-covid-19-has-altered-the-image-of-punjabs-darling-community/390633/.

Neale, W. C. (1979) Land Is to Rule, in R. E. Frykenberg (Ed.), *Land Control and Social Structure in Indian History*, Delhi: Manohar Publishers.

News18.com (2020, May 24) Managing Incoming Migrants Biggest Challenge in Covid-19 Containment for Punjab and Chattisgarh, Accessed at https://www.news18.com/news/india/managing-incoming-migrants-biggest-challenge-in-covid-19-containment-for-punjab-and-chattisgarh-2635353.html.

O'Neill, T. (2003, June) India's Untouchables, *National Geographic*: 2–31.

Oommen, T. K. (1968) Strategy for Social Change: A Case Study of Untouchability, *Economic and Political Weekly*, 3(25): 933–936.

Punjab COVID-19 Response: Initiatives and Policy Measures, Department of Governance Reforms and Public Grievances, Govt. of Punjab, Accessed at http://www.covidhelp.punjab.gov.in/COVID_RESPONSE_PUNJAB.pdf.

Rajivlochan, M. (2018) The British Seeds of Succession in *Outlook* https://www.outlookindia.com/magazine/story/the-british-seeds-of-secession/299757#:~:text=By%201912%2C%20Sikh%20soldiers%20constituted,were%20doggedly%20courageous%20and%20loyal%E2%80%9D.

Ram, R. (2007, October) Social Exclusion, Resistance and Deras in Punjab: Exploring the Myth of Casteless Sikh Society in Punjab, *Economic and Political Weekly*, 42(40): 4066-4074.

Rohini, M., Chitra, R., and Geetika, V. (2020, May 14) Return Migration and COVID-19: Data suggests Kerala, TN, Punjab, UP, Bihar May Be Future Red Zones for Contagion Risk, *First post*, Accessed at https://www.firstpost.com/health/coronavirus-outbreak-return-migration-and-covid-19-in-india-data-suggests-kerala-tamil-nadu-punjab-up-bihar-may-be-future-red-zones-for-contagion-risk-8221531.html.

Sandhu, A. (2019) *Panjab: Journeys Through Fault Lines*, Chennai: Westland Publications.

Sarukkai, S. (2009) Phenomenology of Untouchability, *Economic and Political Weekly*, 44(37): 39–48.

Shah, G. et al. (2006) *Untouchability in Rural India*, New Delhi: Sage.

Singh, S., and Shruti, B. (2020) Punjab's Agricultural Labourers in Transition: A Longitudinal Study of Three Decades, *Economic and Political Weekly*, LV(26 & 27): 21–28.

Sugimoto, D. (2014) Impact of Non-Farm Employment on Landholding Structures in Punjab: Comparison of Three Villages, in U. Shuji (Ed.), *Industrial*

Clusters, Migrant Workersand Labour Markets in India, Hampshire: Palgrave Macmillan.

The Statesman. (2020, May 6) Capt Warns of Covid-19 Spike as NRIs, Migrants Set to Return to Punjab, Accessed at https://www.thestatesman.com/cities/chandigarh/capt-warns-covid-19-spike-nris-migrants-set-return-punjab-1502885016.html.

Thorat, A., and Omkar, J. (2020, January 11) The Continuing Practice of Untouchability in India: Patterns and Mitigating Influences, *Economic and Political Weekly*, LV(2): 36–45.

Tylor, S., Manjit, S., and Deborah, B. (2015) The Ambiguity of Punjabi Transnationalism: Caste and Development within a Transnational Community, in S. Rajan, Irudaya et al. (Eds.), *Immigration, Mobility and Multiple Affiliations: Punjabis in a Transnational World*, Delhi: Cambridge University Press.

Vatta, K. (2014) Patterns of Rural Livelihoods in Punjab: The role of industrial and Urban linkages, in U. Shuji (Ed.), *Industrial Clusters, Migrant Workers and Labour Markets in India*, Hampshire: Palgrave Macmillan.

Livelihood of Agricultural Labourers in Punjab: Emerging Policy Issues

Sukhpal Singh

India is an agrarian economy as over half of the total workforce is engaged in agriculture either as cultivators or agricultural labourers. The capitalistic development model initiated in mid-1960s in selected areas of India linked the farm inputs and farm produce with the market economy. As a result, the subsistent economies of these areas have transformed into a commercialised one. Initially, farm mechanisation led to an increase in labour-intensive shifts in the crop-mix which increased cropping intensity and generated employment in farm sector. But after mid-1980s, farm mechanisation has displaced human labour in agriculture (Sidhu and Singh, 2004). This process has pushed the peasantry and agricultural labourers towards severe crisis in which many of them took the step of self-killing. During last two decades, more than 3.50 lakhs farmers committed suicide in India but it is unfortunate that plight of agricultural labourers are unnoticed by the media, policy makers and the state. For instance, the data of suicides of agricultural labourers was not published and available till 2013. In India 6750 agricultural labourers committed suicides in 2014, their number declined to 4595 in 2015 and exhibits a rising trend thereafter to 5019 in 2016 (NCRB, 2020).

S. Singh (✉)
Punjab Agricultural University, Ludhiana, India

S. Singh et al. (eds.), *Covid-19 Pandemic and Economic Development*,
https://doi.org/10.1007/978-981-16-4442-9_13

In Punjab, the prevailing model of development remained unable to exhibit developmental transition of human resources, according to which the surplus labour from agricultural sector should be pulled towards secondary or tertiary sector. Out of total workforce of 99 lakh in the state, over one-third is engaged in agriculture either as cultivators or agricultural labourers, which is much lower than that for India as a whole (54.6%). Among the total agricultural workforce of 35 lakh in the state, 15 lakh (43%) are agricultural labourers. The mechanisation of agriculture although enhanced crop productivity but reduced the work opportunities in farm sector, thereby generated surplus labour in the state. The capital-intensive farm technologies displaced human labour, consequently the employment elasticity in agriculture has declined. The demand for labour in the state reduced by 12% from 479 million person days in 1983–1984 to 421 million person days in 2000–2001 (Sidhu and Singh, 2004). The surplus labour was forced to hiring-out their labour in low paid menial jobs. As a result, the problems of unemployment, under-employment and low earnings have grown among this poor stratum of the state. These very reasons necessitated a comprehensive study for probing the plight of agricultural labourers in so-called agriculturally developed economy of the state. In this backdrop the present study has undertaken to examine the socio-economic conditions of agricultural labourers and the suggestive policy measures for improving their livelihood.

1 Changing Structure of Workforce

Punjab state, popularly known as 'food bowl' of country, has been passing through the difficult phase of employment generation. Table 1 observed that the total workforce in the state was 39.12 lakh in 1971 which increased to 49.27 lakh in 1981 and further increased to 98.97 in 2011. There were 7.87 lakh agricultural labourers in 1971, which almost doubled to 15.88 lakhs in 2011. But there is an ironical twist in the whole scenario that the share of the workers engaged in agriculture in the total workforce declined from 62.27% in 1971 to almost half (35.59%) in 2011.

It is significant to note that the share of cultivators and agricultural labourers in total agricultural workforce fell from 67.91% in 1971 to 54.93% in 2011 and from 20.11% in 1971 to 16.04% in 2011, respectively. Out of the total agricultural workforce, cultivators and agricultural labourers accounted for 54.92% and 45.08%, respectively. These facts reveal that although the number of agricultural labourers has increased

Table 1 Changing structure of workforce in Punjab (Lakh)

Sr No	*Particulars*	*1971*	*1981*	*1991*	*2001*	*2011*
1	Total cultivators	16.65	17.67	19.17	20.65	19.35
2	Total agricultural labourers	7.87	10.92	14.52	14.89	15.88
3	Total agricultural workforce (1 + 2)	24.52	28.59	33.69	35.54	35.23
4	Total workforce	39.12	49.27	60.98	91.27	98.97
5	Share of agricultural workforce in total workforce (%)	62.67	58.02	55.26	38.95	35.59
6	Share of agricultural labour in total agricultural workforce (%)	32.09	38.2	43.11	41.61	45.08
7	Share of cultivators in total agricultural workforce (%)	67.91	61.8	56.89	58.09	54.93
8	Share of agricultural labour in total workforce (%)	20.11	22.16	23.82	16.32	16.04
9	Share of cultivators in total workforce (%)	42.56	35.86	31.44	22.96	19.55

Source Statistical Abstract of Punjab, Various issues

over time but the proportional share of these labourers in the total workforce of the state has declined.

2 Process of Depeasantisation

Punjab agriculture in general and small farming in particular is becoming a less profitable occupation due to rising fixed and variable input costs and non-remunerative sale prices of farm produce. Unable to afford sufficient earnings due to capital-intensive technologies, small farmers have been leaving farming. As a result, around two lakhs small farmers, who were operating 2 hectares of land, left farming in Punjab during 1991–2011. A study was undertaken by Punjab Agricultural University, Ludhiana in 12 villages from six districts in Punjab state (Singh and Bhogal, 2014). All the farmers in the selected villages who left farming were taken for the study. There were a total of 2002 farmers in the selected villages. Out of these, 288 (14.39%) farmers had left farming since 1991. This proportion was very high in case of marginal (26.49%) and small (18.27%) farmers. However, a relatively small proportion of semi-medium (3.29%), medium (4.74%) and large (4.23%) farmers left farming in the state.

Leaving farming is a healthy trend, if a person joins more lucrative profession, whereas, it becomes disastrous if a person joins low paid profession. Of the total sampled farmers who left farming, about 25% started working as labourers. This proportion was very high among marginal (about 40%) and small (23%) farmers. This transformation of peasantry into wage labour is painful in the context of socio-cultural traditions and psychological conditions of the Punjab farmers. Likewise, 16% of marginal and 18% of small farmers started their own petty business. The study brought out that not even a single farmer, who operates more than 5 acres of land, became labourer. On the other hand, none of the marginal farmer became dealer or commission agent. This process shows that the capitalistic farming model has pushed many marginal and small farmers towards wage labour either in agriculture or non-farm sector.

3 Transformation of Agricultural Labourers

Based on the longitudinal study of 100 agricultural labour households during two time periods i.e. 1987–1988 and 2018–2019 in Punjab, an occupational shift among these households was observed during three decades (Singh and Bhogal, 2020). As much as 88% of households were solely agricultural labour households whereas, the remaining 12 households were mixed households comprising of at least one family member engaged in non-farm activities in 1987–1988. However, the proportion of solely agricultural labour households declined from 88% in 1987–1988 to just 7% in 2018–2019, while for mixed households this increased from 12% in 1987–1988 to 37% in 2018–2019. The shift of labour from farm to non-farm sector is quite robust since over three decades as 56% of these households turned as solely non-farm households with none of the workers of these households engaged in agriculture.

The changing scenario of prospects of a generation of livelihood from agriculture alone induced the transition of the rural economy. The details of the magnitude of shift, of total agricultural workforce towards other sectors, over a period of three decades is shown in Table 2. Of the total workers, about 92% were engaged in agricultural activities during 1987–1988 which reduced to 33.7% in 2018–2019. The shift of employment was seen in favour of menial jobs generally in private sector as the members of agricultural labour households engaged in this sector increased from 2.31% to 10.50%. None of the family members of the sampled agricultural labour households were engaged as industry and construction labour, helpers in shop/workshop and brick kiln workers in 1987–1988; but as many as 14.92, 9.39 and 9.94% of the labourers

Table 2 Distribution of shift of agricultural labour workforce in Punjab (%)

Type of labour/work	*1987–1988*	*2018–2019*
a. Permanent labourer in agriculture	35.83	1.10
b. Casual labourer in agriculture	56.07	32.60
I Total farm workers (a + b)	91.91	33.70
c. Industry / construction labourer	–	14.92
d. Serviceman	2.31	10.50
e. Domestic labourer	1.16	7.18
f. Workshop/shop helper	–	9.39
g. Brick kiln labourer	–	9.94
h. Self-employed[a]	4.62	4.42
i. Others (sale of manure, MGNREGA)	–	9.94
II Total non-farm workers (c to i)	8.09	66.30
Total (I + II)	100.00	100.00

Note [a]Includes activities like dairy and poultry, street hawking, petty-shops
Source Singh and Bhogal (2020)

from these agricultural labour households were found to be engaged in the respective employment activities in 2018–2019.

The proportion of workers engaged as self-employed was found to be almost the same during both the periods of study. Over a period, the non-farm sector has absorbed more of the working population of these households as compared to the farm sector as the proportion of workers engaged in this sector increased from about 8 to 66% from 1987–1988 to 2018–2019.

4 Income Level of Agricultural Labourers

A field survey of 180 agricultural labour households from three agro-climatic regions of the states during 2017–2018 was conducted to estimate their income and debt position. The survey concluded that by virtue of being agricultural labourers, the major source of their income is wage labour in agricultural sector. However, these households enhance their income through other sources. Table 3 clearly depicts that an average agricultural labour household earned Rs. 108,404 annually from all the sources. Income from the casual labour in agriculture is the highest (81.96%) followed by the permanent labour (6.81%) in agriculture. Income from industrial labour, service sector, brick kiln, domestic

Table 3 Income level of agricultural labourers in Punjab, 2017–2018 (Rs./Annum)

Occupation	*Average income*	*% age*	*Per capita income*	*Per worker income*
Permanent agril labour	7380	6.81	1597	4241
Casual agril labour	88,850	81.96	19,232	51,063
Industrial labour	3860	3.56	1084	2218
Service sector	4134	3.81	895	2376
Brick kiln	2235	2.06	484	1285
Domestic servants	975	0.90	211	560
Livestock	970	0.90	210	557
Total	108,404	100.00	23,464	62,301

Source Field survey, 2017–2018

service and livestock rearing contributed towards the total income of the labour households.

On an average per capita income of agricultural labour household was Rs. 23,464 in 2017–2018. Per capita income shows a similar pattern with the total income as per the proportion of the income from different sources is concerned. The main source of per capita income was the income from the casual labour in agriculture. Similarly, as the average number of worker in the family was 1.74 against the family size of 4.62, per worker annual income was Rs. 62,301 in the state during 2017–2018.

5 Indebtedness of Agricultural Labourers

An attempt was made to examine the debt position of the agricultural labourers in the Punjab state. Table 4 shows that as much as 80% of agricultural labour households were indebted in the state. If we take a look at the debt position per sampled agricultural labour household and per indebted agricultural labour household, the average amount of debt was Rs. 81,470 and Rs. 101,837, respectively. The composition of the debt with respect to its sources reveals that 6.78% of the overall debt amount was from institutional sources and 93.22% was from non-institutional sources. The purpose for which a loan was taken is an important indication of its potential to be repaid. The agricultural labour households

Table 4 Debt position of agricultural labour households in Punjab, 2017–2018

Particulars	
Indebted households (%)	80
Debt per sampled household (Rs.)	81,470
Debt per indebted household (Rs.)	101,837
Source of credit (%)	
Institutional Source	6.78
Non-institutional Source	93.33
Purpose of credit (%)	
Productive purpose	8.13
Consumption purpose	91.97

Source Field Survey, 2017–2018

took loan for both productive and consumption purposes. On an average about 92% of the total loan was used for consumption purposes whereas just 8.13% of the total loan was used for the productive purposes.

6 Policy Suggestions

Agricultural labourers play a key role in the economic growth and development of the rural economy. Unfortunately, these labourers are always forgotten and overlooked in the economic policy paradigms of the state. They have been passing through the phase of under-unemployment, low earnings and indebtedness. In such a situation, it is important to address their problems and improve their livelihood.

First of all, the problem of indebtedness of agricultural labourers should be addressed. In Punjab, as much as 80% of the agricultural labourers are indebted to the tune of Rs. 81,470 per household. Most of these households took loans from non-institutional sources, particularly from landlords. It is urgent to waive off the debt amount of formal as well as informal sources of credit. In future, these households should be provided loans from institutional sources at low rates of interest with easy repayment facilities.

Secondly, the large number of agricultural labourers committed suicides during the last two decades. The government of Punjab has formulated the policy to provide relief in case of suicidal deaths of farmers and farm labourers due to indebtedness. The policy included compensation of Rs. 3 lakh along with rehabilitation and preventive measures of support to the distressed family (GoP, 2015). But, the agricultural labour families in which suicide happened due to economic distress are unable to get compensation. Even many families wherein suicide happened due to indebtedness are deprived of this compensation due to lack of some documents, like loan documents (particularly in case of non-institutional loans), post-mortem report, etc. as a large number of labourers are unable to produce these documents due illiterate and many other reasons. Therefore, the compensation should be provided to all deceased labour families wherein suicide happened due to indebtedness or economic distress with the attestation of the village panchayat.

Thirdly, as the employment situation of the agricultural labourers is very restricted and grim, the alternative employment through non-farm activities should be provided to these people. Moreover, MGNREGA scheme should be made effective by enhancing actual days of employment under this scheme from existing 100 days to 300 days annually for every worker. The prevailing wages in the rural economy and MGNREGA scheme are not sufficient for the minimum desirable level of living. Therefore, these wage rates should be increased and an effectiveness of stipulated wage rates should be ensured and constantly enhanced.

Fourthly, the land-related legal entitlements of the landless labourers must be safeguarded. As per Punjab Village Common Lands Regulation Act, 1961, one-third of the cultivated common land should be leased-out to schedule castes/backward class. But in practice they are being deprived of this right. Similarly, the Punjab Land Reforms Act, 1972 stipulates maximum permissible irrigated land owning of 7 hectares only but this is often defied as many farmers in the state owned more than the permissible limit of land. Therefore, it is urgent to distribute/ lease-out one-third of common property land and surplus land with the landlords, on nominal rates, among landless labourers to empower them with means to earn their livelihood.

Fifthly, generally there is hue and cry over the increase in wage rates in the peak season in agriculture. Due to mono-cropping pattern of wheat and paddy, the work opportunities have squeezed. As a result, the agricultural labour demand for higher wages, which are opposed by the farmers. This phenomenon sharply happened during Covid-19, wherein the agricultural labourers demanded higher wages due to shifting of migrant labourers in the lockdown. This act has created social tension in many villages, while the large number of village panchayats have passed resolutions for the fixation of wage rates. In such a situation, it is imperative that farm operation-wise wage rates should be fixed in such a manner that these workers may get desirable level of living.

Sixthly, the housing conditions, healthcare and education of the labour families are in a pathetic state. Therefore, the government should take effective steps through massive investment, institutional set up and policy initiatives for the improvement of living and working conditions of the rural labour class. Moreover, for organising social ceremonies, the community centres equipped with catering facilities should be set-up in every village of the state so that the working class can solemnise the minimum required social functions with their limited means.

Lastly, the agricultural labour households are undergoing a process of transformation wherein they are leaving the agricultural wage market due to crisis-led push factors. In such a situation it is important to make transformation through development-oriented pull factors. For this purpose, there is a need to develop rural industrialisation with special emphasis on agro-based industries. This strategy will be useful for generating ample employment opportunities at their door-steps along with optimum use of time and local resources. For an enduring solution to their problems and healthy livings, the right to work and old age pension should be ensured for this working class.

References

GoP. (2015) *Policy for Relief to Families of Farmers/Farm Labourers Affected by Suicides*, Government of Punjab (GoP).

NCRB. (2020) *Suicides in Farming Sector*, New Delhi: National Crime Records Bureau (NCRB), Ministry of Home Affairs, Government of India.

Sidhu, R. S., and Singh, S. (2004) Agricultural Wages and Employment in Punjab, *Economic and Political Weekly*, 39(37, September 11): 4132–4135.

Singh, S., and Bhogal, S. (2014) Depeasantization in Punjab: Status of Farmers Who Left Farming, *Current Science*, 106(10, May 25): 1364–1368.

Singh, S., and Bhogal, S. (2020) Punjab's Agricultural Labourers in Transition—A Longitudinal Study of Three Decades, *Economic and Political Weekly*, 55(26 and 27, June 27): 21–27.

COVID-19 and Health Care Services in Punjab: Consequences and Challenges

Varinder Sharma

1 Introduction

Indian economy was overwhelmingly rural at the time of independence and around 70% of the population was dependent on agriculture and residing in rural areas. Mass communicable diseases were widespread in the absence of effective health care services. The health survey and development committee headed by Sir Joseph Bhore (1946) recommended the establishment of a well structured and comprehensive health care services system with a sound primary health care infrastructure. During the period of sixties, it was emphasised that economic growth is possible only with the development of useful abilities of human beings and particularly in terms of education and health. At this time various protective and preventive health care measures were taken. From the First five year plan to Eleventh Five year plan expenditure on health remained below 4% out of total plan outlay. Moreover, the demand of effective good health care services increased tremendously.

Health has only use value and may not be exchanged. Contrary to this health care is a commodity but not the health. People want good health and demand health care services. In the normal times the medical

V. Sharma (✉)
Institute for Development and Communication (IDC), Chandigarh, India

S. Singh et al. (eds.), *Covid-19 Pandemic and Economic Development*,
https://doi.org/10.1007/978-981-16-4442-9_14

professionals supply the information of the treatments, this information influences what treatments are demanded (Arrow, 1963). At the time when diseases are life threatening, e.g. Covid-19, the clinicians cannot supply the information of treatments; rather they are decision maker for the demand of the treatments. In such situations the health care is a social good and need arises what types of health care facilities exist and are rationed. In this article we have focussed on the consequences met by present health care services due to Covid-19 and challenges posed for future health care services. The article is descriptive in nature based on the secondary data and personal experiences of field research.

2 History of Infectious Diseases in Punjab: Epidemics to Covid-19

The colonial period health records and literature brings out the history of many epidemics in this region. The period of 1850–1947 brought out frequent epidemics like malaria, smallpox, cholera and the plague. Out of all these epidemics the mortality rate for the plague was the highest. The epidemic malaria occurred fifteen times in this region from 1850 to 1947 and claimed around 52 lakh lives. The high rainfall regions were worst affected due to high breeding of the mosquitoes. Similarly, the smallpox caused deaths of 9 lakh people from 1868 to 1947. Next the cholera occurred twelve times from 1866 to 1921. This epidemic broke out due to contamination of water and insanitary conditions and almost 2.50 lakh people died due to this epidemic.

The most dreaded epidemic out of all the epidemics was a plague. The phase of this disease remained from 1897 to 1918 and mortality touched to 60% of this epidemic. The first case of this epidemic was noticed in Khatkar Kalan village in Banga circle during 1897 (Tandon, 2013).

The mortality from all the epidemics increased during the particular months of the year. The maximum deaths due to malaria occurred during the month of October. The maximum cases of plague were reported during the months of March and April.

The prevalence of the epidemics was high in the rural areas due to insanitary conditions and low standard of living relatively to urban areas. The high prevalence rate of epidemics resulted into high mortality in the rural areas.

The plague and the present pandemic Covid-19 have some commonalities and differences. The corona and the plague are both infectious diseases. The medical experts accept the two diseases spread to humans from certain animals, i.e. Zonotic. However, corona is caused by a virus, a tiny bit of nucleic acid and protein that needs a living host, the plague is caused by bacteria which are single celled organisms. Further, whole antibiotic work on bacteria, they do not work on viruses. The impact of plague was so drastic that many times villages were totally evacuated. The British officers' sincerity to tackle the epidemic plague was remarkable. Presently the state facing the Corona/Covid-19 which is pandemic. On March 9, 2020, the state recorded first case of Corona and which originated from Italy. In the last of month July, 2020, the number of cases has touched to more than ten thousands. The high number of the Corona cases remained in the Central Punjab districts like Amritsar, Jalandhar and Ludhiana. Similarly, the plague disease remained highly concentrated in the districts: Jalandhar, Hoshiarpur, Gurdaspur and the princely State of Kapurthala (Wikinson, 1903). The reason may be there people always remained highly mobile than other districts people and always linked to outer economies as well as dense in population.

From the epidemics to pandemic the worst affected class remained of workers and especially the agricultural population. The historical records highlight the plague affected labourers even worked in fields for the survival. The misery of workers, farmers and migrant labourers is visible at this pandemic period too. At the time of plague, the inoculation of plague was widely accepted and sometimes resisted by the villagers. Historical records support the Muslims never raised voice against the inoculation. The attacks on the medical teams out of frustrations and ignorance were common as are going on today. Health professionals always performed efficiently in past and present to serve the humanity. The state interventions at this time more important than the colonial period to protect the economy and to provide the health services to the people.

In the next section, we will discuss the overall health profile of the state and facilities available in the health institutions to cop up with the Covid-19.

3 Health Profile and Availability of Health Care Facilities

The birth rate and death rate over the years have fallen in Punjab and there is no big difference in these two indicators in rural and urban areas. The birth rate is low in comparison to major states like Haryana, Gujarat,

Rajasthan and Uttar Pradesh, etc. In these four states the birth rate is around 20 and above. Similarly, the death rate in Punjab is 6 which is quiet near to the other major states like Gujarat, Haryana, Kerala, Madhya Pradesh and Karnataka.

The infant mortality rate in Punjab is 21 which is quiet less in comparison to big states like Odisha, Rajasthan, Assam and Madhya Pradesh. In these states the infant mortality is almost double than the Punjab. In Kerala it is 10 which is quiet lower than Punjab. It means there is still a need of state intervention to improve this. The maternal mortality ratio in Punjab is 122 which is far better in comparison to Assam, Madhya Pradesh, Rajasthan, Uttar Pradesh and Bihar. But still high relatively to Kerala where this is 46 (Table 1).

Next, the focus is on the pattern of communicable and non-communicable diseases. Globally, the non-communicable diseases relating to cardiovascular and diabetes are the main cause of deaths. Annually, the cardiovascular diseases kill around 17.3 million people and diabetes kill 1.3 million people. In Punjab the pattern of non-communicable diseases

Table 1 Birth rate, death rate and infant mortality: a comparison of Punjab and other major Indian states (year: 2017)

States	*Birth rate per thousand*	*Death rate per thousand*	*Infant mortality rate per 1000 live births*	*Maternal mortality ratio*
Punjab	14.9	6.00	21	122
Assam	21.2	6.7	44	237
Bihar	26.4	6.0	38	165
Haryana	20.5	5.9	33	101
Gujarat	19.9	6.1	30	91
Kerala	14.2	7.1	10	46
Karnataka	17.4	6.7	24	108
Madhya Pradesh	24.8	7.1	47	173
Orissa	18.3	7.8	44	180
Rajasthan	24.1	6.1	41	199
Uttar Pradesh	25.9	6.9	43	201
India	20.2	6.4	34	130

Source National Health Profile, 2019, Directorate General of Health Services, Ministry of Health and Family Welfare, GoI is near to the global pattern. Out of total non-communicable diseases around 60% of the diseases are cardiovascular and diabetes. Around 20% of the diseases relating to the lung diseases. In comparison to India, the percentage of cases of cardiovascular and diabetes diseases are more in Punjab. These patients are highly prone to corona virus due to low immunity.

Out of the communicable diseases, 62% of the diseases relate to the respiratory infections and 19.77% are diarrhoeal diseases. The enteric fever or typhoid touches to 14.41% out of total communicable diseases. The viral hepatitis is around 1.59%, but the viral hepatitis has significantly increased in Punjab. The statewise data for hepatitis is not available. The studies conducted by medical doctors accepted the hepatitis-C virus (HCV) has significantly increased in districts of Punjab and in rural areas (Sood et al., 2018). In comparison to total India enteric fever cases are on a higher side in Punjab.

Presently Covid-19 is a major viral disease in the state and it needs critical care which is no more available in all the health institutions. We will discuss later in this section about the availability of critical care in health institutions. First, we are going to discuss the number of public medical institutions at the grass root level in the state (Table 2).

The number of SCs is 2950 in the rural areas which is 1% of India and quiet high in comparison to the urban areas (Table 3). The number of PHC is 416 which is four times more than the urban areas but just 1% of nation. Similarly, the CHC are 89 in number in rural areas and 63 in the urban areas. The main problem of these state run health institutions is the institutions have not adequate manpower and specialists to provide proper medical facilities to the people. Moreover, many of them are not functioning it needs a special study on the functioning of these institutions. At this time of pandemic the institutions are not well equipped to treat the patients.

In Table 3, we have discussed the number of primary health institutions in rural and urban areas. Here in Table 4, it has described the average number of villages and population served by these institutions. It is interesting the average number of villages and population served by these institutions are more in Punjab relatively to all India level.

Out of the eleven major states, the number of private hospitals is more than the public hospitals in nine states (Table 5). It means the privatisation of health services is fast going on in each state. Moreover, the private hospitals at the time of pandemic are not cooperating with the

Table 2 Health profile: Punjab and India

Sr. No	*Indicators*	*Year*	*Punjab*	*India*
1	Birth rate per thousand per annum	2017	14.9	20.2
2	Death rate per thousand per annum	2017	6.0	6.4
3	Infant mortality rate per thousand live birth per annum	2017	21.0	34
4	Maternal mortality ratio per lakh live birth per annum	2014–2016	122	130
5	Percentage of cardio vascular diseases out of total NCD diseases	2019	39.29	25
6	Percentage of diabetes mellitus out of total NCD diseases	2019	24.90	29
7	Percentage of lungs diseases out of total NCD diseases	2019	20.91	25
8	Percentage of psychiatric disorder out of total NCD diseases	2019	5.88	20
9	Percentage of acute diarrhoeal diseases out of communicable diseases	2019	19.77	21.83
10	Percentage of acute respiratory infection out of communicable diseases	2019	62.78	69.47
11	Percentage of enteric fever out of communicable diseases	2019	14.41	3.82
12	Percentage of viral hepatitis (C, D and E) out of communicable diseases	2019	1.59	1.80

Note NCD stands for non-communicable diseases in case of India percentage out of four diseases
Source Statistical Abstract of Punjab

Table 3 Number of public medical institutions at grass root level in Punjab and India (2019)

Sr. No	*Type of institution*	*Rural*	*India*	*Urban*	*India*
1	SC (Sub Centre)	2950 (1.87)	157,411	87 (2.63)	3302
2	PHC (Primary Health Centre)	416 (1.67)	24,855	115 (2.22)	5190
3	CHC (Community Health Centre)	89 (1.66)	5335	63 (18)	350

Note Special institutions not included and figures in brackets are percentage out of total India
Source Statistical Abstract of Punjab

Table 4 Average number of villages and population serviced by SC, PHC and CHC in rural area

Indicators	*Punjab*	*India*
Average number of villages covered by SC	4	4
Average number of villages covered by PHC	30	26
Average number of villages covered by CHC	141	120
Average population covered by SC	6039	5616
Average population covered by PHC (In Thousands)	43	36
Average population covered by CHC (In Lakhs)	2.00	1.66
Hospital beds per thousand population	0.59	0.71

Source Rural Health Statistics, 2019, Directorate-General of Health Services, Ministry of Health and Family Welfare, GoI

Table 5 Number of estimated government and private hospitals in major Indian states

States	*Number of government hospitals*	*Number of private hospitals*
Punjab	682 (2.65)	1638 (3.77)
Andhra Pradesh	258 (1.00)	670 (1.54)
Bihar	1147 (4.45)	1887 (4.34)
Chhattisgarh	214 (0.83)	182 (0.42)
Maharashtra	711 (2.76)	2492 (5.73)
Haryana	668 (2.59)	1480 (3.40)
Kerala	1280 (4.97)	2062 (4.74)
Himachal Pradesh	801 (3.11)	235 (0.54)
Madhya Pradesh	465 (1.80)	506 (1.16)
Rajasthan	2850 (11.06)	2794 (6.42)
Uttar Pradesh	4635 (17.98)	12,468 (28.67)
India	25,778	43,487

Note Figures in brackets are percentage

Source Covid-19 in India: Statewise Estimates of Current Hospital Beds, Intensive Care Unit (ICU) Beds and Ventilators, CDDEP, Princeton University 2020

state governments and are charging exorbitantly from the patients. The intensive care unit (ICU) beds and Ventilators are essential part of the critical care and have importance to take care of the critically ill corona patients (Table 6).

Now we briefly discuss the status of ICUs in hospitals. An ICU is defined as a specially staffed, equipped, separate section of a hospital dedicated to the observation, care and treatment of patients with life threatening illness, injuries, or complications from which recovery is possible. The global history of ICU care goes back to the polio epidemic

Table 6 Number of estimated ICU beds and ventilators in government and private hospitals

States	*ICU beds in govt. hospitals*	*ICU beds in private hospitals*	*Ventilators in govt. hospitals*	*Ventilators in private hospitals*
Punjab	897 (1.31)	2153 (1.30)	448 (0.65)	1077 (0.66)
Andhra Pradesh	1157 (4.48)	3005 (4.49)	578 (2.24)	1502 (2.24)
Bihar	583 (0.50)	960 (0.51)	292 (0.25)	480 (0.25)
Chhattisgarh	471 (2.2)	401 (2.20)	235 (1.09)	200 (1.09)
Maharashtra	2572 (3.6)	9015 (3.62)	1286 (1.80)	4507 (1.80)
Haryana	562 (0.85)	1241 (0.83)	281 (0.42)	623 (0.42)
Kerala	1900 (1.48)	3061 (1.48)	950 (0.74)	1531 (0.74)
Himachal Pradesh	620 (0.77)	182 (1.34)	310 (0.39)	91 (0.39
Madhya Pradesh	1555 (3.34)	1692 (3.34)	778 (1.67)	846 (1.67)
Rajasthan	2353 (8.40)	2306 (0.83)	1176 (0.41)	1153 (0.41)
Uttar Pradesh	3813 (0.82)	10,257 (0.82)	1907 (0.41)	5129 (0.41)
India	35,699 (1.38)	59,262 (1.36)	17,850 (0.69)	29,631 (0.68)

Note Figures in brackets are ICU and ventilators per hospital
Source Covid-19 in India: Statewise Estimates of Current Hospital Beds, Intensive Care Unit (ICU) Beds and Ventilators, CDDEP, Princeton University 2020

in 1950s. The ICU at that time assumed the role in prevention of irreversible organ failure. More than 88% of the hospitals in the United States have one or more ICUs, having 5% or less of the total hospital beds.

In India the critical care units started in private hospitals. First coronary care unit started in 1968 at the King Edward VII Memorial Hospital, Mumbai. In India the ICU beds are just 5% in the leading hospitals out of total beds which needs to be raised upto 10% of the total beds (Yeolekar and Mehta, 2008).

The number of ICU beds per government hospital is highest in Rajasthan and this number touched to 8.40. After this in Andhra Pradesh, the number of ICU beds in government hospital is 4.48. After these two states come to Maharashtra and Madhya Pradesh where the number comes around near to 3. In Punjab and Kerala per government hospital, the number of beds is around one. In remaining states in all the government hospitals, the position of ICU beds is quiet abysmal.

The position of ICU beds in the private hospitals in all the states is also not satisfactory. Except Rajasthan where the ICU beds are more in government hospitals than private hospitals. In the remaining states, the number of ICU beds are almost same in government and private hospitals.

Next the position of the ventilators in the government and private hospitals in all the major states is not satisfactory. In three states Andhra Pradesh, Maharashtra and Madhya Pradesh, the number of ventilators per government and the private hospital is around one or two.

From the above discussion, it may be concluded that the position of critical care at this time of corona is not satisfactory in government and private hospitals. Moreover, the acute shortage of the manpower prevails to manage the critical care at this present time.

In the next section, we will discuss the position of health workers but before going to discuss let us have a look at the position of existing labs to test the Corona virus.

In Table 7, the density of health workers has depicted. The density of health manpower per lakh of the population is quiet grim in all the states. In one group of states the density is around one hundred forty to one hundred sixty. The highly populated state Uttar Pradesh fails in this category. The density of allopathic and all doctors are highest in Punjab but the density of all health workers is 394 in Kerala which is more than all other states. The density of nurses is again highest in this state. No doubt this state at this pandemic time performed better in controlling the

Table 7 Number of labs to test Covid-19 in major states

States	*Private labs*	*Government labs*
Punjab	07 (1.83)	20 (2.24)
Andhra Pradesh	07 (1.83)	60 (6.73)
Bihar	04 (1.05)	44 (4.93)
Chhattisgarh	23 (6.02)	34 (3.81)
Maharashtra	57 (14.92)	73 (8.18)
Haryana	10 (2.62)	16 (1.79)
Kerala	27 (7.07)	26 (2.91)
Himachal Pradesh	–	22 (2.47)
Madhya Pradesh	10 (2.62)	73 (8.18)
Rajasthan	11 (2.88)	26 (2.91)
Uttar Pradesh	26 (6.81)	120 (13.45)
India	382	892

Note Figures in brackets are percentage
Source CovidIndia.org

corona virus than all other states, the reason may be adequate availability of health manpower and health facilities in this state. The lowest density of nurses is in Bihar and Haryana.

Another challenge at this time of pandemic is the insufficient number of testing labs to test the corona virus. In all the states, maximum labs to test this virus are in Government Sector. In Punjab and Haryana the number of Government labs are quiet less in comparison to other big states (Table 7). Moreover, in the private Sector number of labs except Maharashtra are quiet less. The credibility of the tests of the private labs is not satisfactory. The Government has fixed the rates of corona virus tests of these labs but many labs are charging above the fixed rates and this is extra burden on the pockets of patients. Due to less number of labs and manpower the speed of tests of corona virus is quiet slow in each state in the government labs.

4 Status of Health Manpower

Health manpower means those professionals who are trained to promote health, to prevent and cure disease and to rehabilitate the sick (Hogarth, 1975). Mainly, the health manpower includes doctors, nurses, pharmacists and lab technicians, etc.

In Table 8, the density of health workers has depicted. The density of health manpower per lakh of the population is quiet grim in all the states. In one group of states the density is around one hundred forty to one hundred sixty. The highly populated state Uttar Pradesh falls in this category. The density of allopathic and all doctors is highest in Punjab but the density of all health workers is 394 in Kerala which is more than all other states. The density of nurses is again highest in this state. No doubt this state at this pandemic time performed better in controlling the corona virus than all other states, the reason may be adequate availability of health manpower and health facilities in this state. The lowest density of nurses is in Bihar and Haryana.

Next, Table 9 highlights the ratio density in urban and rural areas. In all the states except Kerala the number of health workers is more in urban areas than rural areas. In Kerala, the number of health workers

Table 8 Density of health manpower per lakh of population

States	*Allopathic doctors*	*All doctors*	*Nurses*	*Pharmacists*	*All health workers*
Punjab	111.5	134.6	64.8	33.3	271.3
Andhra Pradesh	77	86.1	55.5	24.0	212.70
Bihar	83.9	107.30	38.1	29.7	204.80
Chhattisgarh	41.2	53.8	50.0	12.4	165.30
Maharashtra	78.4	114.8	102.9	25.8	292
Haryana	83.9	107.3	38.1	29.7	204.8
Kerala	61.3	99	185.3	36.6	394
Himachal Pradesh	58.8	87.5	68.4	52.6	259.20
Madhya Pradesh	50.6	65.1	44.3	22.5	163
Rajasthan	41.0	55.1	48.9	25.5	143.7
Uttar Pradesh	63.5	76.7	24.1	18.8	134.6

Source Sudhir Anand and Victoria Fan: The Health Workforce in India, 2016, WHO

Table 9 Ratio of urban density to rural density of health workers

States	*Allopathic doctors*	*All doctors*	*Nurses*	*Pharmacists*	*All health workers*
Punjab	3.0	3.9	2.6	2.4	2.9
Andhra Pradesh	2.6	2.6	3.9	2.7	3.1
Bihar	4.5	4.8	7.9	5.3	5.7
Chhattisgarh	3.6	3.6	5.4	4.4	3.6
Maharashtra	4.0	3.5	4.6	3.6	3.8
Haryana	2.9	3.2	4.5	2.5	3.4
Kerala	4.6	3.1	1.2	1.4	1.7
Himachal Pradesh	6.2	5.1	6.2	2.1	4.5
Rajasthan	6.0	5.3	4.6	3.6	4.6
Madhya Pradesh	4.6	4.9	6.3	4.3	4.8
Uttar Pradesh	3.5	3.8	5.0	4.0	4.1

Source Sudhir Anand and Victoria Fan: The Health Workforce in India, 2016, WHO

seems equal in rural and urban areas. Moreover, again number of allopathic doctors are more in urban areas. Similarly, the number of nurses and pharmacists are more in urban areas than rural areas except Kerala. The availability of less health workers in rural areas is a major problem to the rural people to get the treatment in time. At this pandemic period the corona patients from rural areas have to go to major cities to get treatment and no facility is available even in small towns near to villages.

Lastly, we have discussed the gender of health workers. From Table 10, it seems a majority of the health workers in all states except Kerala are males. Especially doctors are male and nurses are predominantly female in all the states. Historically, the female health professionals faced many difficulties to get entry into this profession. The Christian missionaries and the progressive like Brahmo samaj in India played a pivotal role to promote the female medical health professionals. The female doctors are only in specific specialisation gynaecology and paediatric, etc. The ILO studies find the wages of female health professionals are less than male. At this pandemic time the services of female health workers have well appreciated even by the Prime Minister, Mr. Narendra Modi who telephonically conversed with a female nurse at Pune Hospital.

After discussing the status of health manpower the question arises why the casualisation of services is going on of the services of health workers

Table 10 Female health workers (percentage out of total health workers) (percentage)

States	*Allopathic doctors*	*All doctors*	*Nurses*	*Pharmacists*	*All health workers*
Punjab	15.5	15.6	89.6	15	15.6
Andhra Pradesh	14.4	14.4	80.5	8.7	32.4
Bihar	6.5	5.9	91.0	1.2	22.3
Chhattisgarh	12.0	11.2	81.0	7.3	33.4
Maharashtra	26.2	26.8	79.3	19.1	44.4
Haryana	13.3	13.7	90.9	6.8	27.5
Kerala	34.1	32.8	92.5	42.4	64.5
Himachal Pradesh	17.0	14.9	93.0	9.3	37.9
Madhya Pradesh	13.6	12.3	82.4	4.9	31.5
Rajasthan	14.0	11.8	69.9	2.1	30.0
Uttar Pradesh	7.6	7.2	70.9	3.3	19.9

Source Sudhir Anand and Victoria Fan: The Health Organisation in India, 2016, WHO

in public sector. Many times, the female health professionals protested to regularise their jobs and for other decent working conditions and faced state brutalities in Punjab (*Hindustan Times*, 2016). At the pandemic time the health professionals performed far better than private health manpower without proper-protective equipments. In the next section, we will discuss the health expenditure in India which we already discussed has not increased in all five year plans.

5 Health Expenditure

The per capita expenditure in developed state like Punjab is around Rs. 1173 and in Madhya Pradesh it is Rs. 716 and Uttar Pradesh is around Rs. 733. In any state health expenditure out of total GDP has not crossed more than 1%. Out of total state expenditure in all the states the per cent share on health is between 3 and 5%. In the high income countries 5% of GDP is spent on health (Table 11).

In the present circumstances, the state has to raise health expenditure to create health infrastructure and on the medical education and to recruit

Table 11 Health expenditure and per capita health expenditure

States	*Health expenditure as percentage of total state expenditure (%)*	*Health expenditure as percentage of GSDP (%)*	*Per capita health expenditure (Rs.)*
Punjab	5.87	0.87	1173
Andhra Pradesh	4.70	0.82	1013
Haryana	3.59	0.63	1119
Himachal Pradesh	6.67	1.68	2667
Maharashtra	5.08	0.60	1011
Bihar	3.94	1.33	491
Kerala	5.85	0.93	1463
Chhattisgarh	5.28	1.33	1354
Rajasthan	5.66	1.44	1360
Madhya Pradesh	4.17	1.64	716
Uttar Pradesh	5.07	1.42	733

Source National Health Profile, 2019, Ministry of Health and Family Welfare, GoI

health manpower in state health institutions. Moreover, the state objective under Atmanirbhar Bharat to create infection control hospital at each district level needs huge investment (Dash, 2020).

6 Socialised Medicine and Universal Health Coverage

The two terms socialised medicine and universal health coverage are commonly used in the health care system. In the socialised medicine health care services are provided totally free and the health workers are paid by the government. The universal health coverage (UHC) means that all individuals and communities receive the health services they need without suffering financial hardships (WHO). But the UHC does not mean free coverage for all possible health interventions, regardless of the cost, as no economy can provide all services free of charge on a sustainable basis. The health manpower may be managed by the government or not. At national level, the government is trying to popularise the health insurance schemes as universal health coverage. All UN members states have agreed to try to achieve universal health coverage by 2030, as part of the Sustainable Development Goal (SDG). The health insurance and universal health coverage may be effective during normal times. The pandemic has again strengthened the concept of socialised medicine. At this time only the government hospitals and public health workers are providing in majority care to the corona patients especially to rural masses and slum population. The private hospitals either in the panel of insurance companies are not cooperating with the state and the patients are not satisfied with the treatment. In time of disasters it seems the socialised medicine is the hope of common masses and it should be planned in future.

7 Policy Implications

The capabilities of health care services have been put to test by Covid-19 not only in India but around the world. The caveats posed by the pandemic need to be addressed by the effective policy measures.

I. The colonial period health records on the epidemics must be in digital form. Such records will be useful to study the pattern of diseases in past for medical and non-medical professionals;

II. The health card of every citizen with his disease record and identity should be in digital form, it would be useful at time of treatment anywhere in country if the pandemic happens again;

III. The spread of Covid-19 has highlighted some gaps in our health infrastructure preparedness. The average population covered by the CHCs in rural Punjab is 2 lakhs which is more than all India where it is 1.66 lakhs. The availability of hospital beds per 1000 population is 0.59 in Punjab and 0.71 in India. The need is to enhance the infrastructure in rural areas;

IV. The situation of critical care is not satisfactory in the government hospitals. Out of total all India ICU beds and ventilators in government hospitals, the share of Punjab ranges between 2 and 3%. The critical care units must be strengthened at the district level or block level hospitals. Out of total beds some percentage should be reserved for the ICU beds in government hospitals;

V. The health manpower availability is not satisfactory. For example, in Punjab the availability of allopathic doctors per lakh of population is just 111 and of nurses is 64.8. In 2019 there was a shortage of 81.8% of specialists at CHCs against the IPHS (Indian Public Health Standards). The need is to fill the vacant posts of various medical specialists and nurses on the regular basis with decent working conditions;

VI. The effective health infrastructure requires effective investment. The health expenditure data exhibits that India's current health expenditure as a percentage of GDP is 1.58%. Across the states this percentage could not touch 2%. The per capita health expenditure across the states could not go beyond Rs. 2000. The health sector needs at least 2.5% of GDP to be spent on public health expenditure in a time-bound manner, as suggested in the National Health Policy 2017. Also, there is a need to implement the recommendations of Task Force on the National Investment Pipeline that has earmarked Rs. 1.5 lakh crore for the health sector over financial year 2020–2025;

VII. Atmanirbhar Bharat announced certain reforms in health sector by increasing investment in public health sector to meet pandemic in future. The plan is to create in each district infectious disease hospital and integrated public health labs in each district and lab in every block to meet pandemics in future. The centre has announced viability gap funding of Rs. 8100 crore. The reforms are well intentioned and the state governments should try to go ahead with the funds of central governments and own funds;

VIII. Lastly, the telemedicine concept should be promoted and during a month the grass root level health manpower should interact with the experts of tertiary medical institutions on the various medical advancements and to tackle pandemic in future;

8 Conclusion

The epidemic has always remained a part of our history. In nineteenth and twentieth century, the frequent epidemics like malaria, small pox and plague occurred in Punjab. Presently, the pandemic covid-19 has not only hit the economy, but also put at test the capabilities of health care services. The health infrastructure in the rural areas is not fully functional. The availability of health institutions (PHC, SHC, CHC) is in shortage. Along with this the availability of health manpower especially the specialist doctors are in acute shortage. The females are significantly contributing in nursing care. The critical care services in government hospitals are in shambles. The current expenditure on health as percentage share of GDP is just 1.58% in India and in Punjab it is less than 1%. The need is to raise the share of GDP on health sector up to 2.5%. The continuous casualisation of services of health professionals must come to an end. The treatment of the patients especially of poor and middle class should be free at the time of epidemics and pandemics.

References

Anand, S., and Fan, V. (2016) The Health Workforce in India, Human resources Series No.16, World Health Organisation (WHO).

Arrow, K. J. (1963) Uncertainty and the Welfare Economics of Medical Care, *American Economic Review*, 53: 941–973.

Bhore, S. Joseph (1946) Health Survey and Development Committee, Government of India, New Delhi. Available at: https://www.nhp.gov.in/bhore-committee-1946_pg [Accessed September 18, 2021].

Dash, A. (2020) Rural Healthcare & Atmanirbhar Bharat, *The Financial Express*, June 6, 2020.

Hogarth, J. (1975) *Glossary of Health Care Terminology*, Copenhagen: WHO.

National Health Profile. (2019). Ministry of Health and Family Welfare, GoI.

Protesting Nurse Jumps into Bhakra Canal in Punjab, *The Hindustan Times*, November 16, 2016.

Sood, A., et al. (2018) The Burden of Hepatitis C Virus Infection in Punjab, India: A Population Based Sero Survey, *PLOSONE*, 13.

Tandon, S. (2013) Epidemics in Colonial Punjab, *Journal of Punjab Studies*, 20: 217–242.

Yeolekar, M. E., and Mehta, S. (2008) ICU Care in India—Status & Challenges, *Journal of the Association of Physicians of India*, 56(R): 221.

Wilkinson, E. (1903) *Plague Infected Areas of the Punjab and Its Dependencies* (Report), Lahore: Punjab Government Press.

Making 'Quality Education Accessible' to All: Policy Perspective on School Education in Punjab

Kamlesh Narwana and Angrej Singh Gill

1 Introduction

School education, comprising of elementary and secondary levels, is considered as the most significant segment in the overall education system of any country as it dispenses huge positive externalities and is inherently associated with socio-economic development of a nation. It is, therefore, imperative for every country in the world to include the agenda of universalization of school education in their overall development efforts. However, amid four important policy and context changes which have happened in India, viz. neo-liberal economic reforms, a decade of implementation of RTE Act, National Education Policy 2020, and COVID-19 pandemic shocks, the school education system of Punjab is at the crossroads. Punjab, intriguingly, presents a categorically paradoxical position, which while on the one hand has been among the better-off states in India, lags behind in its educational development standing as per Educational Development Index (NUEPA, 2014), on the other hand. This policy brief, on the basis of DISE, NSS, ASER data, critically examines the status of school education with policy implication for future discourse.

K. Narwana (✉) · A. S. Gill
Panjab University Rural Centre, Kauni, Sri Muktsar Sahib, India

S. Singh et al. (eds.), *Covid-19 Pandemic and Economic Development*,
https://doi.org/10.1007/978-981-16-4442-9_15

Drawing on 'Access, Quality and Equity' framework, this brief highlights that Punjab has many feathers to its cap in quantitative terms, e.g. in the context of enabling access to schools and providing basic infrastructure. Nevertheless, the school education is suffering from several issues like poor quality of education, unwarranted magnitude of privatization and commercialization of school education culminating into reproduction of social inequalities in the state. The next section briefly looks at recent developments in Punjab school education. While focussing on accessibility, the third section elaborates on achievement and gaps in this context. Section four delineates on quality concern while analyzing the learning achievements and challenges related to teaching. The fifth section attempts to analyse the challenge of equity in the context of the size of the private sector and its impact on social inequality. Section Six deals with the impact of corona pandemic on school education in Punjab. The last section summaries the policy briefs while recommending policy implication for revamping the school education.

2 Recent Developments in the School Education Arena

Punjab government has recently initiated few interesting measures to address the challenges state school education system has been grappling with. 'Padho Punjab-Padhao Punjab' (Learn Punjab, Educate Punjab) an activity-based learning enhancement programme for improving reading and learning levels in elementary classes stands as one such important step. Understanding the concern of dwindling enrolment in Government schools, 'Each one, Bring one' enrolment drive has been undertaken with the collaboration of different stakeholders (Goyal, 2019). To raise the educational standards of public school vis-à-vis their private counterparts, the government started English medium instruction in more than 2700 schools since 2018. Punjab claims to be the first state in India which has started 'pre-schooling classes' in Primary schools (*Hindustan Times*, 2019). In another move to update government schools with aesthetic buildings and child centric 'Teaching Learning Material', 13% of government schools are claimed to have been converted into smart schools (Goyal, 2019). For making education technologically updated and to inculcate employment skills in students, the digitalization of education has been undertaken, which becomes more relevant and welcome move in the current educational crisis due to corona shocks (Department of School

Education, 2019). To reinvigorate the school education, a committee has been set up for framing a 'New Education Policy' for the state which is yet to submits its report (Goyal, 2019). This succinct outline of recent happenings in school education arena underlines the state's commitment to fulfil its promise of 'Universalisation of Quality Education'. Nonetheless, these efforts are yet to produce desired results. Against this background, this brief undertakes the discussion forward while analyzing 'where Punjab stands.' In the context of 'Access, Quality and Equity' in school education and underpin the policy implication for moving forward.

3 Enabling Access: Achievements and Gaps

In Punjab, several positive developments have been witnessed in school education in terms of enabling accessibility by providing basic infrastructural facilities and enrolling children in schools.

3.1 Basic School Infrastructure

As per NSS data (75th Round), to comply with RTE norms, 90.7% and 97.8% of the households have a primary school and upper primary school, respectively, within a physical distance of one kilometre and three kilometres from home in 2017–2018. Same is true with regard to physical infrastructure at schools, e.g. 99.98% of the schools have drinking water facility and 99.55% school have functional toilet facility. Furthermore, the school buildings are equipped with electricity connection (99.94%) and library facility (96.87%) as per reported by DISE 2016–2017. However, the percentage of schools with computers in working condition is quite low (i.e. 42.64%).

3.2 Enrolment, Attendance and Progression

A glance at net enrolment ratio (NER) highlights that Punjab still lags behind in achieving the goal of universalization of elementary education as NER stands at 91.89% for elementary classes in 2016–2017 (District Information System for Education (henceforth DISE). The proportion for secondary level was reported 65.23%. To make the accessibility meaningful, it is important that students attend school regularly, progress through grades with little or no repetition and attain the expected learning outcome. Otherwise a vicious circle of frequent absenteeism from school, which causes poor performance, which further led to dropping out can end in 'silent exclusion' (Lewin, 2007). Net attendance rate (NAR) reported by NSS 75th round data (89% at primary, 78% upper primary, 65% at secondary and 48% at higher secondary level in 2017–2018) underlines the concern of student absenteeism in this context. Nevertheless, 97.02% progression rate at the elementary stage and 88.73% at secondary stage (DISE 2016–2017) can be seen as a positive development for meaningful access. Inspite of considerable rate of students progressing from one stage of education to the next, research studies report the poor learning achievement in terms of attaining basic language and numeracy skill indicate the pathetic state of the quality of school education.

4 Challenges of Ensuring Quality Education

Before delineating on concerns with quality education, it needs to be acknowledged that quality education is a broader concept with multiprone facets such as relevant curriculum, learning environment, child centric pedagogy and reflective assessment to list a few and it goes beyond attaining just learning skills. Given the paucity of space, this brief examines only the most glaring aspects relating to the quality of education.

4.1 *Alarming Learning Levels*

Understanding the current learning crisis, the NEP 2020 states that ability to read and write, and basic numeracy skill is a necessary foundation and an indispensable prerequisite for all future schooling. The poor quality of education in Punjab raises concern as ASER report 2018 informs the dismal state of learning levels. As per ASER 2018, 46% children from class 3rd, 20% from class 5th and 11% from class 8th cannot read basic text from class 2nd in rural Punjab. In numerical literacy, situation is even worse as 70% students from class 3rd, 46% from class 5th and 39% from class 8th cannot perform basic division sum.

4.2 *Teachers at the Core of Quality Education*

The challenges of learning achievements directly indicate the problems with the teaching–learning process. Before looking at the problems related to teaching, we need to acknowledge that teachers need not to be seen as only problematic spoke in wheel. Nevertheless, concerns related to teachers need to be treated with utmost priority. The problems concerned with teaching need to be visualized from a multi-prone perspective.

Burden of Non-academic Duties

With the lack of administrative support staff at schools, the teaching community keeps undertaking all the administrative non-academic work which, many times makes their primary duty i.e. 'teaching the students' secondary and neglected tasks.

Quality Comes with Quantity

Quantity reciprocates quality up to a certain extent as a school without sufficient teaching staff crunches cannot provide quality education. In Punjab schools, 26% of total teacher workforce in government schools and 53% in private schools are engaged as contractual staff (DISE 2016–2017) and 10.1% of total sanctioned post kept lying vacant in Elementary schools (*Financial Express*, 2020). This crunch of sufficient teaching staff indicates that teachers have to teach across-grade, but most of them have no training in multi-grade pedagogy and the curriculum is geared towards mono-grade schools, where there is at least one teacher per grade (NUEPA, 2009). Even after a decade of RTE Act 2010, 5.15% Primary and 6.70% Upper Primary school (State Report Cards 2016–2017) are functioning with single teacher which needs to be visualized as violation of fundamental right of many children. Further, it is not surprising to note that the districts with poor availability of teachers in schools are the districts where the private sector has done reasonably well in terms of expansion of educational provisions and enrolment share (Sinha, 2012).

Teacher Education in Shambles

The teacher education in India is in shambles and Punjab is not an exception. With the neo-liberal reforms, the teacher education has come under the institutes functioning as private shops which sell B.Ed. degree at fixed prices and many times, even without requiring the trainees to attend the course. Any reform in school curriculum, learning enhancement programme or any rhetoric about 'child centric education' or 'experiential learning' does not stand ground until Teacher Education is not revamped completely. In the absence of any training which can equip future teachers with recent technique in pedagogy, any progressive scheme like Continuous and Comprehensive Evaluation can fall flat.

5 Challenges to Equitable Learning Opportunity: The Blooming Private Sector

The proliferation of Private schools in the neo-liberal period presents the biggest challenge to the goal of equity of opportunity in school education. Out of the broader three types of schools in Punjab, viz. government, government aided and private unaided (henceforth private schools), the third category, i.e. private schools remain an area of concern with its rising presence in last two decades. The present section deals with the extent of privatization of schools in the state and iniquitous effects thereof.

5.1 *The Magnitude of Private Sector*

The private schools, with a share of 24.30% in total schools have steeply grown in the state during the neo-liberal economic reforms. Looking at the share of private school enrollments, as per DISE 2016–2017, the private schools have registered 41%, 36% and 33% of the students at elementary, secondary and higher secondary levels. This clearly establishes that much of the achievements in school education in Punjab in terms of increase in enrolment and attendance rates are due to considerable participation of private sector. Moreover, this flight of students from the government to private schools leads to sharp increase of 29.2% in 'government schools with 20 of fewer pupils' which underlines the struggle of government school in retaining their students (Table 1).

Table 1 Impact of growth of private schools on government school enrolment

No. of 'tiny' govt. schools	*2010–2011*	*2015–2016*	*Increase in number of 'tiny' govt. schools*	
			Absolute increase	*% of increase*
With 20 or fewer pupils	1077	1392	315	29.2
With 50 or fewer pupils	5865	7162	1297	22.1

Source Kingdon (2018)

5.2 *Household Expenditure on School Education*

Given the predominance of non-state providers in school education in the state, it becomes pertinent to examine: what is the magnitude of household expenditure on school education in private schools (vis-à-vis their government counterparts) and is it possible to designate private schools unaffordable? Moreover, also given that the emergence of private sector in Punjab during neo-liberal reforms is amid a deregulated environment (Brar, 2016), and it is also argued that the private institutions in eduation in India per se, 'though de jure, are described as charitable or not profit-seeking institutions, are de facto profit-making institutions' (Tilak, 2011), it can be expected that these schools charge extorbitant fees and are quite unaffordable for the households in the state. In this context, previous studies (Gill, 2017a, b, 2019) established that the burden of the private school education in terms of household expenditure, is very high (vis-à-vis government schools) and this burden increases with the level of school education. While pursuing primary education in private schools was 9.75 times costlier via-a-vis that of the government schools in the state, it was true at higher levels of school education as well. To put it differnetly, in order to pursue primary education in purely private schools, the households have to incur 9.85% of their annual consumption expenditure (Gill, 2017a), and, as such they are increasingly becoming unaffordable. And, the point is: This is the cost of education for one child at primary level only.

One can effortlessly visualize the situation at higher levels of school education. Moreover, it can also be well imagined how much costlier will it be for educating more than one child in private schools in the state. Moreover, it is also important to examine the break-up of household spending on school education into various components, e.g. school fee, non-fee components (like books/stationery/uniform and conveyance), private supplementary coaching. The largest cost component in private unaided schools at primary level is course fee, which constitutes 54.20% and 63.20% share in rural and urban Punjab respectively. It is followed by the non-fee components of books/stationery/uniforms. Moreover, similar patterns could be seen at higher levels of school education.

Due to the heavy costs of pursuing private education in Punjab coupled with perceived poor quality of education in government schools and perceived quality English medium educaton in private schools, the households with limited income started resorting to 'Low Fee Private Schools' which has serious equity concerns which will be dealt at length in next sub-section.

5.3 *What It Means for the Most Marginalized Sections*

The cost of attending private school keeps the marginalized sections (girls and scheduled castes) largely outside the ambit of privatized education which raise challenge to the government promises of equity. The government schools remain the most accessible educational choice of the downtrodden section as only 36.80% of total enrolled girls (DISE 2016–2017) and 36.41% of total enrolled SC students (Singh, 2019) got enrolled in different private schools. The differential learning levels of students in private and government schools point to the widening social gap where marginalized section keep lagging behind. ASER report 2018 highlights that students enrolled with private schools have better learning competencies than their government counterpart. As per ASER report 2018, only 36.8% of 3rd grade students in government school can read basic text from 2nd grade, while 41.8% of their private counterpart can perform this task. The situation in performing arithmetic skills is more glaring as in comparison to 57% of 3rd standard students in private schools, only 40.5% government school students are able to do subtraction. Nonetheless, it needs to be cautioned that learning outcome concern cannot be simply brushed under the carpet by assuming that there is a huge gap between public and private schools (Nawani, 2018). Different studies have noticed the poor quality of education in certain private schools (especially low-cost category) which definitely is not better than the government schools (Kaur, 2017).

5.4 *Teacher as the Scapegoat of Private Model of Education*

Equity concern does not only end with social divide among students, but it percolates at all level, especially the teacher, whose pitiable working condition with meagre salary make the private school earn more profits. With growth of private sector, these schools have become significant teacher employers as 44.70% of total teacher force in Punjab work in private schools. A private school teacher is paid an average salary of 1925 Rs. per month in rural Punjab (Antony and Chaudhuri, 2014), which is only about 3.2% of government teacher salary in rural Punjab (who got paid Rs. 59654 Ramachandran, 2015). This 'low salary of teacher model proves workable given the high graduate unemployment rate in India which means the private schools take advantage of this low market-clearing wage (Kingdon, 2018). Besides earning less, they are less likely to have formal job contracts and benefits like paid leave and pension which definitely have negative consequences for teacher morale and attrition (Chudgar, 2020).

6 Pandemic Shocks to School Education: Learning Crisis, Digital Divide and Social Equity

As discussed above, Punjab has been suffering from the problem of learning gaps and social equity challenges even in the pre-COVID-19 pandemic era, the pandemic situation with closure of physical classroom, has further accentuated this crisis. It is apprehended that it can lead to huge drop out from the school, who may never return to fold of education again which results in permanent learning losses if students remain away from school for longer period.

Different models of coping programmes have been put in place by government and private schools in the state to minimize the damaging impacts of school closures on schoolchildren. In the absence of basic access to technological infrastructure, the government schools are majorly resorting to measures like DD-Broadcasts on Television which is more available to even poor households. The government school students facing the challenges posed by online education as the NSS data noted that only 39.4% of the rural household in Punjab and 57.1% of their urban counterparts had internet facility (NSS 2017–2018). Moreover, given that laptop/computers are considered to be better way of online education, the poorest 20% households in the state suffer at this end also as only 2.2% such households at the rural Punjab, and 5.2% their urban counterparts had computers in 2017–2018. Private schools, on the other hand, are using diverse platforms like google meet, Cisco webex, etc. to provide online teaching to the students. These measures are well taken up by parents with resources and educational capital, while in the absence of educational capital, parents belonging to marginalized sections, majorly catered by 'low fee private schools' are struggling to provide learning opportunity to their ward given their limited resource and technological knowledge. This learning scenario during the pandemic lockdowns further deepens the existing equity challenges.

Nevertheless, this particular situation has a silver lining for reviving the crumbling government sector in Punjab. With major setback to economy during lockdown period, the employment crisis has severely impacted the household capacity to spend on privatized education. Consequently, with the closing down of many small private schools, Punjab has witnessed 2.1 lakh new admissions to government schools. This 'back to government school' scenario, needs to understood as an opportunity to behold the public trust in government schools and shrink the neo-liberal sector to its margin.

7 Revamping the Future Discourse of School Education in Punjab: Policy Implication

- First, there is urgent need to improve the quality of education at government schools so that the children of the socially underprivileged, who are predominantly enrolled in these schools, could improve their learning outcomes. To achieve the goals of quality, it is important that the state government adopts a multi-pronged strategy after duly taking into account ground level problems connected with lower levels of learning outcomes. For this, the most important requirement is to increase public spending on education in general and school education in particular, which are insufficient vis-à-vis norms (Gill and Brar, 2010). Furthermore, it is also important that a detailed research should be conducted by a team of academicians in collaboration with different stakeholders with exposure to grass root issues of school education in Punjab, to recommend locally appropriate strategy in this direction.
- There is a need to recognize that the teaching community is not well equipped to meet different challenges. Non-teaching work burden on teachers need to be minimized so that they could concentrate on teaching by providing enough administrative staff to ease their burden of administrative duties. To protect the fundamental right of every child i.e. Right to Education, there is most urgent need to resolve the challenge of multi-grade teaching by filling all the sanctioned vacant posts at the earliest.
- Teacher Education is one area which demands paradigm shift if government seriously think of improving teaching standards. Considering 'Teacher Education' a standalone specialization for study, a four year integrated undergraduate programme needs to be

designed under the guidance of prominent educationist. The 'Bachelors of Elementary Education' under 'University of Delhi' is one progressive model which can be studied for such restructuring.

- There should be an effort of developing a network of school mentors for providing continuous support to teachers. A platform needs to be created where school mentors, school leaders academicians at university, educationist working with civil society organisation can work together to help school teacher and schools to more effectively transmit the school education to students.
- As 'Common School' policy is nowhere in sight, the presence of 'non-state actor' in education cannot be negated. However, to bridge the emerging social inequalities as well as to ease the middle class households who feel the heat of high costs of private schools, it is important to regulate these schools, which, by exploiting excess demand phenomenon, have largely become commercial houses, making school education a 'commodity'. The state needs to tighten the control over private schools in terms of fee structure, standard of curriculum and protecting the teachers in private schools with minimum standard salary and benefits. A comprehensive policy specifying stringent guidelines and regulations, as well as effectual apparatuses of authority to implement them realistically is highly important in this context. Moreover, pre-emptive steps should be taken to resolutely implement the clause of '25 per cent reservation of Economically Weaker Section students in private schools' which has been adversely diluted in Punjab.
- In order to pursue education in private schools, the students/households have to incur several forms of expenditures. Some such expenditures, like costly books/stationery (as prescribed by private schools), dresses from designated shops, form the biggest method of exploitation of households by private schools. It has been observed that although the private schools have somewhat rationalized fee during COVID-19, the household expenditure on such sundry items has significantly been dropped. The government should make efforts to keep such expenditure to the minimum possible levels in the post-COVID era also so that the schools do not revert back to such exploitation when the economic situation gets back its normalcy. To meet the challenges emerged during pandemic, there is need to upgrade the school education system by adopting a multi-dimensional strategy with a focus on inclusive

education by addressing the skill gap, bridging the digital divide and equipping teachers with digital skills.

References

Antony, M., and Chaudhuri, N. (2014) *Limiting Choices and Denying Opportunities? The Case of School Closures in Punjab*, New Delhi: Centre for Civil Society.

ASER. (2019) *Annual Status of Education Report 2018*, ASER Centre, New Delhi: Pratham.

Brar, J. S. (2016) Critical Evaluation of Educational Development in Punjab, in L. Singh and N. Singh (Eds.), *Economic Transformation of a Developing Economy: The Experience of Punjab, India*, Singapore: Springer, pp. 291–312.

Chudgar, A. (2020) *Non-state Actors Are Influencing the Teaching Profession: What Are the Implications?*, Oxford: United Kingdom Forum for International Education and Training.

Department of Education. (2019) Four Year Strategic Action Plan (4SAP)—2019–23 and Annual Action Plan—2019–20, Punjab: Government of Punjab.

Financial Express. (2020) Over 10 Lakh Posts Lying Vacant in Government Elementary Schools Across Country: RTI. Available at: https://www.financialexpress.com/jobs/over-10-lakh-posts-lying-vacant-in-government-elementary-schools-across-country-rti/1866947/.

Gill, A. S. (2017a) State, Market and Social Inequalities: A Study of Primary Education in the Indian Punjab, *Millennial Asia*, 8(2): 194–216.

Gill, A. S. (2017b) Developments in Provisioning of School Education in Punjab (India) in the Era of Neo-liberal Reforms: Insights from NSS Data, *IASSI Quarterly*, 36(2 and 3): 228–244.

Gill, A. S. (2019). State, Market and Economic Status Related Marginalization in Access to Higher Education in Punjab: Insights from Recent NSS Data, *Man and Development*, 41(4): 99–118.

Gill, A. S., and Brar, J. S. (2010) Public Expenditure on Education in North-West Region During Reforms Period, in H. S. Shergill, S. S. Gill, and G. Singh (Eds.), *Understanding North-West Indian Economy*, New Delhi: Serial Publications, pp. 235–257.

Goyal, D. (2019) Two Years of Amrinder Singh in Punjab: Education Gets a Primary Makeover. Available at: https://indianexpress.com/article/education/punjab-education-gets-a-primary-makeover-5631483/.

Hindustan Times. (2019) 2750 Punjab Schools to have English Medium from April 1. Available at: https://www.hindustantimes.com/punjab/2-750-pun

jab-schools-to-have-english-medium-from-april-1/story-bP7E6yh9yGLWAkL vKjX3pK.html

Kaur, S. (2017) Quality of Rural Education at Elementary Level: Evidence from Punjab, *Economic and Political Weekly*, 52(5): 58–63.

Kingdon, G. G. (2018) The Private Schooling Phenomenon in India: A Review, *The Journal of Development Studies*, 56(10): 1795–1817.

Lewin, K. (2007) Improving Access, Equity and Transitions in Education: Creating a Research Agenda, CREATE Pathways to Access Research Monograph No. 1, Brighton: University of Sussex.

Nawani, D. (2018) Assessing ASER 2017: Reading Between the Lines, *Economic and Political Weekly*, 53(8): 14–17.

NUEPA. (2009) Educational Access in India, Country Policy Brief, Consortium for Research on Education, Access, Transitions and Equity, New Delhi.

NUEPA. (2014) Report of Workshop on Educational Development Index (EDI), NEUPA: New Delhi.

Ramachandran, V. (2015) Teachers in the Indian Education System: Synthesis of a Nine-State Study, New Delhi: NUEPA.

Singh, P. (2019). Punjab's Failure in Education has Left Scheduled Caste Students Stranded, *The Caravan*.

Sinha, S. (2012), Status of School Education in Punjab, Institute for Development and Communication, Chandigarh.

Tilak, J. B. G. (2011) Education for Profit, *Economic and Political Weekly*, 46(9): 18–19.

COVID-19 Pandemic and the Service Sector in Punjab: An Assessment of Impact and Policies for Revival

Manjit Sharma and Pushpak Sharma

1 Introduction

The current global pandemic has genesis in the extreme exploitation of both human and natural resources. The on-going ecological and social crisis, emerged out of the market logic of profit-oriented production system has challenged the viability of the economic ecosystem. Modern epidemics of various kinds could be traced to the fact that the "source of the problem lay in a world dominated by "markets" and "cosmopolitan dealers in finance" (Lankester, 2011, as cited in Editorial notes of Monthly Review, 2020, pp. 31–33). Scientists have been raising the alarm for decades that the industrialization, deforestation and corporate consolidation of meat production have increased risks for the emergence of global pandemics such as COVID-19. In this context; Bhaduri (2007), Bhaduri and Patkar (2009) and Kumar and Prakash (2017) rightly argued that the current pattern of growth is anti-development in nature. The

M. Sharma (✉)
Department of Economics, DAV College, Chandigarh, India

P. Sharma
Department of Economics, Panjab University, Chandigarh, India

S. Singh et al. (eds.), *Covid-19 Pandemic and Economic Development*,
https://doi.org/10.1007/978-981-16-4442-9_16

current public policy scenario widens the income gap between poor and rich and leads to income inequality in the economy.

Since the meltdown of 2008 and amidst all sorts of trade wars among the major economies of the world, the sudden outburst of the Novel Corona Virus (COVID-19) has been an unprecedented shock across the globe. According to the World Bank estimates, the world's GDP has shown a negative growth of 5.2% in 2020–2021 and the global north lost more human lives as compared to the global south (worldometers. info). The economic impact of the pandemic has been largely disruptive as India's economy contracted by 23.9% in the first quarter and the overall GDP also dropped to the figure of 7.7% in the fiscal year 2020–2021. Punjab being an integral part of the Indian economy is going to experience a contraction of 3% in the gross state domestic product in the current fiscal year due to the pandemic (India Ratings and Research, 2020). Punjab economy which has already been suffering due to the prevailing agrarian crisis and jobless industrial growth, further jolted by the shock of demonetization and Goods and Services Tax (GST), now suffered from the demand drought due to the pandemic. The service sector turns out to be the dominant sector in Punjab in terms of both gross value added and employment during the last decade. The employment data is available for NSSO's rounds only, hence data for gross value added is taken for the same period just to make compatibility between these two variables.

The service sector contributes half of the state's gross valued added and grew at a higher rate (6.4%) as compared to agriculture (2.1%) and the industrial sector (4.3%) over the period 2011–2020 (see Table 1). Apart from that, Punjab's service sector contributes nearly 40% of the state's total workforce which is higher than agriculture (24.7%) and the industrial sector (35.3%) in 2018–2019. Moreover, the share of the service sector in employment has increased (3.0%) at a higher pace viz-a-viz industry which experienced a slow increase (1.6%) and the agriculture sector which faced a decline (−4.6%) in the study period.

The service sector of Punjab holds a key position in share and growth trajectory of output and employment of the state. It prompted us to examine the performance of the service sector during the COVID-19 period. The main objectives of this paper are to understand the composition of the service sector of Punjab in pre-pandemic period, to do the preliminary assessment of its sub-sectors during the pandemic period and to propose policy suggestions for its revival in the post lockdown period.

Table 1 Sector wise share of GSVA and employment in Punjab at constant (2011–2012) prices (in %)

Output[a]	*2011–2012*	*2017–2018*	*2018–2019*	*2019–2020 (A)*	*CAGR (2011–2020)*	*Employment*[b]	*2011–2012*	*2017–2018*	*2018–2019*	*CAGR (2011–2018)*
Agriculture	30.8	25.7	25	24.6	2.1	Agriculture	36.5	26	24.7	−4.6
Industry	25.4	25.1	25.2	24.6	4.3	Industry	31.5	33.1	35.3	1.6
Service	43.8	49.1	49.8	50.7	6.4	Service	32	40.9	40	3.0

Source [a]Various National Accounts Publications, Ministry of Statistics and Programme Implementation; [b]Various NSSO's Employment-Unemployment Survey and PLFS Labour Force Surveys

This paper has been divided into four sections. First section deals with the introduction. The second section examines the composition of service sector of Punjab in pre-pandemic period. The third section analyses the service sector of Punjab during the COVID-19 period and the last section discusses the conclusion and policy prescription for the revival of state's economy.

2 Service Sector of Punjab Before COVID-19 Period: An Overview

The services sector comprises a wide variety of activities such as trade, hotel and restaurants, transport, storage and communication, financing, insurance, real estate, business services, community, tourism, social and personal services, and services associated with construction. At the intra-sector level; sub-sectors, trade and hotel (23.2%) and real estate (20.3%) are among the major contributors in the output of the service sector of Punjab. Transport and communication (11.4%), public administration (11%) and financial services (10.8%) have comparatively lesser share to the total gross state value added of the service sector. "Other services" (including activities like the repair of computers and personal and household goods, personal services, households as employers of domestic personnel etc.) (Table 2).

contribute 23.3% to gross state value added. These sectors witnessed decent growth during the study period.

Labour is a primary factor of production and its demand being derived in nature, have a pivotal role in the logic of production and production structure. In this context, the employment share of the sub-sectors of the service sector is discussed (Fig. 1). In Punjab, trade and hotel hold prime importance as both contribute to 41.3% of the total service sector's workforce in 2018–2019. Employment share of Trade has increased whereas the share of other sectors has decreased during the time period of 2011–2012 to 2018–2019 (Fig. 1). Trade and restaurant and other services hold more than 3/4th of the total employment in the service sector of Punjab. Other services contribute 31.8% in employment within the service sector followed by transport and communication sector (14.3%). Public administration, Financial Services and Real estate contributes 5.1%, 3% and 2.9%, respectively, to the total employment generated in the service sector of state's economy.

Table 2 GSVA share of sub-sectors in Punjab's service sector (in %)

Sub-sectors	*2011–2012*	*2017–2018*	*2018–2019*	*2019–2020*	*CAGR 2011–2020(in %)*
Trade, repair, hotels and restaurants	22.8	23.3	23.2	23.2	6.6
Transport and communication	11.9	11.6	11.5	11.4	5.9
Financial services	13.2	11.2	11.0	10.8	4.1
Real estate	20.5	20.1	20.2	20.3	6.3
Public administration	11.4	11.2	11.1	11.0	6.0
Other services	20.3	22.6	23.1	23.3	8.0
Total	100.0	100.0	100.0	100.0	6.4

Source Various National Accounts Publications, Ministry of Statistics and Programme Implementation, New Delhi

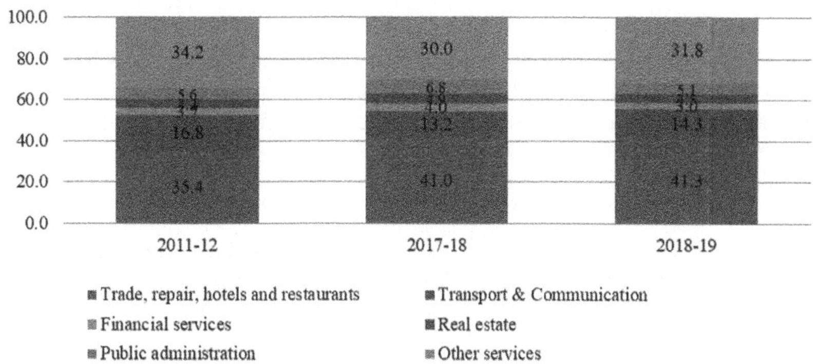

Fig. 1 Employment share of sub-sectors in Panjab's service sectors (in %) (*Source* Various NSSO's Employment-Unemployment Survey and PLFS Labour Force Surveys)

3 Service Sector of Punjab During COVID-19 Period: Preliminary Assessment

Punjab is suffering from a revenue loss of Rs. 22,000 crores in FY 2020–2021. Further, the Goods and Services Tax (GST) revenue collection stands at Rs. 7881 crore for the period April to December, 2020 in comparison to Rs. 9851 crore for the corresponding period of last year, thereby denoting a fall of 20% (Rs. 1971 crore). Punjab Taxation Commissioner's Office targeted the State GST collection as Rs. 15,859 crore for fiscal year 2020–2021. Under the given circumstances, it seems difficult to achieve the targeted amount.

Though health and safety concerns during the pandemic led to a boom in online marketing and e-commerce activities yet the fall in the Purchasing Manager Index (PMI) of the service sector during the lockdown has become a policy concern. Personal services that cannot be availed and provided through digitalization; like physical examination and surgery, physiotherapy, barbers, domestic workers, and drivers, etc. and can neither be exported nor imported (Mazumdar, 2020). Centre for Monitoring Indian Economy reported that the recovery of job loss due to lockdown continued to evade the service sector at the end of the third quarter of 2020–2021. In this context, the sub-sectors in the service sector of Punjab are discussed during the pandemic period.

3.1 Trade, Hotels and Restaurants

The jolt of pandemic altered the whole outlook of Punjab's trade sector during COVID-19. Uncertain scenarios and a broken supply chain affected the trade resulting in a higher unemployment level. This sector's dismal performance arrested employment opportunities and revenue generation which further led to the slump in the retail demand (70% drop in orders for winter wear in Punjab) and consequently resulted in the surplus stock with the traders (Press Trust of India, July 22, 2020). The lockdown affected the availability of labour for loading and unloading of consignments and the implementation of protective measures for workers raised the cost of labour.

The case of the hotel and tourism sector is not very different from the trade sector. Around 20–22 lakh people are directly or indirectly employed in the Punjab's hotel industry. President of Punjab Hotel and Resort Association shared with *The Tribune* that around 5,000 small, medium and large hotels and restaurants, including national and international chains, have suffered a monthly loss of Rs. 960 crore in the state (Paul, 2020).

Punjab tourism witnessed expansion at an impressive rate of 29.5% between 2010 and 2018. Amritsar city accounts for more than 59% of the total tourist inflow in the State (Economic Survey, 2019–2020). *Jallianwala Bagh*, *Wagha Border*, Golden Temple and *Virasat-e-Khalsa* museum in Anandpur Sahib have witnessed a reduction in daily footfall of 70% in the unlock period.[1] According to the conservative estimates, there is a monthly loss of Rs. One crore during the lockdown in the state. As per axiomatic considerations and common understanding, the sudden loss of tourists resulted in both backward and forward multiplier effects; income loss of other small self-employed enterprises, transporters, hotels, *dhabas* and *pheri walas*. The small own account workers which depend on the daily inflow of tourists were the worst affected during the lockdown.

3.2 *Financial Services, Transport and Real Estate*

Banks played a crucial role in the transfer of financial benefits of government-led schemes through Direct Benefit Transfer (DBT). There is a steep fall in usage of banking through physical mode and people had to resort to online mode of banking or they preferred digital banking system during lockdown. The credit misallocation, increasing non-performing assets (NPAs) and credit losses may lead to banking sector at risk. Bankers discussed during focussed group discussions that the risk may aggravate if the borrowers who availed the moratorium are unable to pay interest and instalments promptly. The Non-banking financial companies (NBFCs) which give loans to informal workers and small businesses (micro finance) are under threat, as repayments cannot be estimated in this uncertain situation.

During the period of lockdown; road, rail and air transport were completely halted the intra-state and inter-state mobility of Punjab. Almost one lakh bus drivers and conductors of private buses had to face income and employment loss during the lockdown. In addition to other losses that cannot be measured directly, the government also suffered the loss of tax revenue worth Rs. 66 crore due to exemption in Motor Vehicle tax to private bus operators.

Due to Covid-19 pandemic, the housing sales are estimated to possess plunged by about 75% forcing developers to offer discounts to boost sales

(*Hindustan Times*, June 13, 2020). Reasonable housing, however, has been the worst hit as a result of a majority of potential consumers have suffered job losses, cut in wages and financial hardship quite three months of the lockdown across the country with the COVID-19 showing no signs of abating. The potential homebuyers are treading with extreme caution because of uncertainties. Liquidity crunch, inflation of construction material and exodus of migrant workers from the state are contracting supply creation. Builders have lost 50–100% of their migrant workers since interstate transport was allowed. Despite the very fact that labourers want to return now, it'll take a while before construction schedules normalize (*Hindustan Times*, June 13, 2020).

3.3 Social Security, Health and Education

During the pandemic period, the Punjab government announced various social security measures such as special health insurance cover of Rs. 50 lakh each for those who were in the frontline of the fight against COVID-19. In addition to it, Finance Department released Rs. 296 crore for social security pensions to 24.70 lakh beneficiaries during the pandemic. Further, Punjab Land Development and Financial Corporation have issued a subsidy to the tune of Rs. 140.40 lakh for SC beneficiaries to help them recover from the COVID-19 crisis (Department of Governance Reforms and Public' Grievances, 2020). Monetary grant was given to women account holders of *Jan Dhan Yojna* of Rs. 500 per month and Rs. 1000 per month to senior citizens, widows and disabled persons for 3 months. All the above measures proved far from being satisfactory and put a question mark on the welfare perspective of the state. This neoliberal mind set can be clearly understood as empirical evidence has shown expenditure on social security, medical and public health and education, sports and culture witnessed a decline during the last decade (see Table 3).

The health services being a public good must be provided by the modern welfare state to shape human capital formation. World Economic Forum estimates that the cost of prevention of pandemic will always be a fraction of the cost of dealing with it. The shortage of Personal Protective Equipment (PPE) kits, ventilators, doctors, nurses and paramedical staff in the public sector is a glaring loop hole to tackle any pandemic like COVID-19.[2] The private health sector (which has an 80% share in beds and doctors) closed their hospitals under panic in the beginning period of the pandemic but later on fleeced the skin of

Table 3 Expenditure on education, health and social security (figures are as % of total revenue expenditure)

Expenditure head	*2011–2012*	*2017–2018*	*2018–2019*
Education, sports, art and culture	16.0	14.9	13.5
Medical and public health	4.2	4.1	3.7
Social security and welfare	3.1	1.6	1.2

Source State Finances: A study of Budgets, RBI

COVID-19 patients.[3] Both public and private hospitals kept their OPDs closed without taking concern for the ailing patients with other chronic diseases. This entire situation had put tremendous physical and mental pressures on the patients particularly; children, pregnant women and other aged persons with serious health issues who required immediate medical service.

Education which is a great human resource investment too was not duly addressed by the state. The COVID-19 pandemic ranging across the globe has led to the eventual closure of educational institutions. The alternative measure through online education was used to fill the deficiency of classroom teaching.[4] Finance capital grabbed the opportunity and the online education appreciated by the middle and upper class[5] but it excluded the downtrodden section of the society. The huge digital divide emerged as a big challenge to the tech-based teaching learning processes. The Annual Status of Education Report (ASER, 2021) shows that 38.2% of children do not have access to smart phones. Further, the education ministry's budget for digital e-learning was slashed to Rs. 469 crore in 2020–2021; from Rs. 604 crore of the previous year, puts a question mark on scope, effectiveness and future of digital learning. Due to sudden loss of livelihood and income, parents were unable to pay the fees of private schools. Approximately 1,60,372 students of the private school shifted to government schools in Punjab in session 2020–2021 (Bariana, 2020). The public education sector which was willingly weakened by the neo-liberal policies came to rescue the poor students from the eventual educational exclusion. India is estimated to lose $440 billion in possible future earnings due to the impact of school closures, as per the "Informality and COVID-19 in South Asia" report.

The emerged urban–rural divide in healthcare and education is another cause of concern and needs to be addressed. To augment the education and health facilities at the ground level, the state created an institutional mechanism. To achieve this objective, *Aganwadi* and ASHA workers (Accredited Social Health Activists) acted as a connecting link between the community and government. The pandemic has given visibility to nearly 20,000 ASHAs workers and 26,656 *Anganwadi* workers and a similar number of helpers of the State[6] but the irony of the situation is that they are classified as "honorary workers" and are denied minimum wage.

4 Conclusion and Policies for Revival

This pandemic has unfolded the structural inequalities that human civilization face across the globe. The economic malaise which was deep even before the pandemic is further provoked by the pandemic. The dismal performance of trade, hotel and restaurants, transport, real estate and tourism arrested employment opportunities and revenue generation. The hotels and restaurants have suffered a monthly loss of Rs. 960 crore in the state during the pandemic period. Almost one lakh private bus drivers and conductors had to suffer loss of income and tourism sector have witnessed a reduction in daily footfall of 70% in the unlock period in the state. The state undergone 20% (Rs. 1971 crore) loss of tax revenue of GST during April to December, 2020 viz-a-viz the corresponding period of last year. The loss of government revenue results in interaction of multiplier and accelerator which leads to fall in consumption and investment level. The degeneration in economic activities, fall in public expenditure for social security, health and education facilities will reduce the efficiency and welfare activities. The huge digital divide and rural–urban dichotomy reflects structural oppression which excluded the vulnerable section from education and health sector. One can imagine the predicament of rural areas with its fragile health resources in case of pandemic emerges in rural areas. Macro level studies had already pointed out a deeper crisis of female employment in the state. The present status of "honorary workers" of *Aganwadi* and ASHA workers (Accredited Social Health Activists) and denial of minimum wages will further raise unemployment level among the women. Approximately 80% (67.2 lakh as per PLFS, 2018–2019) of the employment in Punjab is in the informal sector, which is low-paid and unskilled. The loss of livelihoods reflects fault lines of class nature of political and administrative clumsiness. Hence, the pandemic has exposed the labour market regime.

The response of the state to the pandemic is ill conceived and public policy has an inbuilt bias against inclusive development. COVID-19 catastrophe has compelled a re-imagination of the development paradigm. In this context, policy making requires deep down micro understandings, public policy and discourse must be recalibrated to make it more inclusive. The broken supply chain affected the trade. Huge losses were incurred by the traders due to low demand in the market. Hence, the traders must be given tax exemption and an extension in the payment of loans. The hotel industry must be granted extra time for payment of annual licence renewal fees and property taxes. It will enable the small hotel owners to revive their business and also to maintain the employment level in the industry. Moreover, small and medium level hotels should get support from the government for the payment of employees' salaries at least for six months. The governments need to develop a strategy for the promotion of tourism along with safety protocols, i.e. by stimulating domestic travel while international travel bans are still in place. Domestic tourism may be promoted upon the easing of travel restrictions within the country. Relief measures are required for the transport sector and the drivers of private buses, cars and trucks must be given at least six month salary. Permit of buses must be given to unemployed youth for improving their livelihood opportunities.

Steep fall in the demand for property resulted in income loss to small and medium builders and dealers. The real estate sectors should be given an extension in payment of instalments and extension in the permissible period of construction of projects respectively. Government should regulate rent of houses by cancelling the increase in annual rental payment during short period and providing the low-cost housing to the downtrodden section of the society in the long run.

There must be MGNREGA like scheme for informal workers in urban areas, regulated labour market regime, decent working conditions and social security for informal workers. The number of working days must be increased to 200 under new proposed scheme. The workers in the informal sector who suffered from COVID-19 must be given a minimum of one month of paid leave and the government must bear the treatment cost of these workers. These workers must be given a decent amount of Rs. 6000/month for six months for maintaining their health after recovering from COVID-19. The dearness allowance which was freezed by government from January 1, 2020 to June 2020 must be restarted immediately and its arrears must be given immediately to government employees. Sixth pay commission which is much delayed and long pending demand of employees must be released immediately. In addition to this increased public sector expenditure, employees of private sector should be protected by providing one-time bonuses to vulnerable workers. Skill development schemes like Pradhan Mantri Kaushal Vikas Yojana (PMKVY) and Punjab Skill Development Mission (PSDM) should be given a boost so that more young workers can get vocational training. Migrant's nightmare exposed the fault lines of the Indian labour market. The government must facilitate them with food and shelter and also assure their proper rehabilitation after the lockdown period. Hence, the major emphasis must be on increasing the aggregate demand along with strengthening the supply side in the economy.

Females in Punjab have a low and declining work participation rate which made them more vulnerable to poverty during the pandemic period. There must be a separate MGNREGA like a scheme for female informal workers. Anaganwadi' and "ASHA workers" must be paid minimum wage rather than honorarium. Unpaid work is a privately produced public good and subsidizes the government by taking care of the old, sick and disabled. Government can also recognize the unpaid workers in the national database by a sound database survey and use the data in national policies (Hirway in *The Hindu*, March 22, 2021).

On the financial front, the states must be compensated by the Centre. The Cess and surcharge share of the Central Government has increased from 10.4% to 19.9% from 2011–2012 to 2020–2021, which are not shared with state governments. GST is not shared as per commitments. Financial federal relations were weak already, are under strain and central government is not honouring the commitments made with state governments. Government must increase the transfer of funds through a higher grant in aid to compensate for lower tax devolution to states.

The COVID-19 crisis is a wake-up call for strengthening public healthcare systems, and the nationalization of private healthcare facilities is the need of the hour at least during pandemics; on the pattern of France, the UK and Spain. There is an urgent requirement of up gradation of the capacity of government medical colleges and primary health centres at the village level, as its need has been felt acutely during the pandemic. The government should provide universal health coverage. Education and health should be treated as a public good rather than a market good.

Countries such as the United States and the United Kingdom that were typically lower spenders on the social contract before the pandemic have raised their expenditure by significantly more than economies such as Denmark, which previously had ranked among the higher spenders (Madgavkar et. al in McKinsey, 2020). Hence, government should learn the lesson from the developed countries in tackling COVID-19 crisis.

Notes

1. 10 million visitors have visited the museum so far in a short span of eight years of its opening. During unlock period, the average daily footfall in the museum has reduced to 1,000 visitors daily which was 4000–5000 visitors before lockdown.
2. Punjab lost human resources (5,473 deaths due to COVID-19 as per covidindia.org).
3. In Punjab, the private hospitals have been charging anything between Rs. 30,000–50,000 a day while the treatment is free of cost in government hospitals and around Rs. 6,000 a day in semi-government or charitable hospitals (*The Week*, June 18, 2020). https://www.theweek.in/news/india/2020/06/18/flooded-with-complaints-of-high-bills-haryana-and-punjab-to-rein-in-private-hospitals.html.
4. The online teaching can't substitute classroom teaching, the teachers and students lack the sufficient internet speed, the skills and equipment for effective online education.
5. It is noteworthy that, between 11th March and 5th April, Zoom (online meeting application used by academic institutions for teaching, companies for office meetings and professionals) reported 1.28 crore downloads in India.
6. State Government pays honorarium of Rs. 7500 and Rs. 3500 per month to Anganwadi Workers and Anganwadi helpers respectively. Punjab's ASHA workers are voluntary health workers and are denied minimum wages.

References

ASER Centre. (2021) *Annual Status of Education Report (Rural)*, New Delhi, India, p. 33.

Bariana, S. S. (2020) 1.6 Lakh Students Move from Private to Government Schools, *The Tribune*, September 6. Available at: https://www.tribuneindia.com/news/punjab/1-6-lakh-students-move-from-private-to-government-schools-137483 [Accessed 02 January 2021].

Bhaduri, A. (2007) Development or Developmental Terrorism, *Economic & Political Weekly*, 42(7): 552–553.

Bhaduri, A., and Patkar, M. (2009) For the People, By the People, Of the People, *Economic & Political Weekly*, 44(1): 10–13.

Department of Governance Reforms and Public' Grievances. (2020) Punjab COVID-19 Response—Initiatives and Policy Measures.

Economic Survey of Punjab. (2019) *Tourist Footfall in Amritsar Vis-a-Vis Punjab*, Chandigarh: Economic and Statistical Organisation of Punjab. Government of Punjab.

Hirway, I. (2021) How to Treat Unpaid Work, *The Hindu*, March 22. Available at: https://www.thehindu.com/opinion/op-ed/how-to-treat-unpaid-work/article34125020.ece [Accessed 23 March 2021].

India Ratings and Research. (2020) State-Wise Estimated GSDP Growth in FY21. Available at: https://www.indiaratings.co.in/PressRelease?

Kumar, D., and Prakash, V. (2017). Poverty and Condition of Employment Among Social Groups in India, *International Journal of Social Science*, 6(2): 125–135, https://doi.org/10.5958/2321-5771.2017.00014

Lankester. (2011) Notes from the Editors (2020), *Monthly Review*, 72(1): 31–33. Available at: https://monthlyreview.org/2020/05/01/mr-072-01-2020-05_0/#lightbox/0/.

Madgavkar, A., Tacke, T., Smit, S., and Manyika, J. (2020) COVID-19 Has Revived the Social Contract in Advanced Economies—For Now. What Will Stick Once the Crisis Abates?, *Mckinsey*. Available at: https://www.mckinsey.com/industries/public-and-social-sector/our-insights/covid-19-has-revived-the-social-contract-in-advanced-economies-for-now-what-will-stick-once-the-crisis-abates.

Mazumdar, S. (2020) COVID-19 and the Industrial and Services Sectors, *Corona Policy Impact*, July 24. Available at: https://coronapolicyimpact.org/2020/07/24/covid-19-and-the-industrial-and-services-sectors/ [Accessed 05 January 2021].

Paul, G. S. (2020) Hospitality Industry in Punjab on Verge of Collapse, Demands Relief, *The Tribune*, April 7. Available at: https://www.tribuneindia.com/news/punjab/hospitality-industry-in-punjab-on-verge-of-collapse-demands-relief-67062 [Accessed: 05 January 2021].

Press Trust of India. (2020) Covid-19: Punjab's Garment Industry Sees 70% Drop in Orders for Winter Wear, *Business Standard*, July 22. Available at: https://www.business-standard [Accessed 05 January 2021].

Singh, G. (2020) Realty Market Dives in Mohali as Covid-19 Blues Hit Home, *Hindustan Times*, June 13. Available at: https://www.hindustantimes.com/cities/realty-market-dives-in-mohali-as-covid-19-blues-hit-home/story-n7Lv6HHlSy4acInwpvSwDM.html [Accessed 06 January 2021].

Worldometers. (2021). Coronavirus. Available at: https://www.worldometers.info/coronavirus/.

Basic Human Needs and Non-state Actors in Punjab: Understanding the Lives of Poor Amidst the Covid-19 Pandemic

Baldev Singh Shergill

1 Introduction and Problem Setting

The Indian state has taken an authoritarian measure by directing lock-down of the entire country in the last week of March 2020. The strategy adopted by the state during Covid-19 has thrown the working poor below survival and the question of subsistence has cropped up. Because a complete economic shutdown, complete income loss and having negligible savings among the working poor households left them without food and other essential items as their life always been hand-to mouth existence. It also steered to distress, scarcity, and the social exclusion of the poor households and they survived on the mercy of Non-state actors: socio-religious institutions, social and political organizations, and individual volunteerism without any state support.

There have been few essential commodities and services which are necessary for the survival of humans in a society. Economists, anthropologists, sociologists, scientists, engineers and other professionals have been engaging themselves to find solutions, policies, approaches. In 1970, various reports from ILO on employment-oriented programmes which

B. S. Shergill (✉)
Guru Kashi College, Punjabi University, Talwandi Sabo, Punjab, India

S. Singh et al. (eds.), *Covid-19 Pandemic and Economic Development*,
https://doi.org/10.1007/978-981-16-4442-9_17

focussed on to generate employment for the masses to get income to meet basic needs. The basic needs approach was presaged by the committee for development planning's attack on mass poverty and unemployment of United Nations in 1972. Thus the basic needs approach enables targets to be stated a physical rations of the specific goods and services, having universal validity instead of the abstract monetary aggregates making up gross national product (GNP) estimates. It emphasizes the necessaries of life in place of the values of the market place (Rimmer, 1981). Meeting basic needs was on the proposed strategy of the ILO as a priority objective to satisfy the basic needs of each country's population. It is further specified that basic needs should be understood to include certain minimum requirements of a family for the private consumption, such as adequate food, shelter, and clothing as well as certain household equipment and furniture, as well as certain essential services, such as safe drinking water, sanitation, public transport and health, education and cultural facilities (ILO, 1977; Srinivasan, 1977). In addition, International Covenant on Economic, Social and Cultural Rights, 1966 (ICESCR), a core instrument of the UN Charter of Human Rights, which recognized the right to food, clothing and shelter as a core element of the right to an adequate standard of living and social security (Lambie-Mumford and Silvasti, 2020).

The continuing development processes and welfare policies has been failed to provide minimum level of living and unable to meet minimum needs. At the policy level, it had little influence on Indian policy until 1972, when the approach paper on the fifth five-year plan included a minimum needs program as part of the plan that was quietly dropped in the draft as well as the final version of the plan (Srinivasan, 1977).

The income poverty of the working poor arises from unfair and avoidable differences which are manifested through socio-economic factors, low level of education attainment, low wage and insure occupations, household wealth, geographical location, gender and caste. Thorat (2006) in his study tries to find who the rural poor are and why. As Srinivasan (1977) argues that a development strategy cannot be fully articulated on the basis of the need to provide a limited set of goods and services to a part to the population. Nor can any success achieved in the provision of basic needs be sustained in the future without growth. On the other hand, McHale and McHale (1979) argue that modernization and various necessary stages of technological development and national economic growth were largely viewed as inevitable processes whose benefits would trickle down bringing material progress, social justice and freedom to all. In the past several years, the inevitability of these processes has been called into question. Wealth has not trickled down and poor has become poorer and material growth has not necessarily been accompanied by social progress and justice. In addition, Rimmer (1981), the reaction from the single-minded pursuit of economic growth came when it was apparent that recorded rates of growth in many developing countries exceeded expectations, belied prognoses, and even defied prescriptions such as the necessity for central planning. By 1970 the international agencies badly needed a new challenge; they found it unemployment and underemployment, the persistence of poverty, the tendency for development to bypass the masses, inequality and unsatisfied basic needs. The fundamental question after the neoliberal regime in the context of macroeconomic policies is why public spending has been on sharp decline. As Streeten (1995) argued that the ratio of public expenditure to national income, the ratio of social expenditure to public expenditure and the ratio of priority social expenditure to social expenditure are not sufficient for the desired results.

In this vacuum, when state has been continuously failed to provide basic minimum needs, socio-religious institutions, political organizations and individuals are frequently seen as first respondents to the needs of the poor at international, national, regional level and across geographical distribution. The Punjab state which is in question has been a long tradition of charity and philanthropy by the non-state actors since non-existence of modern state and the role of non-state actors were prominent as moral responsibility.

The poor households do always efforts to meet their very basic needs in normal days with household income, dependent on social welfare activities, subsidies, socio-religious charity, and individual charity. Adequate income of the landless households and unmet basic human needs is the result of development processes in the economy. Many developing and developed countries have been failed to provide or full filling basic human needs of the poor households.

During this covid-19 pandemic, poor households had been the sole sufferers which did not able to meet their basic needs. It is high time to rethink the strategies and policies adopted by the state because state and state policies have been responsible for their living conditions in a Sovereign Socialist Secular Democratic Republic. The successful countries adopted different strategies lead to success or failure in fulfilling basic needs in three regimes the socialist strategy—China, Albania and

Cuba, the capitalist market economic system—Taiwan and Hong Kong and welfare state or mixed economy—Sri Lanka and Costa Rica (Stewart, 1989).

During the lockdown, the challenge was to deliver food to every person in every corner of the country. Also, the amount of food grains provided to eligible beneficiaries under NFSA and other welfare schemes was doubled as under PMGKAY and the Atmanirbhar package announced by the Prime Minister (Agarwal, 2020c). Ministry for Consumer Affairs, Food and Public Distribution announced that the beneficiary population under NFSA was 81.3 crore people and 25 crore additional population over and above NFSA under own Ration Card Scheme of different state covered linked to census of 2021. In the case of Punjab, 1.41 crore (1,41,44,291) beneficiaries comprising of almost 50% of the state population is covered under the ambit of NFSA, PMGKAY and other schemes by the state. This population depends on these schemes for food security. When lockdown was announced, this section of society deprived from food and other essential commodities because of complete loss of their income. While state did not have any roadmap how to provide food for the people, non-state actors: socio-religious institutions, social organizations and individuals came forward to provide food to the poor.

This research policy brief is based on case studies of four socio-religious institutions from three districts Bathinda, Sangrur and Faridkot and primary survey at the household level from Talwandi sabo of Bathinda District to analyze the state of basic human needs of the poor during Covid-19 pandemic in Punjab. The detailed household information collected from fifty households. These households were those which completely lack resources, lost employment and work, weak social and family support and networks. All the households belong to schedule caste and backward caste and across from all religions- Sikh, Hindu, Muslim, Christen and other sects. The occupation of the surveyed households comprising of agriculture labourers, construction workers, other informal labourers working on different categories of shops, self-employed workers like rickshaw pullers, delivery service workers and other salaried workers working in nearby cities.

2 Empirical Evidence and Discussion

The Indian state implements massive food, livelihood and social security programmes which theoretically support vulnerable people from even before their birth to their survivors after death. According to Mander et al. (2011) these programmes are plagued by corruption, leakages, errors in selection, delays, poor allocations and little accountability.

Many organizations had begun its relief service/charity by providing meal or packed grocery kits to the poor and needy. Several studies and field observations regarding food charity indicate that there have been several potential barriers to access food aid: limited operating hours and inadequate & non-suitable assistance. The case studies and household survey indicated that there were approximately half of the individuals who were needed special needs born out of disability, illness, age and gender. But all were ignored by providing same meals to households. A large number of individuals reported that due to loss of income, we could not fulfil our special needs and nobody helped us in this regard. One committee argues that we provided food and milk feeders and fruits for the children which we got from donors. Case studies also revealed the fact that organizations themselves realized that food charity is not designed to meet such dietary needs for instance people suffering from allergies and diseases across gender and age.

It is no doubt that concerned administration and media smear a positive image of charitable food aid. The analysis of case studies about charity food distribution by the socio-religious institutions, voluntary organization and individual donors reflects that charitable responses constrained by limited resources, ad-hoc and un-coordinated provision, the continuous risk of withdrawal of donors and other organizations, dependence on the availability of volunteers and personnel and coverage. The case studies revealed the fact that all organizations and individuals served meal or distributed food kits only for a month. After that they also faced a deep crisis and deprived from food and many respondents told that we made only one meal in a day and were suffered from sickness and other diseases.

Do the efforts by the social organization sufficient? Our empirical evidence did not support this question. Majority of the households received cooked meal or grocery kit for only one month. The respondents told us that food aid provided by the social organization without any discrimination and on secular lines. One of the volunteer answered that we distributed food to all whether they belong to lower caste or whatever religion they followed. We distributed food by keeping in mind that they are poor. If we don't provide food aid and they will ultimately die because nobody was ready to come out from their houses due the fear of covid-19. Many respondents responded that we felt bad to take food or grocery kits from individuals, social organizations and religious institutions. But we did not have any option left.

It is found that state support was inadequate and ridden by delay and insufficient ration with leakages. State did not provide rations during the first month of lockdown, but the main objective of PDS have been to provide rations during scarcity, to control private trade, to maintain stable prices and to improve the well-being of the poor by the provisions of basic foods and other essential commodities at reasonable prices (Swaminathan, 2000).

Household survey also indicated that the actual consumption of staple consumer goods declined across households. It led to increased penury and the real burden increased on the head of family and other adults. Moreover, this crisis in the household would not only mean short rations; the price of eating might be the humiliation of an onerous dependence or the sale of any asset or livestock which reduced the odds of achieving an adequate subsistence the following year.

The current Covid-19 pandemic may provide religious institutions a window of opportunity to expand their poverty alleviation and charity activities. Guruduwara also played an important role to distribute to the needy irrespective of caste, religion. But the church in the village distribute food kits only to the followers of Christianity.

It is to be found that socio-religious institutions, civil society organizations and individual donors provided only two meals or grocery kit only. Respondents reiterated that we have had other basic needs which were unmet. The response of state was remorseful in this regard and people who donate us food, they could not meet other essential needs. We also required other commodities like soap, milk and other essential items which were not realized.

Food charity has a partial capacity to respond the needs of the clients. If the religious institutions and civil society organizations have the capacity to combat transnational poverty, why working poor have been suffering with the lack of basic needs in the south and even in the global north which is so called developed world. All the charities done by the religious institutions and social organizations were limited to providing meal not even other basic needs during the crisis and normal days. Many researcher pointed out that they can divert attention away from the state's duty to provide income and food security for the poor and needy. As empirical evidence suggests that this work like providing food does not extend to political issue such as redistribution of wealth, economic inequality, and economic and social justice which are closely related to poverty reduction and alleviation. As we understand the situation, faith-based institutions frequently serve as a front-line response, after governments leave many of the basic needs of the poor to individuals and non-governmental agencies. It is the fact that it is a paradigmatic shift in the responsibility of socio-religious institutions, social organization and individuals (including NRIs) to the poor in an organized manner performed a function in altruism in a broader sense but state which is constitutionally responsible, it is necessary to ask where the political responsibility lies. According to Scott and Cnaan (2018) the drawback of poverty alleviation from a congregational perspective is that it is a process that takes time and can often fail. In contrast feeding poor people is immediate and instantly gratifying.

Increasing evidence proved that food charity by the social institutions, NGOs and other voluntary organizations and registered social clubs are being formalized as part of denuded state welfare system both the provisions of direct funding from the local authorities and local community grants and by active engagement of the local administration and police personals.

In the case of education, there has been high drop rate among the students across gender due to various reasons in the surveyed households. Only a very few among them could pursue higher education and secure employment. Education is the sole tool for the upward economic and social mobility of the marginalized sections of the society. It can still be considered educationally backward section of the society comprising only four mean year of schooling of all fifty surveyed households. There was a list of reasons but three are main reasons: rural disadvantage, income poverty and cultural backwardness.

Health of an individual is a function of various socioeconomic considerations: good diet, awareness, safe drinking water and hygiene and medical facilities, facilities at the household level. Even seventy four Anganwari and school going children did not get mid-day meal due to shut down of schools during lockdown. All the households have been in lack all kind of considerations which led to poor health of the larger section of the society. All the households did not have their own water resource; they depend on the tap water supply and were mutually dependent. The irregular water supply had been the common problem.

During the field work we noted that conflicts between family members, domestic violence on women and aged family members, violence on children increased than before as many respondents admitted that. In this regard, Acs and Desai (2007) argue that social problems in the developing world are deeply entrenched and compounded by lack of knowledge, lack of resources, lack of priority and insecurity.

It can be conferred that approximately all surveyed households faced many difficulties to access public social welfare facilities- education, health and safe drinking water. Having low income overtime, they also live in dearth of less food (two meals a day only), poor housing condition and derisory clothing. Above all, hunger or surviving without food is an extreme form of marginalization and evidence provided the fact that working poor has been suffering from starvation, malnutrition and food inadequacy.

3 Broad Conclusions and Policy Implications

Empirical evidence verify that the poor lives close to margin in a hierarchical society and unable to meet basic human necessities often limit their meals.

Why this situation arises? It is evident that this situation emerges due to income poverty which is manifested by lack of physical assets, poor education attainment and poor conditions of work availability in the informal sector and insecure self-employment occupations without social security.

According to Dowler (2002), food should be considered as constitutional responsibility of the state as right to food than a charitable concern for a democratic state (cited in Cloke, 2016). In this regard, central government, concerned ministries and respective governments of the different state have failed to offer meal and other basic human needs to the marginalized sections of the society. The role of bureaucracy and local administration put them into question for their poor performance during economic lockdown.

State has no remorse in failing to provide very basic needs of the poorer section of the society. If any citizen who is eventually would be a poor die without food then who is responsible- state, socio-economic system, policy failure, bureaucracy, legislature, judiciary, civil society or individual himself. Moreover, various studies indicate that there is no lack of food availability in the context of buffer stack at the national level. It is a case of distributional injustice. Whatever the efforts done by the social organizations and volunteer organization are appreciable but not sufficient and enough. There is a need to question the economic development processes adopted by the Indian state and state governments and the political economy of supranational institutions, international collaborations and agreements which are selective and biassed in nature. Academia and policy makers have failed to understand the sociopolitical characteristics of the development process comprising of the local, regional, national and international level.

In the village economy, economic and social dominance due to caste and landownership. To break this socio-economic and cultural dominance, the common land should be converted into cooperative land pool for the landless communities and the rent should be spent on the local development projects. Rural economy requires productive activities which would generate decent employment opportunities that would lead to migration of poor who earned a meagre wages and forced to live in slums in the cities overtime. It is a time to decentralize the production system comprising of what to produce, how to produce and for who to produce to keep in mind the local resources and local endowments.

At the local, regional and national level, substantial investment should be continued in decentralized infrastructure. Rural industry should be encouraged to develop rural-industrial estates. Within agriculture, the allied sectors should not be considered as allied. There should be different policy on livestock, piggery, poultry, goat rearing and fishery. Assistance and extension services should be monitored by the committed barefoot agricultural extension officials. Agriculture production should be on the basis what is required at the local level. Micro level and local planning for agriculture and other sectors is required to value community worldview, their organization and dietary behaviour and ethno-medicinal practices which should be based on the local and regional needs Social agriculture-livestock linkage programmes must be taken into account to fulfill the food requirements of the households. State employment policy should be framed. Registration of the each worker should be a necessary step for making policy and identification is required who is vulnerable and marginalized. PACSs can be used as multifunctional and multipurpose. Some action plans of the governmental agencies with local volunteerism should be initiated. Sector with potential should be identified- development of clusters, development of rural town as market centres, focal points for village industries development. There is a need to change the character of livelihood and develop livelihood options at the local, block and district level to curb distress migration. It is a need to change the character of economic policy which is mainly based on corporate's profit. Shift from corporate to people centric and from global to local should be the strategy of regional planning. Such an understanding is the first step on the road towards a framework for defining and evaluating alternative development strategies for the intra and inter socio-economic class balances with social justice and freedom.

The decentralization is the basic tool of local development and local development institutions need to be established. Gram Panchyat with the fixed framework of bureaucratic control allowed for little autonomy for the overall welfare of the village community. State has always been in favour of top-down approach to development which minimizes the role of Gram Sabha and strengthen the bureaucracy and landed community that ultimately edges the marginalized sections of the society and inhibits people's participation. Village development councils should be developed to look at the development programmes in the village. Community organizing concept should be on the priority in the policy which helps to identify and create a plan to address the needs of the community.

In emergency situations, there is need to develop local food management system which particularly focussed on storage facilities at the block level in the state under public distribution system. During the crisis, the public distribution system should be universalized. The distribution of essential commodities should be broad based. Primary agricultural cooperative societies should be used for storage and distribution. There is a need to strength the diversification of food and cropping pattern at the local level to avoid food miles. There is need to build a strong confederation at the village level, town level and city based to strengthen the ties between them to face the challenge and respond adequately.

At least one qualified doctor should be employed at the village level to meet the basic health facilities. A common schools system should be implemented by the state to provide free education from preschools to high education for the vulnerable sections of the society. Universal food system and housing cooperative society at the village level need to be established. Promoting various aspects of health, hygiene and education across gender and age should be undertaken on the priority as constitutional mandate. Public spending on basic human needs should be increased.

What can the state do to promote that will contribute to rural growth and diversification without agony? The revolutionary changes regarding rethinking development are required without pain and nonviolent processes as we heard that revolutionary changes always painful and violent. New criteria of development must be taken as their universally accepted valuation the Gandhian idea of the realization of the potential objective of human personality and found conditions for achieving this objective in the satisfaction not only of such physiological needs as food, shelter and clothing but also of psychological needs including employment, political participation, nationalism and possibly equality (Seers, 1972, Adelman, 1975 cited in Rimmer, 1981).

The satisfaction of basic human needs should be central to all development processes and should be a unifying framework and integrative orientation. Greater self-reliance both individual and collective should be a major thrust of development policy not wholly in terms self-sufficiency but towards broader diversification of resource use. There is need to engage communities and individuals, organizations for transformative initiatives can come from anywhere, from civil society and communities, from government officials and research institutions, from social enterprises and business. It is need to create forums for people to meet, share, jointly create, and transmit further and trust that something good will come out of it (Kothari, 2019).

The persistence of and vulnerability to hunger and malnutrition on a mass scale is the fundamental justification for maintaining and strengthening a system of food distribution such as PDS. A striking feature of the functioning of PDS is the diversity across states with the Kerala having the most effective and extensive system both in terms of coverage or participation and in terms of quantity of food grain distributed (Swaminathan, 2000). It is no doubt that providing food and ration to the poor and needy serves as a guide for the policy making and how do they work, it is a learning chapter for the state, bureaucracy, administration and politicians. It can be argued on the basis of above discussion that ongoing development process at the national level throws up full of contradictions and conflicts. At one hand the majority of the asset less section of the society have not been able to secure their basic human needs with dignity.

References and Supplementary Bibliography

Acs, Z. J., and Desai, S. (2007) Democratic Capitalism and Philanthropy in a Global Economy, Jena Economic Research Papers-056, Friedrich-Schiller-University and the Max Planck Institute of Economics, Jena, Germany. www.jenecon.de.

Agarwal, K. (2020a) Interview | India Has Enough Food Grains For Two Years: Ram Vilas Paswan, The Wire Responds, June 30. https://thewire.in/.
Agarwal, K. (2020b) Food Ministry Denies Shortfall in Lockdown Ration Distribution, The Wire Responds, June 5. https://thewire.in/.
Agarwal, K. (2020c) PM Garib Kalyan: 144 Million Ration Card Holders Not Provided Grain in May, The Wire Responds, June 4. https://thewire.in/.
Agarwal, K. (2020d) Coronavirus Lockdown: As Hunger Grows, the Fear of Starvation Is Real, The Wire Responds, April 16. https://thewire.in/.
Agarwal, K. (2020e) How Have the Centre's Food Distribution Schemes Performed So Far?, The Wire Responds, July 1. https://thewire.in/.
Arrow, K. J. (1974) *The Limits of Organization*, New York: W. W. Norton.
Booth, W. J. (1993) A Note on the Idea of the Moral Economy, *The American Political Science Review*, 87(4): 949–954.
Brocheux, P. (1983) Moral Economy or Political Economy? The Peasants Are Always Rational, *The Journal of Asian Studies*, 42(40): 791–803.
Cloke, P. (2016) The Geographies of Food Banks in the Meantime, *Progress in Human Geography*, 41(6): 703–726.
Crosswell, M. (1978) Basic Human Needs: A Development Planning Approach. A.I.D. Discussion Paper No. 38, Agency for International Development, Bureau for Intergovernmental and International Affairs.
Guardiola, J., and Garcia-Munoz, T. (2009) Subjective Well-Being and Basic Needs: Evidence from Rural Guatemala.
Heikki, H. (2012) Rethinking the Role of Church in a Socio-Democratic Welfare State, *International Journal of Sociology and Social Policy*, 32(7/8): 401–414.
International Labour Organisation (1977) *Meeting Basic Needs*, Geneva: ILO.
Kothari, A. (2019) Collective Dreaming: Democratic Visioning in the Vikalp Sangam Process, *Economic and Political Weekly*, LIV(34): 70–76.
Lambie-Mumford, H., and Silvasti, T. (2020) *The Rise of Food Charity in Europe*, Policy Press, University of Bristol, UK.
Mander, H., et al. (2011) *Living with Hunger*, New Delhi: National Book Trust.
Martin, J. P., Chau, J., and Patel, S. (2007) Religions and International Poverty Alleviation: The Pluses and Minuses, *Journal of International Affairs*, 61(1, Fall/Winter): 69–92.
McHale, J., and McHale, M. C. (1979) Meeting Basic Human Needs, *The Annals of the American Academy of Political and Social Sciences*, 442: 13–27.
Mylek, I., and Nel, P. (2010) Religion and Relief: The Role of Religion in Mobilizing Civil Society Against Global Poverty, *Kotuitui: New Zealand Journal of Social Sciences Online*, 5(2): 81–97.
Nissan, E., and Niroomand, F. (2005) Convergence and Divergence of Basic Needs and Income: An International Comparison, *The Journal of Developing Areas*, 39(1): 151–167.

Raftopoulos, B. (1992) Beyond the House of Hunger: Democratic Struggle in Zimbabwe, *Review of African Political Economy*, 19(55): 57–66.

Rimmer, D. (1981) "Basic Needs" and the Origins of the Development Ethos, *The Journal of Developing Areas*, 15(2): 215–238.

Salonen, A. S. (2016) Locating Religion in the Context of Charitable Food Assistance: An Ethnographic Study of Food Banks in a Finnish City, *Journal of Contemporary Religion*, 31(1): 35–50.

Salonen, A. S. (2018) Religion, Poverty and Abundance, *Palgrave Communications*, 4(27).

Salonen, A. S., Ohisalo, M., and Laihiala, T. (2018) Undeserving, Disadvantaged, Disregarded: Three Viewpoint of Charity Food Aid Recipient in Finland, *International Journal of Environmental Research and Public Health*, 5: 1–15.

Scott, J. C. (1977) *The Moral Economy of the Peasant: Rebellion and Subsistence in Southeast Asia*, Yale University Press.

Scott, M. L., and Cnaan, R. A. (2018) Religious Congregations and Poverty Alleviation in the Age of New Public Governance, *Nonprofit Policy Forum*, 8(4): 391–410.

Silvasti, T., and Riches, G. (2014) Hunger and Food Charity in Rich Societies: What Hope for the Right to Food?, in G. Riches and T. Silvasti (Eds.), *First World Hunger Revisited. Food Charity or Right to Food?* 2nd Edition, Palgrave Macmillan.

Srinivasan, T. N. (1977) Development, Poverty, and Basic Human Needs: Some Issues, *Food Research Institute Studies*, XVI(2): 11–28.

Stewart, F. (1989) Basic Needs Strategies, Human Rights and The Right to Development, *Human Rights Quarterly*, 11(3): 347–374.

Streeten, P. (1995) The Political Economy of Fighting Poverty, Discussion Paper on Issues in Development, Development and Technical Cooperation Development, ILO, Geneva.

Stuart, H. (1985) Community Justice, Capitalist Society, and Human Agency: The Dialectics of Collective Law in the Cooperative, *Law & Society Review*, 19(2): 303–327.

Stuart, H. (1987) The Political Economy of Informal Economies, *The Annals of the American Academy of Political and Social Science*, 493: 137–153.

Swaminathan, M. (2000) *Weakening Welfare: The Pubic Distribution of Food in India*, New Delhi: LeftWord Books.

Thapar, K. (2020) Coronavirus Lockdown: 'Food Riots Are a Very Real Possibility,' Says Pronob Sen, The Wire Responds, March 27. https://thewire.in/.

Thorat, A. (2006) Rural Poor: Who Are They and Why? A Case Study of Madhya Pradesh. *Journal of Social and Economic Development*, 1(41): 1–26.

Times of India. (2019) Punjab to Replace Blue Cards with Smart Ration Cards by September, June 23.

Primary Sources-Interviews

Case study of Sri Damdama Sahib—This case study is based on an interview with the Manager, S. Parmjit Singh, Head Priest S. Gurjant Singh and media reports on June 10, 2020.

Case study of Ha Da Nahra Sahib—This case study based on an extensive interview with the Manager on June 25, 2020.

Case Study of Guru Harkrishan Gurudwara Sahib—This case study is based on an interview with Manager, on June 27, 2020.

Case study of a church- based on an interview with the priest at Talwandi Sabo on July 2, 2020.

Punjab's Migration Crisis Under Lockdown and Beyond: Some Suggestion for Public Policy

Lakhwinder Singh

1 Introduction

COVID-19 pandemic and lockdown decision was taken by the governments of India and Punjab on March 24, 2020, to save the population from the spread of the infection. The lockdown shut all economic activities and also stopped all kinds of transportation means for not allowing any movement of the humans. The lockdown decision announcement and its implementation with the gap of few hours without taking into consideration how to ward off the adverse impact on the lives and livelihood of the daily wage earners working in the informal sector of the economy. A large number of labourers who have migrated from rural to urban areas and were engaged in economic activities of various kinds turned out to be without income and employment all of a sudden. The type of information spread and stringent lockdown has created high degree of uncertainty about the survival of humans. The migrant (circular labour) workers not only lost their employment and income earnings but also

L. Singh (✉)
Commerce, Management and Economics, Khalsa College, Punjabi University, Patiala, Punjab, India
e-mail: lakhwindergill@pbi.ac.in

S. Singh et al. (eds.), *Covid-19 Pandemic and Economic Development*,
https://doi.org/10.1007/978-981-16-4442-9_18

abandoned by the employers along with non-payment of wages earned in the past. Given the high degree of uncertainty, fear of life and without any institutional support, some of them started walking back to their respective villages from where they had come to work in the cities. Since the government machinery was busy restricting the movement of the humans, the migrants started walking on roads where police were not visible and off the road and along railway tracks to reach their respective villages. However, the desperate workers in mass started visiting bus stands and railway stations to press the government to start transportation for their safe travel back home. Social media and played an important role to bring to the fore the misery and sufferings of the migrant labour. Some voluntary organizations and prominent individuals also played an important role to press the government to restart train service as a special arrangement for the travel of the migrant workers. This exodus of reverse migration has raised a number of questions about the working and living conditions of the migratory workforce. Their ability to move on the ladders for making their working and living conditions better. The COVID-19 shock has also raised several questions regarding inadequacy of existing public policy, regarding the governance mechanism in the normal and at the shock times. This chapter based on field survey provides evidence regarding the working and living conditions of the migratory workforce that comes from rural areas to urban cities in Punjab. It also provides empirical evidence regarding the upward mobility that is usually predicted both by the economic theory and public policy. The chapter is organized into six sections. In section two, the main concerns of economic theory of rural–urban migration have been examined. The working and living conditions of rural–urban migrants of Punjab are examined in section three. The empirical evidence regarding upward mobility based on the primary survey of rural–urban migrants of Punjab are analysed in section four. In section five, the public policy dealing with rural–urban migration has been examined and new measures for alleviating the misery of the rural–urban migrants of Punjab are suggested. The major conclusions that emerged from the study are presented in the final section.

2 Key Concerns of Economic Theory of Rural–Urban Migration

Migration is a core theme in the theories of structural transformation of a capitalist economy (Szirmai and Foster-McGregor, 2021). Migration in economic literature is positively associated with economic growth and development. W. A. Lewis (1954), in his 'Economic development in the unlimited supply of labour' argued that the process of transformation of an economy from a traditional sector to modern (industrial) sector triggers rural–urban migration. The modern urban industrial sector provides higher wages and generates unlimited employment opportunities for the workforce employed in the traditional sector. It was also asserted that the workforce working in the agriculture sector has nearly zero marginal productivity and does not affect the output of the agriculture sector. The stylized facts of rapid urbanization were reported during the process of the first Industrial Revolution by Kuznets (1966). On the basis of examining nearly two and a half century experience of industrialization in the industrially advanced countries, Kuznets has argued that a major shift of both income and labour force has happened from traditional (agriculture) to modern (industrial) sector. However, in the post-world war two economic development experience of the developing countries showed that the urban centres could not develop the kind of dynamism of economic activities that have been witnessed in the industrially advanced countries. Therefore, the rural–urban migration results in high degree of unemployment or underemployment of the workforce in the cities. The Harris-Todaro (1970) model of rural–urban migration has addressed this gap in the literature of rural–urban migration. The authors have argued that despite urban unemployment the migration has been taking place while taking into account the lifetime possibilities of expected income. So the change of place of work is determined by the probability to succeed to be employed and expected lifetime income. Therefore, it is suggested that the decision to migrate from rural areas to urban locations is a rationale decision. It also implies that the migration decision is determined by the expectation of upward mobility that has been confirmed by several studies that had examined the long-term transformation of the industrially advanced countries of the world (Kuznets, 1966; De Haas, 2010). It is argued by several studies on migration (King and Skeldon, 2010; McAlister, 1995; Sabirianova, 2002) that economic development is the main reason for employment and occupation mobility of the migrants.

An important fact revealed by empirical literature on migration is that the occupational mobility is 'U' shaped (Srivastava, 2012; Srivastava and Pandey, 2017; McAllister, 1995). It is expected that there will be a decline in occupational status of the migrant compared with the occupation at the place of origin. It is precisely because of the major reasons of cultural differences, inadequate knowledge of labour market, lack of education and skills and inadequate social networks. As the migrant gain experience of longer stay at the destination, the migrant has bright chances of moving upward in terms of earnings and occupation. Human capital formation both at the place of origin and destination plays an important role in determining the probabilities of progress. The migration policy both at the place of origin and destination also plays a catalytic role in determining the mobility of occupation and earnings. There is a dearth of studies that provides empirical evidence in terms of occupational and earning mobility of agriculturally advanced region of India such as Punjab. This study is an attempt to fill this gap in the empirical literature.

3 Working and Living Conditions of Migrants

Punjab state has remained one among the high migrant-receiving states of India (Rajan and Mishra, 2020). The lockdown started on March 25, 2020, and remained enforced till May 30, 2020. The total days of lockdown were 68 and the first easing was done on June 1, 2020. During this period, the migrant workers have moved to their respective native places popularly called 'reverse migration'. As per the claim of the government of Punjab, the expenditure on the safe travel of the migrants incurred was Rs. 30 crore. It is claimed that 5 lakh migrants were travelled back to their respective homes while requisitioned 375 trains and 725 special buses by the state government (GoP, 2021). The micro containment jones announced by the Punjab government in the month of April 2021 and strict restrictions imposed in May 2021 to control the spread of the second wave of the COVID-19 pandemic with infection and fatality rate rising at a fast rate, the migrant workers are hiring private buses for their safe travel back to their respective native places. The pandemic shock has once again generated high degree of uncertainty and reduction of employment opportunities showed a failure of the state that triggered crisis for the migrant workers.

It is important to understand how the migrant workers working and living in the urban locations of Punjab even during normal times. A survey of 1567 migrant workers working in the urban location in Punjab was conducted in 2016–2017 to ascertain information regarding their working and living conditions (Singh et al., 2018). A migrant worker shifted from rural areas to urban areas at least one year before the time of survey up to twelve years was included in the sample as a rural to urban migrant. Among the 1567 migrant workers surveyed, 29.87% migrated from rural areas of Punjab, 69.18% from other states and less than one per cent of the migrants were from Nepal.

So far as the educational qualifications of the migrant workers were concerned, a majority of the migrants, that is, 36.95% were having education up to middle class. Up to matriculate, there was only 15.06% of the sampled migrant workers. There were 12.50% migrant workers having educational qualifications plus two or higher. An important fact that emerged from the analysis of the sampled migrants is that 35.48% of the migrant workers were illiterate. Age wise distribution of the sampled migrant workers clearly shows that 62.03% among them were in the age group of 26–45 years. This indicates that the migrant workers shifted from rural locations to urban locations at the time of a most productive age group. Occupational division shows that 53% of the migrant workers were self-employed and 47% were salaried/wage earners. 79.11% self-employed migrant workers were engaged in economic activities in open spaces or in the public shelter.

The access to basic amenities like housing, safe drinking water, sanitation, clean cooking fuel and durable goods are necessities for living a quality life. The analysis of the survey data shows that 89.60% of migrant workers were living in pucca houses. There were 6.96% migrant workers were stay in semi pucca houses and 3.45% of the migrants were staying in the temporary/kutcha houses. It is important to note that migrant workers employed and paid salary/wages a higher proportion, that is, 91.96% were living in pucca houses as compared to self-employed, that is, 87.52% were living in pucca houses. The facility of electricity supply in the houses was as high as 96.68%. The water supply within the premises and that too of tap water was available in 84.81% houses in which migrant workers were living. Out of this, 77.15% of the migrant houses were using untreated but tap water within the premises. The supply of filtered water was available to as low as 14.04% houses of migrant workers. This implies that safe drinking water is available to a small proportion of the migrants. The toilet facility with flush system was available to 81.94% of the migrants. However, 1.91% of the migrants were using open spaces for toilets. Food preparation requires proper kitchen facility. The analysis of the survey data shows that only 33.63% of the sampled migrants were able to cook food in a proper kitchen and a vast majority, that is, 66.37% did not possess such facility. The fuel used for cooking is LPG by 48.17%, nearly 24% were using firewood/dung cakes and 25% were using kerosene. Only 2.86% migrants were using electricity for cooking food. The communication services are an important source for migrants to remain in touch with their family members, co-workers and also helpful in searching work-related opportunities. There were 73.07% of the migrant workers who have been using mobile telephone for communication. A good number of migrant workers (26.23%) did not have an access to either landline or mobile phone connection. The survey analysis revealed an important fact that nearly one-fourth of the migrant workers owned motorcycles/scooters for their travel from home to workplace. 22.85% migrant workers were using bicycles for the purpose of mobility. Those who did not have any means of transportation were 31.01%.

The analysis of the survey regarding consumer durables amply shows that the most common item possessed by the migrants was electric fan (82.26%) followed by TV (56.60%), Refrigerator (30.57%), Radio (20.87%), Electric cooler (17.10%), Computer (3.96%) and air conditioner (3.83%).

The livelihood of a migrant is dependent on the capacity to earn income. The estimated per month income of the 58.65% of the sampled migrants was less than Rs. 8000. There was 19.97% of the migrants who have been earning between Rs. 8001 and Rs.10,000 per month. Only 14.36% of the sampled migrants were earning between Rs. 10,001 and Rs. 15, 000. The above facts clearly bring out the existence of wide variations in the earnings of the migrants. Moreover, it implies that the migrants are engaged in low-paid economic activities. When we examine the social security benefits given to the migrant workers, it amply shows a very poor state of affairs. There were only 5.55% migrants who have been able to receive EPF/CPF benefits. A very low proportion of migrant workers who are able to get the benefit of weekly off days or casual leaves (18.39%), medical leave (21.25%) and earned maternity leave (33.24%). There were only 31.33% migrants reported that they receive extra payment for extra work. The above analysis shows that the working and living conditions of the rural to urban migrants were not very conducive.

4 Empirical Evidence on Upward Mobility of Migrants

The analysis of the primary survey has revealed an interesting empirical evidence with regard to upward mobility of the migrant workers. In economic theory, it has been claimed as well as predicted that the migrant workers shift their location of work due to occupational mobility and lifetime expected earning potentials. An important fact can be noticed from the distribution of current work and nature of employment of the migrant workers is that the migrant workers were engaged in unskilled manual work were as large as 55.90%. Nearly 33% of the migrant workers were engaged in skilled manual work. There were only 5.62% migrant workers who have been engaged in economic activities that required high educational skills. As for as the supervisory and managerial work-related economic activities were concerned, there were only 1.32% of the migrant workers employed in them. On the job training is an important source of upward mobility of the migrant workers. The primary survey results revealed that only 11.23% of the sampled migrants were able to gain/improve their skill base while working. The majority, that is, 88.77% of the migrant workers could not able to improve up the skill base which they have already possessed. The stability of the economic activity, in which the migrant workers had been engaged, can be observed from the fact that 60.66% of the migrant workers that lie between six and twelve years in the same job. An examination of the survey data regarding economic activities and the number of years engaged in that activity and per month earning shows that there is a positive correlation between the number of years in the job and economic activity. Two professions, that is, lawyers and doctors, have provided the highest monthly income of the order of Rs. 35,143. Those migrants engaged in their own business, were able to earn an income of the order of Rs. 25,871. The other economic activities where the average monthly income lies between Rs. 19,862 and Rs. 8591 were taxi operators, mechanics, office work, shopkeepers, autorickshaw, tailoring, construction work, street vending, cobblers and sweeping. When we analyse the number of years put in a particular occupation, it is observed that those migrant workers who have spent six years or above in the economic activity had earned higher than the per month average income compared to those below the experience of six years. But the differences in income earnings across economic activities are quite large but the gain of experience has marginal improvements. This implies that the upward mobility of the migrant workers is very limited and that too confined to highly skilled migrant workers.

5 Public Policy for Regulation of Migrant Labour in Normal and Shock Times

Public policy for facilitating migration, regulation and saving them from exploitation has remained grossly inadequate even in normal times. The shock times such as Covid-19 pandemic has not only exposed the inadequacy of public policy for migrant workers but also showed a non-responsive attitude of both the employer and the state. However, the philanthropy and general public have remained very handy during the crisis but still remained inadequate to meet the basic needs of the vulnerable migrant workforce especially when the lockdown turns out to be pretty long (Shergill, 2021). Still, the social media and desperate attempt of the migrants to save themselves from this unprecedented crisis of humanity has forced the government to arrange for their safe travel back home during the first wave of lockdown. In the peak of the second wave of the COVID-19 pandemic and consequently, the select lockdown has again brought the matter of safety, security and livelihood of the migrant workers in the public domain. In an interim order, the supreme court of India directed the union government and also of various state governments to ensure two basic meals in a day for the migrants, ensure the supply of raw food under existing schemes and adequate transportation facilities for their travel back home if demanded by the migrants (FE Bureau, 2021). This amply shows that neither the central government nor the state governments have any policy put in place for the migrant workers who are suffering from the lockdown and consequently non-availability of work and income to the migrants. In the absence of daily wage income, the migrant workers are in a state of misery. This misery forced the supreme court of India to pass the directions to the central and state governments to care for the migrant workers who are without work due to lockdown imposed in the context of controlling the second COVID-19 pandemic wave.

Historically speaking, there have been some pieces of public policy revolved around the organized industrial sector where large amount of migrant workforce was expected to be absorbed. It is significant to note that India has enacted legislation on internal migration in the form of

Interstate Migrant Workmen Act, 1979. This act protects and regulates the recruitment and working and living conditions of the migrant workers. It has been widely recognized that it is a good legislation but has remained poorly implemented. Moreover, it is argued that the legislation is biased towards formal and organized sectors (Borhade, 2014; Srivastava, 2012; Sethi and Kundu, 2020). Obviously, the legislation does not regulate the informal sector and circular migrant workers. It has also failed to provide social protection to the migrants. However, the public policy approach has remained mainly to mitigate push factors and control the rural outmigration such as Mahatma Gandhi National Rural Employment Guarantee Act (MGNREGA) and the rural housing scheme-the PM's Awas Yojana. If one examines the five-year plan documents right from seventh to eleventh plan, it is amply evident that the strategy and public policy has been working to reduce the pressure of the migrants on the metropolitan centres (Sethi and Kundu, 2020). During the pandemic times, the same policy has been pressed into service especially to retain the returnee migrants in the villages. It is significant to note that migrant workers exposed to urban life and enjoyed better than village level opportunities in the urban centres, they had slowly returned to the urban centres again for a better livelihood. This shows that public policy is working contrary to the natural flow of human population from rural to urban and the law of capitalist economic development and transformation.

The migrant workers are citizens of India. When they work in any state such as Punjab, it is important that each and every migrant worker should be registered (formal and informal sector) by their mobile telephone number. So the information and communication technology should be pressed into service to make registration of the migrant workers possible. All the registered migrant workers should be provided comprehensive social security including provident fund, health insurance, maternity benefits, paid leaves, pensions and write to vote in each and every local elections. They should be entitled to all kinds of public distribution system facilities on the basis of simple registration or with the mobile telephone number. It is suggested that each migrant worker should be provided with six basic facilities, that is, safe drinking water, toilet facility, electricity, cooking gas and street lighting. Since the migrant workers are working in the highly productive age group, their skill base needs to be upgraded keeping in view the emerging new employment opportunities. It is important that their wards should be provided a minimum level of education and training to be prepared for future employment opportunities. Therefore, it is suggested that the children of the migrant workers needs to be incentivized so that they should continue to remain in school. For contingency such as COVID-19 lockdown in the first and now in the second wave, the urban employment guarantee programme should be launched and minimum number of days work should be provided to the migrant workers. As suggested by the supreme court of India, migrant workers should be provided basic needs for food, shelter and travel. Along with this, a minimum one-time cash transfer on the basis of average monthly income earned by the migrant workers as reported in this study or using a rule of thumb, it is suggested that government should transfer Rs. 10,000 per month per family during the period of lockdown. The urban planning should be done in a manner so that in each of the new urban locality, a space for migrant workers should be reserved. This will not only ensure the basic urban facilities to the migrant workers but there will be easy access to the local citizens of the migrant workers services. Among the migrant family members, the female workforce has low level of education and skills. The female workforce must be accord high priority for providing them basic education and skills. The skill imparted to the female migrant workers generates capabilities and saves them from dual exploitation as well empower them. It is well known that education and skill development has a capacity of upward mobility in terms of social and economic status. However, equally important is financial literacy. The opening up of a saving bank account and operating it helps especially the female workforce to realize the uses of their income for changing the consumption pattern of the family for maintaining better nutrition and health care. The two-pronged literacy, that is, education and skills and financial literacy will help the female migrant workforce to jump the ladders of upward mobility. To reduce the uncertainty in the life of the migrants, the law and order implementing agencies such as police need to be educated to respect the human rights of the migrant workers. The above suggestion will not only reduce the discrimination against the migrant workers and but also will ensure the safety and security of the migrant workers.

6 Conclusion

This study has examined the plight of the migrant workers during the times of COVID-19 pandemic as well as in the normal times. It is well known that large number of migrant workers faced misery in the first lockdown that lasting more than 68 days. In the initial phase, the migrant workers and their family members travelled back home with their own meagre transport facilities such as bicycle and barefoot. Some died on the way due to lack of food and water and other lifesaving facilities. The government of Punjab has claimed that the migrants travel back home, while hiring buses and trains, was supported and paid from the government sources. The support of the Punjab government has been remained crucial but it was too late and too little compared to the contribution of the migrant labour to the economy of the state. The empirical evidence based on survey of 1567 migrant workers conducted during the period 2016–2017 clearly brings out the fact that the working and living conditions on the basis of multiple indicators show the plight of migrant workers. The migrant workers possessed very low level of educational qualifications and skill base. A large chunk (35.47%) of them was illiterate. The access to basic amenities like housing, safe and portable drinking water, sanitation, housing and kitchen facilities, transport and recreations facilities, and the poor household assets were not satisfactory. They are largely employed in the urban informal sector and their working conditions are poor and unregulated. The migrants are engaged in low productivity activities and therefore, their income earning capacity is relatively low. The variations in income across economic activities as well as number of years spent in the economic activities have remained very high. Thus, it is safe to conclude that their upward mobility is quite limited. Keeping in view the crisis faced by the migrant labour both in the times of COVID-19 pandemic and normal times, there is an urgent need to frame a comprehensive public policy that can ensure decent work and upward mobility of the migrant workforce. It is thus suggested that a compensation of Rs. 10,000 per month per family of the migrants should be provided by the government of Punjab for the lockdown period of 2020 and a similar compensation should also be provided for the current lockdown imposed to control second wave of COVID-19 pandemic during the April–May 2021. Furthermore, if the government of Punjab would like to draw full benefits of the young migrant workforce working in the urban locations of Punjab, it should provide them education and skills keeping in view the emerging new employment opportunities. The female migrant workforce should be imparted two-pronged literacies, that is, education and skills and financial so that they can not only be saved from double exploitation but also empowered and ensured upward mobility.

While formulating public policy for the migrant labour, the contradictions between the economic theory of transformation and urban development policy should be resolved. The resolution of elimination in theory and practice will not only have an enduring impact on the migrant labour but will help the smooth transition of the economy from low level of economic equilibrium to self-sustained economic development.

References

Borhade, A. (2014) Urban Migration Trends: Challenges and Opportunities in India, in *World Migration Report, 2015*, Geneva: International Organization for Migration.

De Haas, H. (2010) Migration and Development: A Theoretical Perspective, *International Migration Review*, 44(1): 227–264.

FE Bureau. (2021) Give Ration, Two Free Meals a Day to Migrant Workers, SC Tells Centre, Delhi, UP, Haryana, *Economy* 2, *Financial Express*, Friday, May 14, New Delhi.

GoP. (2021) *Budget Speech 2021–22*, Finance Minister, Chandigarh: Government of Punjab.

Harris, John R., and Todaro, Michael P. (1970) Migration, Unemployment and Development: A Two-Sector Analysis, *American Economic Review*, 60(1): 126–142.

King, R., and Skeldon, R. (2010) Mind the Gap! Integrating Approaches to Internal and International Migration, *Journal of Ethnic and Migration Studies*, 36(10): 1619–1646.

Kuznets, S. (1966) *Modern Economic Growth: Rate Structure and Spread*, New Haven: Yale University Press.

Lewis, W. A. (1954) Economic Development with Unlimited Supplies of Labour, *The Manchester School*, 22(2): 139–191.

McAilister, I. (1995) Occupational Mobility among Immigrants: The Impact of Migration on Economic Success in Australia, *International Migration Review*, 29(2): 441–468.

Rajan, S. I., and Mishra, U. S. (2020) Migration and Financial Transfers, in S. I. Rajan and M. Sumeetha (Eds.), *Handbook of Internal Migration in India*, Thousand Oaks, CA: Sage, pp. 780–790.

Sabirianova, Z. K. (2002) The Great Human Capital Reallocation: A Study of Occupational Mobility in Transitional Russia, *Journal of Comparative Economics*, 30(1): 191–217.

Sethi, M., and Kundu, D. (2020) Migration Policy: Where Do We Stand? in S. I. Rajan and M. Sumeetha (Eds.), *Handbook of Internal Migration in India*, Thousand Oaks, CA: Sage, pp. 685–702.

Shergill, B. S. (2021) Basic Human Needs and Non-State Actors in Punjab: Understanding the Lives of Poor amidst the Covid-19 Pandemic, in S. Singh, L. Singh, and K. Vatta (Eds.), *Covid-19 Pandemic and Economic Development: Emerging Public Policy Lessons for Indian Punjab*, Palgrave Macmillan

Singh, L., Singh, S., and Kumar, D. (2018) *Rural-Urban Migration, Informal Sector Employment and Income/Earning Differentials: Reflections from Two Indian States-Punjab and Haryana*, Patiala: Centre for Development Economics and Innovation Studies (CDEIS), Punjabi University.

Srivastava, R., and Pandey, A. K. (2017) Internal and International Migration in South Asia: Drivers, Interlinkage and Policy Issue, *Discussion Paper*, New Delhi: UNESCO.

Srivastava, R. (2012) Internal Migration and Social Protection in India: The Missing Links, in *National Workshop in Internal Migration and Human Development in India*, New Delhi: UNESCO/UNICEF.

Szirmai, A., and Foster-McGregor, N. (2021) An Introduction to New Perspectives on Structural Change, in L. Alcorta, N. Foster-McGregor, B. Verspagen, and A. Szirmai (Eds.), *New Perspectives on Structural Change: Causes and Consequences of Structural Change in the Global Economy*, Oxford: Oxford University Press, pp. 1–20.

Diaspora Well-Being and the COVID-19 Pandemic: Some Reflections on Public Discourses on Impacts in the USA and UK

Shinder S. Thandi

1 Introduction

Most narratives on the 30 million strong Indian diasporas acknowledge that, although heterogeneous and diverse, it is relatively wealthy and generally thriving, at least in developed western countries. The rich countries of Europe, especially UK, and North America, particularly USA, are both home and magnets for potential migrants from India. The promise of a higher standard of living in these countries continues to act as a major motivating factor. Although Indian migration to these overseas locations has a long history, mass movements only started in the 1950s to the UK (and to mainland Europe in the 1980s) and to USA and Canada from the mid-1960s when new immigration laws (1965 in USA and 1966 in Canada, respectively) abolished the old zonal quota system and allowed fresh migration based on new points-based selection criteria. This created a brain drain of educated Indian professionals (doctors, dentists, scientists, engineers, academics etc.) especially to USA because of the vast opportunities it offered. There was also a steady

S. S. Thandi (✉)
Department of Global Studies, University of California, Santa Barbara, CA, USA
e-mail: thandi@global.ucsb.edu

S. Singh et al. (eds.), *Covid-19 Pandemic and Economic Development*,
https://doi.org/10.1007/978-981-16-4442-9_19

inflow of migrants who were reuniting with their previously settled families after the quota system was abolished. Although migration patterns between the USA and UK have differed, the UK experience is one of unskilled and low or semi-skilled migration relative to the USA in the earlier years. Both countries now have substantial Indian or Indian-origin populations comprising a mixture of first-generation, second-generation and third-generation Indians. The main objective of this short paper is to provide an overview of their experiences during the COVID-19 pandemic keeping in mind that USA is the hardest hit country in the world and UK, at the point of writing, is the worst-hit country in Europe with over 100,000 deaths so far. The paper demonstrates how their migratory lived experiences and lifestyles bring out both their strengths and weaknesses through discussing a range of indicators: their degree of health vulnerabilities making them more susceptible to contracting or becoming victims of the COVID-19 virus, and their contribution in mitigating the effects of the pandemic. The paper highlights new types of public discourses that have come to the fore, flagging up much-needed attention on neglected aspects of public policy. These varied experiences provide some important lessons and policy implications going forward. The paper is divided into three sections. The first section provides salient features of the USA and UK Indian diaspora communities including their migration history, demographic, socio-economic and labour market characteristics. The second section provides personal observations and critical commentary on public discourses on disproportionate impacts and the final section highlights comparative experiences between USA and UK and identifies some potential policy implications arising from these experiences.

2 A Tale of Two Diasporas

2.1 Indian Diaspora in the USA: A Successful Model?

The Indian population in the USA in 2015 numbered over 2.4 million, rising from just 12,000 in 1960. Indians constitute around 6% of foreign-born immigrants in the USA, compared with only 0.5% in 1960. Migration from India rose rapidly between 1965 and 1990 as immigration rules were relaxed and a variety of visas were introduced to lure talented workers either on temporary or permanent visas. For example, historically, Indians have been top recipients of highly skilled H-1B temporary visas and also form the second-largest number of international students in the

USA (Khadria, 2012). Over time, with stricter quantitative restrictions on visas for family reunions, the number of skilled migrants increased, becoming predominant as recipients of visas issued in the Science, Technology, Engineering and Management (STEM) area in recent years. In fact, young Indian migrants are known to capture a disproportionate number of H1B visas (Kirkegaard, 2019).

However, today the overall Indian diaspora in the USA is considered much larger at around 5 million as this number includes not only those born in India but all those who reported Indian ancestry, ethnicity or race. These would include US-born, second and third-generation Indian Americans and also 'twice' or 'thrice' migrants of Indian origin who migrated to the USA from countries around the world, especially from Africa, the Caribbean and Europe. As a result of this global immigration, a picture that emerges is that of a relatively educated, wealthy and successful Indian American community.

Thus the dominant Indian-American immigrant narrative is one of a successful upwardly mobile community, earning the label of a 'Model Minority', along with American Japanese, Chinese and Korean communities. This means that in terms of key metrics such as level of education, income and wealth, percentage with higher job status, political representation at state and federal levels, level of crime and family stability, the Indian American community scores highly, not only well above the US average but also above the average of other Asian American groups mentioned earlier. A recent report by the National Council from the Asian American Community Development found that the household income of an Indian American family was on average USD 120,000 per annum, surpassing all American ethnic groups. For example, the average for Asians, albeit a very heterogeneous group, was USD 87,194, for Blacks it was USD 41,511, for Latinx USD 51,404 and for White households, only USD 67,937 (National CAPACD, 2020).

This is undoubtedly the outcome of a highly selective immigration system where preference was given only to 'cream of the cream' (Chakravorty et al., 2016). The overall occupational structure of the US Indian diaspora population shows that nearly three-quarters are employed in Management, Business, Science and Arts with the next category being Sales and Office based occupations at 14% (Zong and Batalova, 2017). This certainly affirms the upwardly mobile nature of the community although the label 'Model Minority' is problematic given the large degree of diversity within the community.

After the lockdown associated with the COVID-19 pandemic was declared in different states from the middle of March, we would not have expected members from this 'successful and wealthy' community to be adversely affected. After all, many of those in employment could be considered 'essential workers', while many others were able to work from home rather than become furloughed, or be laid off and forced to sign up for unemployment benefits. But as the lockdown began to take effect, with many retail and leisure and hospitality businesses closed for nearly three months, this had the inevitable impacts on business revenues, jobs and incomes. However, not all Indians were equally impacted. The motel industry, dominated by the Gujarati Patels was particularly hit hard in contrast to the skilled IT workers who could continue working from home. Similarly gas station owners, Punjabi-dominated truckers and Seven–Eleven grocery franchise owners or small grocery store owners could continue trading due to them providing essential services. However, many unskilled and semi-skilled workers were furloughed along with small business owners who had to rely on Government stimulus cheques or subsidies if qualified, to ease financial hardship. On the whole, given the socio-economic characteristics of the community, economic impact was not as adverse as for other American communities, with millions forced to sign up for unemployment insurance.

One sector, however—the health sector—stood out for the role of Indians in interesting ways. The US heath sector is huge as it includes consultants, family physicians, dentists, pharmacists, medical educators, nurses and hospital and insurance company administrators both in the public as well as private sectors. While we have a lot of research which highlights the success and contribution of Indian IT immigrants in the USA, far less is known about the equal success and contribution of Indians working in different segments and at different levels in the US health sector. In fact, the COVID-19 media coverage revealed their significant and important presence and contribution. At the beginning and during the height of the pandemic when the media was still trying to explain the nature of the virus, its possible causes, modes of transmission and effects on the body, one immediate fact would have stood out to an outsider. Many of the experts offering explanations happened to be of Indian origin, whether they were being interviewed as academic researchers, doctors working in emergency rooms, directors of public health research or private medical research institutes, or simply as family physicians. Indians seemed to be continually visible everywhere on cable news media, certainly living up to their label of a Model Minority. Among the many, four names that have been cropping up on a daily basis in the media are that of Dr Sanjay Gupta, a neurosurgeon and CNN's chief medical correspondent, Professor Ashish Jha, Dean and Head of Harvard's Global Health Institute and Dr Seema Yasmin, a CNN Medical Analyst based at Stanford, CA and Dr. Celine Gounder, CNN health commentator and an infectious diseases expert at NYC Health+ Hospitals/Bellevue and a clinical assistant professor of medicine at NYU Grossman School of Medicine and now member of President Biden's team of Advisors on defeating the COVID-19 pandemic. A highly respected physician and former vice-admiral Dr Vivek Murthy was appointed as co-chair of Biden's COVID-19 Advisory Board. Dr. Seema Verma, a health policy consultant who headed the Centers for Medicare and Medicaid Services, was appointed as a key member of President Trump's White House Coronavirus Task Force in March 2020, although her public appearances remained limited. What was also noticeable among the many Indian-origin medical professionals interviewed was their age and specialism range which indicated that many of them appeared to be US-born and trained, an interesting departure from the earlier crop of Indian-trained doctors. Quite clearly these were either children of Indian doctor parents or children of first-generation Indian immigrant families who had nurtured their children to enter the medical or health professions. The COVID-19 pandemic quite clearly demonstrated the strength of the Indian American community and their contribution in mitigating the effects of the pandemic and undoubtedly raised the community's socio-economic profile even further. The discourse in USA has predominantly focused on disproportionate infections and mortalities among African Americans and Hispanics rather than Asian or Indian Americans. In a way, the discourse was merely highlighting what was already well established in medical research: that due to health inequalities there is a considerable gap in life expectancy between Black, Hispanic and White Americans.

2.2 *Indian Diaspora in the UK: Largely a Punjabi and Gujarati Narrative*

The Indian population in the UK 2011 Census was estimated at around 1.5 million, excluding persons with mixed ethnicity. This represents only around 2.3% of the UK population, with the number having risen from

1,053,411 (1.8%) in the 2001 Census. Nearly half of the Indian population is British born but apart from India, there is a sizable number who were born in an East African country. It is worth noting UK is also home to over a million Pakistanis and over half a million Bangladeshis among others, making the South Asian migrant community quite a significant visible minority at 6%.

Although the UK Indian population has become more diverse over the years, historically Punjabis (still constituting around 45% of the UK Indian population) and Gujaratis together comprise the largest component. Most of the Indian population resides in the densely populated London and Midlands metropolitan regions. Data shows that Indians tend to have high employment rates (around 75%) and low unemployment rates, relatively high educational levels, high median incomes and lowest poverty rates among all minority ethnic communities. Thus, as is the case in USA, the Indian diaspora community is also considered upwardly mobile and relatively well-integrated and is often compared to the highly successful Jewish community. However, in terms of occupational structure, the Indian community is distributed more evenly across different sectors of the economy, including a sizable number working in the public sector or are in self-employment, as owners of small and medium-sized businesses (Thandi, 2006).

Yet these impressive metrics can be very misleading and illusory. Despite their relatively higher socio-economic status, it is well documented that members of the Indian community have their own underlying health problems, related both to their ethnicity and lifestyle (Zaman and Mangtani, 2007; Lucas et al., 2013). Research shows that British Indians tend to suffer disproportionately more from chronic health conditions such as Type 2 diabetes, cancer, coronary heart disease, hypertension, strokes and mental illness (Lucas et al., 2013; Bhavsar et al., 2018). With the outbreak of the COVID-19 pandemic it was therefore not entirely surprising that the community became extremely vulnerable and took a severe hit in terms of infection rates and fatalities. In fact, not only Indian but all other Black and Minority Ethnic (BAME) groups were disproportionally impacted by the pandemic due to their higher vulnerability and lack of protective gear and exposure as front-line public sector workers, especially those in the National Health Service and Transport (ONS, 2020).

3 Public Discourses on Disproportionate Impacts

Although the virus was regarded as non-discriminating ('we are all in it together'), media reports began highlighting its disproportionate impacts and this empirical reality—faces of black and brown victims including Asian doctors, nurses and transport workers appearing daily in newspapers and on television screens—generated a vigorous and emotive national debate on the causes and remedies to these disproportionate impacts and there were calls for direct action by the British government. Preliminary reports issued by a number of national bodies, for example, the Office of National Statistics (ONS), the Institute of Fiscal Studies (IFS), the National Health Service (NHS) and Public Health England (PHE) confirmed the disproportionate effects. For instance, the PHE, at an early stage of the pandemic showed that of the 13,918 patients who died in hospitals till April 17, 2020, after testing positive for the novel coronavirus, 16.2% were of Black, Asian and Minority Ethnic (BAME) background and those identifying with Indian ethnicity made up 3% of that—slightly higher than their 2.3% in the UK population. A little later a Public Health England report on disparities in the effects of COVID-19 confirmed that BAME Britons were up to twice as likely as White Britons to die if they contracted coronavirus. As the rates of infections spread and deaths increased, it became more and more clear that BAME communities, including Indians, were the worst affected or over-represented (PHE, 2018). Further reports by major organizations and government-commissioned research have tended to conclude that Indians are 1.5 times more at risk of dying compared with Whites, Pakistanis and Bangladeshis 1.8 times more and Blacks (Afro-Caribbean) 1.9 times more (ONS, 2020; Butcher and Massey, 2020).

So what were the causes of this and how did the media and public discourses explain these disproportionate effects? While observing these public discourses being played out, three sets of explanations or causal factors came to the fore, indicating this to be both a contentious and complex issue. Before discussing the three explanations, it is worth keeping in mind this discourse focused largely on the BAME group in general rather than on any specific BAME community. Given there is great diversity within this general category, it is indeed problematic to generalize. However, despite this limitation, given there are many and sufficient common causal factors among all BAME groups, this allows us to relate the discourse specifically to the Indian and Punjabi community.

We will consider and unpack each one of these three positions carefully in some detail to better understand the nature of the debate, especially as they relate to the Indian diaspora community. An important point to bear in mind is that all the three explanations are chronological and complementary and thus all have contributed in different ways to the ongoing discourse on the varied impacts of COVID-19. Taking them together will give us a better sense of the ground reality and reinforce the point that there are many layers of complexity in understanding this issue.

The FIRST type of explanation came from scientists and some politicians, who tried to use science as a basic explanation. It was suggested that race was a factor as some races may be more susceptible to infection due to genetics and biology. One factor regularly highlighted was lack of Vitamin D deficiency associated with insufficient exposure to sunshine. For example, the Indian (and BAME communities in general) were disproportionally impacted because they have innate qualities given their darker skin. Thus, as the argument went, their low immune system and impaired bodily functions made them more likely to contract the virus and get sick. However, this line of reasoning began to lose potency when it could not explain why a largely White population in the northeast or northwest of England was also greatly affected. Were they also lacking the sunshine nutrient or was something else going on? In any case, the causal link between vitamin D deficiency and susceptibility to COVID-19 has not been conclusively proven. The discourse began to shift towards identifying other factors such as existing health inequalities and poverty rather than race. Since the media was constantly giving voice only to scientists, it was not surprising that genetic explanations overshadowed the long-proven views of social scientists regarding the role of health inequalities and poverty. Although inadequate as an explanation, the only positive that could come out of this discourse may be further research on the medical benefits of adequate levels of vitamin D, especially D3, among the general population.

The discourse in the USA also used similar reasoning but the groups most disproportionately affected there were African Americans and Hispanics/Latinos. But all these groups come from very different populations and ethnic groups and in any case, we also began to see high death rates in Brazil, China, Italy and South Africa which indicates that genetics or race remains a fatally flawed argument.

A SECOND narrative that gained popularity in explaining disproportionate effects was that these were due to the interplay between prevailing health inequalities and ethnicity, with the latter factor emphasizing comorbidities or pre-disposition to certain chronic medical conditions among certain ethnic groups. Health experts regularly highlighted that people who have serious underlying health conditions—respiratory problems such as asthma, diabetes, kidney problems, coronary heart disease, hypertension, obesity, etc.,—were among the most vulnerable given their low level of immunity in fighting the virus. If one also added factors such as greater difficulty among some ethnicities to practice social distancing, given that many live in overcrowded multi-generational households and often in areas that are socio-economically deprived, ethnicity effects become even more pronounced. Of course, Indians and other BAME groups disproportionately display these characteristics, making them most vulnerable. Major organizations and government-commissioned reports in the USA and UK have continued to confirm disproportionate impacts both in terms of infections and mortality rates. This explanation is an improvement on the first one as it can capture the greater infection/fatality rates among White working-class communities who also suffer from similar chronic conditions and economic and health deprivation in their localities.

But what explains the existence of health inequalities among different groups of people in the first place? Here, there has been a considerable debate and disagreement with one camp arguing that poorer living standards and higher poverty levels among minority ethnic groups is a critical factor explaining inequalities whereas the other camp blames these inequalities on institutional or structural racism in society. The latter view is considered in more detail below as the third, but related, explanation in the discourses.

Considering the British Indian community, while they appear to be doing well as a group and are indeed upwardly mobile, there are still large segments of the community that lives in poorer inner-city neighbourhoods alongside other immigrant groups and suffers from multiple deprivations including overcrowding and poverty. These localities do not necessarily offer the best schooling, health care or recreational facilities. Lack of these is often reflected in low life expectancy and these life expectancy gaps could be as large as seven years for women and nine years for men. There is ample literature that has documented income inequalities in general and health inequalities in particular (Postnote, 2007; Bécares, 2013). More recently, results from one of England's largest surveys, covering 1.4 million adults over 55 years between July 2014 and April 2017, found that the average health-related quality of life of a 60-year old from an ethnic minority background was similar to that of an average 80-year old from a White household. This 20-year gap reflects health inequalities arise from some BAME groups not only being income poor, more likely to suffer from underlying health conditions, more likely to report worse treatment when visiting their GP surgery and receiving insufficient support from local services, such as housing and social care (The Lancet Public Health, 2020). Previous UK governments have acknowledged this as well and they have introduced many initiatives to improve inner-city socio-economic deprivations (PHE, 2018). It is also worth noting that these densely populated neighbourhoods are usually the first to attracts new immigrants or retain earlier elderly immigrants due to their inability to move out to the suburbs. These inner-city areas are clearly visible in English cities such as Birmingham, Coventry, Leicester, Smethwick in Sandwell and Wolverhampton. Furthermore, many first-generation migrants who entered the UK as adults or as dependents are also at a greater risk since they may have had fewer vaccinations or have undetected nutritional deficiency related to diet or other latent underlying conditions. This undoubtedly has an impact on life expectancy as well but not acknowledged. So in a way, it should not be surprising to learn that if this vulnerable population was to contract the virus, get hospitalized, there would be a greater risk of mortality. The COVID-19 pandemic had simply laid bare the huge health inequalities existing in these communities. So it seems clear it is the circumstances of their lives that make them more vulnerable.

The THIRD factor highlighted in recent discourses lays the blame for disproportionate deaths on institutional and structural racism. The protracted global protests for racial justice that followed in the aftermath of the murder of George Floyd in police hands added further weight to this narrative. There are several threads to this argument. One thread argues that income and racial inequalities, prevalent for so long, whether in the USA or UK, are manifested directly in health inequalities. The root cause of why minority communities suffer from low income and high poverty, overcrowded or poor housing is due to prevalence of systematic racism or discrimination. Another threat argues that historical racism may make ethnic minority or Indian individuals less reluctant to seek care when needed. This may be related to lack of trust in NHS services because of a previous bad experience, cultural or linguistic communication difficulties, or if they were NHS key employees, because they were less likely to speak up if they had concerns about inadequate personal protective equipment (PPE) or of increased risks (PHE, 2018). The logical argument then is that institutions and governments failed to protect these 'at risk' key workers. Yet another thread emphasizes that the experience of racism, discrimination, stigma, fear and trust among Indians (and BAME communities generally), including key workers within the NHS and transport services, has made them significantly more vulnerable. The logical argument then is that it is not differences in 'race' or 'ethnicity' per se, but racial inequalities resulting from systemic structural racism which makes institutions and governments indifferent in protecting vulnerable 'at risk' key workers and communities.

4 Observations and Policy Implications

In this paper I have attempted to demonstrate that despite living in 'rich countries' and carrying the label of a relatively wealthy diaspora, the COVID-19 pandemic, nevertheless, disproportionally impacted these communities and exposed some of the hyper myths surrounding the relative prosperity of the Indian diaspora in different ways. However the impacts on USA and UK Indian communities have varied, with the latter being more exposed due to both socio-economic, demographic, locational factors and occupational structure. Further, the higher socio-economic status of the US Indian community, especially in the health and medical profession, has given the community greater public exposure in a positive way. The smaller size of the Indian American community relative to the much larger African American and Hispanic communities has also meant impact on them has remained largely invisible and national media discussion highly limited except among the community itself. Although the Indian community is highly represented and visible in the UK's National Health Service, perceptions of public exposure and positive image are more ambiguous. I have also attempted to summarize the public discourses that developed in the media regarding the underlying causes of differential impacts. There appears to be no consensus and it seems that explanations that focus on a single factor fail to capture the multi-layered complexity of issues involved. However, I would argue the three explanations discussed above, when considered together, will go a long way to capture the essence of the debate.

Although it is difficult to make definitive comments at this stage given that the pandemic is still raging in these countries, some tentative observations and policy implications are presented below.

Firstly, although it took a pandemic to finally put the issue of link between ethnic minorities and health outcomes at the top of the policy agenda, it is to be welcomed. It has revitalized an old and forgotten or largely neglected issue with more vigour. In the coming years, both in the USA and UK, extra research funding is anticipated to provide better understanding of the links between ethnicity and health outcomes. A number of new projects are already underway or under discussion in both the USA and UK and the results of these will be helpful in lowering mortality rates in the event of another COVID-19 like pandemic. But it needs to be emphasized that research funding or commissions of enquiry on their own are not going to solve the problem. Only concerted government action which tackles systemic structural racism and which actually alleviates income inequalities and poverty are going to make a material difference to well-being. The real danger is that once the pandemic is brought under control or eradicated all talk of anti-racism and health inequalities will again be forgotten.

On the other hand, if the pandemic is not brought under control and the public health crisis also transforms into a deep and protracted economic recession, persistently high levels of unemployment and income inequalities and poverty levels are the most likely outcomes. In fact, there is already growing evidence of the disproportionate unemployment impacts on Indian communities, almost a year after the first lockdowns. This will over time exacerbate even further existing health inequalities, worsening the situation for Indian and other ethnic minorities, especially in Indian-dominated neighbourhoods in the UK.

Secondly, the pandemic has thrown a positive light on the contribution of the Indian diaspora to host countries and especially in the case of USA raising further the already high profile of the community especially in media representation. In the UK, however, even though the community has been disproportionally impacted compared with the White population, it has been the least adversely affected relative to other BAME groups. This in a way reaffirms the affluent status of the Indian community relative to other BAME groups but at the same time exposing their continuing vulnerability.

Thirdly, in terms of comparative experiences between USA and UK, although both reward meritocracy, in the UK, however, there are still too many glass ceilings and institutional racism holds medical professionals back, preventing them from achieving a high profile and institutional representation whereas no such obstacles exist in the USA. For example, despite the critical role of Indian doctors and nurses in the NHS not many of these professionals have gained as much media and public exposure as in the USA, despite structural racism being a common factor in both countries. The recent US election of President Joe Biden with the Indian heritage Kamala Harris as vice president has provided a further boost. The fact that the Biden and Harris leadership has appointed more than 25 persons of Indian origin to serve in their administration, only reinforces the point about the higher profile and status of the Indian American community.

Fourthly, discourses in USA have focused more on disproportion impacts on African American and Hispanic communities as opposed to South Asians or Indians in particular. This affirms the relative prosperous status of the US Indian community despite the fact that comorbidities cited for higher mortalities among African Americans and Latinos are very much the same. This also seems to affirm that poverty overlaps with race, class and gender. As more survey data comes in, we may see a closer connection between them, in other words, we may find that factors that make ethnic minorities more vulnerable also make certain categories of white Americans and Britons more vulnerable, too.

Fifthly, one noteworthy observation regarding the Sikh community requires a mention. In every location in the diaspora but especially in the USA, UK and Canada, the community has used the opportunity offered by the lockdowns and the pandemic to publicly display their core value of selfless *seva*. As the pandemic led to lay-offs and high unemployment and with more people falling into income poverty and becoming reliant on food banks, many Gurdwaras stepped up to provide *langar* to tens of thousands of people on a daily basis. This public relations activity undoubtedly had a positive impact on public perceptions about the Sikhs, especially in the USA where the community has struggled to escape the curse of mistaken identity (that is, being mistaken for Middle Eastern terrorists) in the post 9/11 period, despite several Sikh awareness campaigns.

Sixthly, one impact of the pandemic which has been commonly felt by Indians in both countries is their inability to travel back and forth between their adopted countries and the homeland. The sudden and early introduction of a strict lockdown in India (combined with subsequent lockdowns in USA and UK as well) left thousands of Indians, especially Punjabis, stranded in India. It was only because of relentless pressure by their families and their representatives back in the diaspora that forced British and American governments and airlines to organize special flights to bring these stranded diasporans back home, sometimes after several months delay. Inevitably this caused considerable anxiety, medical and financial hardship to many families. Needless to say, suspension of flights (only partially lifted even now) led to many postponed travel arrangements for family visits and celebrations, for doing business and undertaking tourism, causing not only inconvenience but also financial ruin for many. The psychological impacts would have been even harsher if not for digital connectivity through social media.

Finally, at the point of writing the pandemic is still raging in the USA, with the death total now exceeding 455,000, while the situation in the UK is still not under control with over 100,000 deaths with severe restrictions in place throughout the country. The only good news has been a breakthrough in vaccines with several now being offered to different segments of the population. While it will still be months before sufficient numbers are vaccinated to generate herd immunity among the population, nevertheless, it is a promising development offering light at the end of a long tunnel. The downside appears to be some anecdotal evidence of vaccine resistance, where some members of BAME in the UK and African Americans in the USA are showing hesitancy because of misinformation circulating on social media, including many false rumours that the vaccine may contain alcohol or pork or unspecified or covered up side effects. These rumours may be difficult to counter along with attempts in overcoming very challenging structural, cultural and language barriers in some locations. With the availability of vaccines, the focus of governments will now undoubtedly shift towards rebuilding economies and pursuing policies to help people in adapting and adjusting lifestyles to the new post-COVID-19 normal. We can only hope that in this post-COVID-19 period there will still be a political desire on the part of present administrations to help rebuild minority ethnic communities. One of the more likely outcomes of this pandemic may be that it leads to an increase in positive discourses within the Indian diaspora communities around health education, diet and lifestyles which may leave the community better prepared and less exposed in case of recurrence. More optimistically, it may even generate greater collective action to mobilize and lobby for more health care facilities and health education in their neighbourhoods.

References

Bécares, L. (2013) *Which Ethnic Groups Have the Poorest Health? Ethnic Health Inequalities 1991 to 2011*, October, ESRC Centre on Dynamics of Ethnicity (CoDE), University of Manchester and Joseph Roundtree Foundation, October. Accessed at https://www.hummedia.manchester.ac.uk/which-ethnic-groups-have-the-poorest-health.pdf.

Bhavsar, V., Ventriglio, A., and Bhugra, D. (2018) The Mental Health of South Asians in the UK, *Mental Health and Illness in Migration*, pp. 1–13.

Butcher, B., and Massey, J. (2020) *Why Are More People from BAME Backgrounds Dying from Coronavirus?* BBC, June. Accessed at: https://www.bbc.co.uk/news/uk-52219070.

Chakravorty, S., Kapur, D., and Singh, N. (2016) *The Other One Percent: Indians in America*, Oxford University Press.

Khadria, B. (2012)*India Migration Report 2010–11: The Americas*, Cambridge University Press.

Kirkegaard, J. F. (2019) *The US H-1B Visa: A Boon for High-Skilled Immigrants from India*, Petersen Institute of International Economics, November

Lucas, A., Murry, E., and Kinra, S. (2013) Heath Beliefs of UK South Asians Related to Lifestyle Diseases: A Review of Qualitative Literature, *Journal of Obesity*, 2013(827674): 13 pages.

National CAPACD. (2020) *The Economic Reality of The Asian American Pacific Islander Community Is Marked by Diversity and Inequality, Not Universal Success.* In Partnership with Prosperity Now, November. Accessed at: https://www.nationalcapacd.org/data-research/inequality-and-diversity-not-universal-success-marks-the-economic-reality-of-the-asian-american-community-2-2/.

Office of National Statistics. (2020) *Coronavirus (COVID-19) Related Deaths by Ethnic Group, England and Wales*, 2 March 2020 to 15 May 2020, 19 June. Accessed at: https://www.ons.gov.uk/peoplepopulationandcommunity/birthsdeathsandmarriages/deaths/articles/coronaviruscovid19relateddeathsbyethnicgroupenglandandwales/2march2020to15may2020.

Postnote. (2007) *Ethnicity and Health*, Parliament Office of Science and Technology, January, Number 276.

Public Health England. (2018) *Local Action on Health Inequalities: Understanding and Reducing Ethnic Inequalities in Health* Ref: PHE publications gateway number: 2018264. Accessed at: https://www.gov.uk/government/publications/health-inequalities-reducing-ethnic-inequalities.

Thandi, S. (2006) Labouring Enterprise and South Asians, in N. Ali, B. Sayyid, and V. Kalra (Eds.), *Post-Colonial People: South Asian Experience in Britain*, London: Hurst.

The Lancet Public Health. (2020) Ethnic Inequalities in Health-Related Quality of Life Among Older Adults in England: Secondary Analysis of a National Cross-Sectional Survey - The Lancet Public Health. Accessed at: https://www.thelancet.com/journals/lanpub/article/PIIS2468-2667(20)30287-5/fulltext.

Zaman, M., Justin, S., and Mangtani, P. (2007) Changing Disease Patterns in South Asians, *Journal of the Royal Society of Medicine*, 100(6, June): 254–255.

Zong, J., and Batalova, J. (2017) *Indian Immigrants in the United States in 2015*, Migration Policy Institute. Accessed at: https://www.migrationpolicy.org/article/indian-immigrants-united-states?gclid=EAIaIQobChMI2JTBjbTD6QIVzz2tBh3XsQkLEAAYASAAEgL-ZPD_BwE.

Governance Structure and Punjab Economy Under and Post-COVID 19 Lockdown

Sucha Singh Gill

1 Governance Structure and Management of COVID-19

The governance structure of economy in Punjab has largely moved from a state-supported system during pre-1991 towards a neoliberal policy regime giving greater role to market forces in the recent period. The government has significantly withdrawn from health and education providing more space to the private players. Even in agricultural marketing the opening has been allowed to the private players. The policy issues are handled largely by politicians and bureaucrats more in consultation with corporate players. Except for power subsidy, public distribution system and a few social security measures like the old age and destitute pension and health insurance, etc., on the Central Government pattern; all other affairs are governed by private players. The governance structure in the state is now dominated by three parties viz; Indian National Congress, Shrimoni Akali Dal, and Aam Adami Party. At present, all the three parties have formally similar agendas for governance and promises for the people as reflected by their manifestos during the 2017 elections to the State Assembly. Media reports indicate that Akali Dal and Congress

S. S. Gill (✉)
CRIID, Chandigarh, India

S. Singh et al. (eds.), *Covid-19 Pandemic and Economic Development*,
https://doi.org/10.1007/978-981-16-4442-9_20

politicians are known to provide patronage to real estate mafia, liquor mafia, and sand mafia engaged in massive tax evasion. Apart from the normal situation, the constitution of the country provides a wide range of powers to the State Governments and Central Government to deal with abnormal situations like threat of spread of COVID-19. In spite of the 73rd and 74th amendments of the constitution, the third tier of democracy, i.e. the village panchayats and urban local bodies have not been devolved enough power to play any significant role in the governance structure of Punjab State.

The government of Punjab fearing the threat of spread of COVID-19-imposed curfew in the entire state from 20th March 2020. In the first phase from 20th March to 30th April, the strict curfew was imposed in the state. The movement of public and private transport was banned except for vehicles on official duty or those engaged in supply of medicines and essential eatable commodities of household use. The supply of essential commodities such as milk, vegetables, fruits, items of daily use, and medicines were allowed through authorised persons or curfew pass holders. Except for the supply of essential goods and ICT services everything else was closed. People were asked to stay home, maintain social distance and wash their hands frequently. All the educational institutions from schools to colleges and universities were closed, all shopping malls, all shops, and markets were closed. All modes of transport from two-wheelers, to three-wheelers, buses, and passenger trains were suspended. All the offices, hotels, restaurants, dhabhas, sweetshop, and tea stalls were closed. All the factories, repair shops, banks, and business enterprises were also closed. As the people were stopped from going outside their houses, all economic activities came to a grinding halt. The State was handed over to the police and later on, the paramilitary forces were also deployed at some places to help the police to enforce curfew. Doctors, nurses, and paramedical staff in the state-run hospitals and other medical institutions were put on duty to identify the suspected corona-positive cases and put them on fifteen days quarantine and seriously affected persons to the hospitals for treatment. The ASHA (accredited social health activist) workers were sent to seriously affected rural and urban areas to identify the suspected cases for admission to hospitals or to be quarantined. The private clinics, nursing homes, five-star private hospitals, and clinical diagnostic centers had put down their shutters. In spite of appeal of the Chief Minister that the private health care should also join in the fight against COVID-19, it did not open up to the affected/suspected COVID-19 patients. Rather they started demanding Rs. 4500 for testing corona patients. They did not attend even the non-corona affected patients in the first phase of curfew. It is after 1st May 2020, i.e. in the second phase of curfew that the private health care began to open up. This happened only when the Chief Minister threatened to cancel the licenses of those private hospitals which do not open up for the patients.

The Prime Minister and Chief Minister appealed to the private sector employers not to retrench or terminate services of the workers employed by them. At the same time, they were also told to make payment of wages and salaries to the workers and employees during the curfew/lockdown period. But most of these employers in Punjab did not pay their workers. Within a week or so the workers in private sector or daily wage earners began to face crunches in their financial resources and were without food to feed themselves. Initially, some philanthropic and non-government organisations (NGOs) undertook the responsibility of feeding them. Soon it was realised by the administration that these organisations were not able to follow the required protocol of social distancing. This task was handed over to the Red Cross in every district under the supervision of the district administration. At the same time, the food packets began to be distributed to the poor by the State Government. All this was being handled by the government and political leaders of all the parties withdrew to their homes to remain safe from the virus threat. With a few exceptions of BKU leaders, voluntaries of Gurdwaras and local committees, the task of feeding the people in distress was handled by the civil and police administration. The employers in the private sector completely abdicated their responsibilities towards their workers. The migrant workers and daily earners like rickshaw pullers or auto drivers or petty shopkeepers were hit hardest. In fact, in spite of positive efforts, the Punjabi society could not create emotional security for the migrant workers (Swarajbir, 2020). As the curfew entered the second phase on 1st May restless among the workers to go to their places of origin in UP, Bihar, Madhya Pradesh, Jharkhand, Odisha, etc., became very strong.

2 Strategy towards Migrant Workers and Punjabi Entrapped Outside

With the increase in period of curfew and fear of COVID-19 pandemic expected to continue for a bit longer the migrant workers began to make frantic efforts to reach their native places even when all modes of transport were closed within the state and borders with other states were sealed. At this point of time, the State Government took a decision to list the workers online and the destination where they wanted to reach through the office of district administration. Within a few days, this number reached 9.50 lakh and ultimately crossed 10 lakh. Nearly the halves of the migrants were stationed at Ludhiana. Although migrants are spread all over Punjab but other major places of concentration were Amritsar, Jalandhar, and Patiala. The State Government itself in a financial mess yet decided to send the restive migrants to their native places by special trains known as *Shramik* trains and pay for their fare costing the State Government Rs. 26 crores. The State Government approached the Indian Railways authorities for this purpose and arranged 75 trains from various places in Punjab to the different destinations in India (Kumar, 2020). This also became a moment when the government started opening up various economic activities. This led to some extent a section of migrants to change their decision and stay back in Punjab.

Like many migrant workers, several workers and others from Punjab were trapped at various places outside the state during lockdown. There were two types of persons trapped. One category of persons were pilgrims from Punjab to various places like Nanded in Maharashtra. On the demand of these people, the state transport buses were sent to bring them back during the first phase of lockdown. The expenditure on their transport was born by the State Government. A large chunk among the returnee pilgrims were identified as corona positive cases and they were treated freely in the government hospitals. The second group of persons from Punjab trapped outside consisted of owners along with the workers on harvester combines who had gone to other states for harvesting of wheat and mustard crops on custom-hiring basis. As their number was not very large and they were not concentrated at a few locations they could not be provided any help to bring them back. Generally, the attitude of the State Government towards Punjabi trapped outside was sympathetic and helpful to bring them back and treat them free of cost and put them in quarantine at public expenditure. But the government could not identify other locations such as in Nepal, Uttar Pradesh, Madhya Pradesh, and Rajasthan to help trapped Punjabi migrant workers.

3 Policy Towards Economy

In the first phase of curfew, the priority was to save the life from the threat of coronavirus. People were asked to stay home; borders of the state were sealed. All modes of transport were suspended and all economic activities were stopped except the supply of essential items such as food and medicines which were supplied by designated persons holding passes. All emergencies of health and food were handled by civil and police administration. From 13 April, harvest of wheat crop was expected, the government allowed farmers to harvest their crops from 15 April. As a first step they allowed the farmers to get harvesting machinery ready after repair or oiling from 1stApril. The authorities also allowed the opening of shops, repairing agricultural machinery, and selling spare parts. It was announced that from 15th April the farmers were allowed to bring wheat in the marketing yards. The marketing yards were sanitised and a protocol was developed by the Agriculture Department of the government to maintain social distancing during marketing operations. A limited number of farmers were allowed to bring their produce to the market and they were issued passes through the commission agents under the supervision of the market committees in their areas. Though there were some operational difficulties faced by some farmers, the system worked well and the wheat crop was procured by 30th May 2020. One of the problems faced during the marketing operations was created by unseasonal rainfall both before and after harvesting began. The unseasonal rainfall before the harvesting accompanied by the high-speed winds led to shriveled grain of wheat of some farmers. While rainfall during the marketing season created disruption in the sale and water was collected in some market yards which made the grain wet. When the wheat was dried up after the rainfall the colour of the grain was changed which led to luster loss. The procurement agencies introduced a price cut of Rs. 4.81 for luster loss and Rs. 24.06 for shriveled grain per quintile of wheat. The State Government could not convince the procurement agencies to avoid these price cuts and some farmers suffered loss of their expected income level. But, the State Government did not work out a well thought-out strategy for marketing perishable agricultural produce. It was assumed from day one of the lockdown/curfew that the supply of milk, vegetables, fruits, eggs, meat, and other such commodities would be allowed uninterrupted to consumers through their suppliers at the doorstep of the consumers. But by closing of shops of processors of the products such private milk plants, sweetshops, tea stalls, dhabhas, restaurants, hotels, marriage palaces, etc., and also banning of gathering beyond 20 persons led to shrinkage of demand of these commodities. This led to sharp fall in the prices of these commodities. At the same time, the state boundaries were closed and markets in the neigbouring states of Delhi, Himachal Pradesh, and J&K became inaccessible to the suppliers of these products. The owners of poultry, producers of milk, vegetables, and fruits suffered colossal losses. Our estimates show that the producers of these four groups of commodities suffered a loss of Rs. 1349.90. crore during the first phase of curfew from 20 March to 30 April 2020 (Gill, 2020). In addition to this, the producers of honey whose number is 3000 in the state producing annually 3000 metric tonnes of honey also lost in a big way. The flower cultivators lost the market because all celebrations related to birth, marriage, death, and other social celebrations were almost suspended to maintain social distances. The honey producers immediately lost the export market where they generally unload one-half of their produce and also lost market in other states. They had to hire cold store facilities to keep the honey safe and had to make extra expenditure in the hope of opening up the market. The flower cultivators lost the market because all celebrations related to birth, marriage, death, and other social celebrations were almost suspended to maintain social lost distances. The government began to open up very slowly from 17 May 2020, a few more activities after lockdown-2 but more activities such as shops on rotation basis in urban areas and all shops in the villages and located in isolated localities and factories in the major cities located in the non-containment zones. The shopping malls and religious places are allowed to be open up from 8 June and schools and other educational institutions are proposed to be open in October 2020.

4 Economic Revival Strategy

The State Government has been very conscious and careful in dealing with COVID-19 risk to life and livelihood of the people in Punjab. In anticipation of normalisation of the situation, the State Government appointed 20 members of Expert Group to Shape Post-COVID-19 Economic Revival in Punjab. This group was mandated to submit initial set of recommendations by 31st July 2020 to be followed by two more reports by 30th September and 31st December 2020 (Kirari, 2020). This reflects attentiveness of the State Government to the crucial role of experts to provide it the informed advice. This group has held some online discussions between themselves and some people in the state in May 2020. The first set of recommendations by the Expert Group indicates that it wants increased role of corporate sector in the state.

The Chief Minister of Punjab has submitted a memorandum to the Prime Minister seeking financial aid of Rs 79,460 crores along with non-fiscal assistance on various counts to save lives and livelihood in the state due to pandemic caused distress (Bajwa, 2020). This indicates that the State Government is primarily depending on the Union Government for resources for the revival of the economy. This package from the Union Government may not materialise if the past experience is of any guide. There is no indication that the State Government is seriously making any effort to pull up its socks to internally mobilise its resources. There are media reports that the State is losing several thousand crores of Rupees due to activities of liquor mafia, real estate mafia, and sand mafia which have been operating under the patronage of ruling parties for several decades. Because of lack of commitment to internally mobilise resources the reports of the Expert Group may remain an academic exercise and unimplemented at practical level. At the same time, the state may lose an opportunity to learn from its own experience of dealing with the society during the lockdown period. During the crisis period crucial role has been played by public institutions both in education and health in dealing with COVID-19 with depleted resources. They deserve a greater attention of the governments in the revival strategy. Another important lesson has been that unlike Kerala our village panchayats and urban local bodies could not be involved in handling the pandemic at ground level. This is because these institutions of the third tier of democracy have not been empowered with functions, funds, and functionaries to perform the due role in all situations. In the post-COVID-19, it is an opportunity to correct the distortions which have happened over time in the various segments of governance in the state.

Immediately the State Government needs to identify the loss of producers of perishable crops and compensate them for losses they have suffered. They are those cultivators who are engaged in production of crops other than wheat and paddy. If we don't compensate them, they will also revert back to raising traditional crops and the state programmme of crop diversification will lose attraction for cultivators in general. In this situation the State Government may pick up crops like oilseeds, pulses, and maize for support in terms of payment to the farmers at MSP and assures purchases by the state agencies for agro-processing. The agencies like MARKFED can engage in purchase and processing of oilseeds and maize and Pungrain/PUNSUP for procurement of pulses for PDS under Dal-Atta scheme. This will give a big push to crop diversification programme and also it will also create necessary confidence among the farmers about seriousness of the government in promotion of this programme.

Punjab agriculture is passing through serious crisis and a large number (more than 16,000) of poor farmers and agricultural labourer have committed suicide (Singh and Bhangu, 2016). It is the right time to evolve measures to prevent this agrarian tragedy to happen and start rehabilitation measures for the victim families. This requires institutional reforms such as modern land leasing measures to save the land of poor owners leaving agriculture and reforms towards group cultivation in the form of cooperative farming, formation of farmers' producer organisations (FPOs), self-help groups (SGPs), etc., to move from individual forming to group farming as individual farming has become unviable for small and marginal cultivators. The innovative measures can involve groups of farmers into farming, marketing of farm produce, build storage for farm produce, and do host of other activities including engagement in supply chain of agricultural produce.

Another task which the State Government can undertake is to have a quick survey of micro small medium enterprises (MSMEs). At present, the number of such enterprises is more than 14.65 lakh but only 0.44 lakh are registered. The enterprises not registered are not eligible to access any loans from banks at concessional rates. MSMEs employ nearly 24% of the total workforce (GOI, 2019). This sector is the second-largest employer in Punjab after agriculture. On the basis of survey, a comprehensive programme for their revival needs to be started. This sector has suffered the most but it lacks vocal voice to air its grievances. This is the sector in which future hopes of the state and people fall. For this purpose, the city wise associations of these enterprises can be consulted and their engagement in agro-processing can be advanced to build and strengthen agriculture-industry linkages. The revival of this sector can generate huge employment and also involve them in supply chain and make rural unemployed youth as part of it. It is very critical in view shrinking employment opportunities abroad signified by return of lakh of workers from the Middle East and other countries following the COVID-19 pandemic in the world. The programmes like MGNREGA have to be seriously planned in the rural areas. At the same time, we need to think of such programmes in urban Punjab for the poor daily wage workers in order to provide them minimum earnings for their survival for 100 days.

In the medium term, we need to strengthen public health system and the government-supported public education system by restoring the budgetary support they lost after 1991. The State Government was spending 9.30% of the state budget on health services and 23.66% on education during triennium ending 1980–1981 which has fallen respectively to 4.7 and 16% by triennium ending 2017–2018 (Gill et al., 2010; Government of Punjab 2020). There are indications that these sectors have suffered in terms of resource allocation in the budgets over a period of time. The COVID19 pandemic has shown that during the crisis of serious nature, the private sector closes its shops both for employees as well as for the people. In order to strengthen our human resources, public sector role in health and education has to be increased as private sector players in this area only work for profit.

References

Bajwa, H. (2020) Punjab Seeks over Rs. 80,000 Crore Aid from Centre Save Lives and Livelihoods, *Indian Express* (Chandigarh), June 15.

Gill, S. S. (2020) A Note on Losses of Perishable Crops in Punjab, Unpublished CRRID, Chandigarh, May.

Gill, S. S., Singh, S., and Brar, J. S. (2010) *Globalisation and Indian State: Education, Health and Agricultural Extension Services in Punjab*, New Delhi: Aakar Books.

Government of India. (2019) *Annual Report 2018–19*, New Delhi: Ministry of MSMEs.

Government of Punjab. (2020) *Punjab Economic Survey 2019–20*, Chandigarh: Economic and Statistical Organisation.

Kirari, P. (2020) Punjab Appoints Expert Group to Shape Post Covid Economic Revival, *The Economic Times* (New Delhi), April 26.

Kumar, S. (2020) How Punjab's Farmers Rose to the Challenge, *The Tribune* (Chandigarh), June 3.

Singh, L., Singh, K., and Sharma, R. (2016) *Agrarian Distress and Farmer Suicides in North India*, New Delhi: Sage.

Swarajbir. (2020) Covid 19 Pandemic and Punjab (in Punjabi), *Punjabi Tribune* (Chandigarh), June 19.

Punjab's Post-COVID-19 Economic Policy Under Indian Federalism

Pritam Singh

1 Introduction

The COVID19 pandemic is the worst human health crisis since the 1918 flu epidemic and the worst economic crisis since the Great Depression. The economic crisis caused by COVID-19 is, however, likely to be even more catastrophic than that triggered by the Great Depression because the latter was confined mainly to the advanced capitalist economies while the current crisis is truly global, even if its severity varies regionally (Singh, 2020a). Furthermore, this economic crisis, unlike the Great Depression, is occurring in a period of global climate instability creating an existential crisis for Planet Earth. The Paris Climate Change Accord of 2015, which reflects a consensus that has emerged among international climate scientists, stipulates that if the average global temperature rise is not kept below 1.5 degree centigrade by 2030, in comparison with the average global temperature before the start of the industrial age, the planet will face irreversible and catastrophic changes. Right now, in 2020, there is a window of opportunity of only 10 years left to avoid that catastrophe (Singh, 2019a).

P. Singh (✉)
Oxford Brookes University, Oxford, UK
e-mail: psingh@brookes.ac.uk

S. Singh et al. (eds.), *Covid-19 Pandemic and Economic Development*,
https://doi.org/10.1007/978-981-16-4442-9_21

Any policy response that can be visualised in Punjab has to keep this global scenario of climate crisis and economic crisis in mind and the limitations faced by state governments within India's federal capitalist economy. These limitations can be overcome, partially by extending the policy discourse usually associated with state government power to include the power of other civil society institutions, and partially by using the full potential of what a state government can do within federal limits. Within India as a whole, a political environment must be created in which Punjab plays a crucial role despite its small size and relatively low political bargaining power, in order to encourage state governments to be bold in their efforts to break the stranglehold of central/federal power. An institutionalised centralisation began to increase from the framing of India's constitution onwards, but has become so overwhelming more recently that acquiescence to the central powers has become normalised. Due to this stifling normalisation, all too often state governments hesitate to take the initiative in policy formulation and implementation.

2 Need for New Thinking

We have reached a point due to the COVID-19-caused economic crisis (Singh, 2020a) and to the centralised misgovernance of economy and polity in contemporary India (Singh, 2020b, c) where it is time to dare to think outside the box. The lazy approach of implementing a return to 'business as usual' after the COVID-19 pandemic is over would result not only in utter economic failure but also in ecological and health catastrophes of unimaginable proportions.

Daring to think outside the box involves reimagining economic concepts, paradigms, goals and strategies. Politically, it means abandoning the narrow 'law and order' approach to governance and thinking about people's participation even if that seems sometimes unruly and chaotic. The beauty and creativity of what may seem chaos in democratic participation are any day preferable to the deathly silence that 'law and order' authoritarianism can create.

It is out of the creative synthesis of this new economic and political imagining that a new political economy for our post-COVID-19 era would evolve.

The first casualty of this new political economy must be the concept, goal and strategy of economic growth. Globally, nationally and intranationally, economic growth as measured through increase in GDP has been the mantra of traditional economics—whether capitalist or claiming to be socialist. National and subnational entities measure their own 'progress' or lack of progress by looking at their own GDP over time, and compare their own progress with that of other comparable entities by comparing their own GDP growth rate with the GDP growth rates of others.

It is precisely this obsession with economic growth at the expense of examining its positive and negative consequences critically and holistically, and with celebrating GDP as a measure of welfare without examining its drawbacks—especially the way it is measured—that is at the root of the emergence of the COVID-19 pandemic. Since the beginning of agricultural settlement, human beings have been encroaching upon the living habitats of other non-human living species. This encroachment has been accelerated under capitalism as capital accesses every 'resource' with the objective of maximising profit. Although there is still no scientific consensus on the precise origin of the COVID-19 virus, there is a very high degree of agreement that this virus was transmitted by animals and birds to human beings. This transmission—caused by human domination over other living species—has been significantly and qualitatively heightened by the logic of the capitalist economy. Expanding capitalism is the driving force behind deforestation causing destruction of natural habitats. The profit-driven international meat market, encouraging international trade and transportation of live animals, leads to an accelerated flow of commodities, people and infectious diseases such as COVI-19 (Singh, 2020a).

GDP must be used in a very limited way as a measure of exchanged products and services. It does not include positive products and services that do not enter the market exchange process, e.g. home-grown vegetables and fruits as products, and household work as a service mainly provided by women. It is, undoubtedly, a male-biased measure. On the contrary, it includes many negatives such as the destructive military expenditure incurred mainly by men. Of course, GDP does not measure inequalities and environmental destruction. In fact, the more the environment is destroyed (e.g. through deforestation) to produce commodities which may or may not be useful, the more it adds to the increase in GDP.

The first major implication for Punjab if it follows an ecologically sustainable path of development is to go beyond Central directives which require state governments only to measure those activities which are relevant for the state's GDP. It need not abandon the existing practice of measuring GDP because of its utility in accounting for the value of exchangeable commodities and services in the state, but it can insist on going beyond this to start measuring other indices such as, for instance, air and water quality and public services such as health provision to name a few (see, e.g. Anderson, 1991). This would require an institutional restructuring of Punjab's data collection departments, such as the Directorate of Economics and Statistical Organisation which compiles the annual Statistical Abstract. This is something to which the Centre is unlikely to object, and Punjab may act as an encouragement to other states. To emphasise its dissatisfaction with the GDP measure, Punjab can refuse to participate in the meaningless exercise of inter-state comparison of GDP growth rates.

As a result of this dissatisfaction with the discourse on economic growth, states need to abandon the traditional path trajectory of 'development' from agriculture to industry to services as a matter of urgency. In the context of developing ecological crisis, agriculture must take a larger role. Once the importance of agriculture in ecologically oriented development is recognised, then even the existing model of agricultural development in the state must be abandoned. Punjab's agricultural model of development through the so-called Green Revolution, to meet the Centrally decided objective of national food sufficiency, has damaged Punjab's land, water, air and human health. Once Punjab decides on the alternative, ecologically compatible course of action, it must build ties of solidarity with other states in the Indian federation, and confront the Centre, by choosing cropping patterns that are appropriate for the state's ecological stability and not those that suit the Centre's agenda. Punjab's recent clash with the Centre over its agricultural market reforms may provide inspiration for the upcoming conflicts with the Centre on agriculture, given that the Centre has intruded on the subjects of agriculture, together with industry and state finances, on a regular basis (Singh, 2008b,2020c; Singh et al., 2020).

3 Ecological Perspective

A new path of development built on sound ecological considerations would be possible in Punjab only if there is wide-ranging public pressure from below by farmers' and agricultural workers' organisations working in association with supportive academics, journalists and civil servants. Any government in Punjab, irrespective of the party in power, would feel encouraged to defy directives issued by the Centre which are contrary to ecologically-oriented development if it has mass support and if it remains under continuous and vigilant pressure from mass organisations. Therefore, the options a state government in Punjab can pursue under the Indian federal system go beyond the thinking, policies and actions of Punjabi politicians in power and those of government administrators. For example, the move towards substantial, if not wholly, organic agriculture would require mass education in many creative and diverse ways, and appropriate mass political mobilisation. Similarly, the option of moving from fossil fuel energy to renewable energy would require both technical competence as well as mass participation of stakeholders (Singh and Singh, 2019).

The use of the written and spoken Punjabi language would be of critical importance in ensuring effective mass education on the desirability and sustainability of organic agriculture. This focus on the importance of using Punjabi to equip people with knowledge and confidence about organic agriculture could create tensions with the pro-Hindi policies of the Central government (Singh, 2019b). The likelihood of Centre/state tension on the language issue—which is not merely a cultural issue, as it is often understood, but is linked to development—is especially acute at present due to anti-federal government policies (Singh 2016, 2019c). The state government—with the active support and mobilisation of the people of the state—needs to object to the increase of CBSE schools in the state's school system which plays a covert role in spreading the supremacy of Hindi over Punjabi. The constitutional amendment brought during Indira Gandhi's Emergency (1975–1977) to take out 'education' from the State List and insert it into the Concurrent List (Singh, 2008b: 109), has never been undone by any non-Congress government, because both the Congress and the BJP—the two main parties in the Indian parliament—are supporters of the increasing centralisation of education. This pro-centralisation politics is the driving force behind the increased numbers of pro-Hindi CBSE schools even in the rural heartlands of Punjab (Singh, 2019d).

4 Way Forward for Punjab

Given the level of indebtedness of the state and of the farming community, the state needs to mobilise revenue resources as it is unlikely that central government will do anything substantially either to reduce government debt or to waive farmers' debts even in part. There is neither the political will on the part of the central government nor any economic incentive to deal with these forms of debt. To mobilise revenue internally within the state, the Punjab government will have to think creatively about imposing a form of direct tax on the super-rich in Punjab. Punjab's wealthiest have amassed huge sums through legal and, in several instances, illegal means of extracting surplus from Punjab's land, labour, water, sand, forests and hills—to name just a few of the natural resources—while a substantial section of Punjab's population, especially in the rural areas, is in hardship, which has even led to suicides. The evidence is emerging in the form of trader/money-lender suicides indicating that distress is now spreading to small shopkeepers/money lenders even in urban areas. In the unprecedented circumstances of the COVID-19 pandemic, it is absolutely necessary that the super-rich Punjabis (or non-Punjabis resident in Punjab) share a part of their wealth to help the Punjab state's finances, which can then be used to help the most distressed sections of Punjabi society. As we are now observing the 550th anniversary of the birth of Guru Nanak who is revered by all Punjabis, his moral imperative to *vand shako* (share the fruits of your labour with others) needs to be put into practice (Singh, 2018a, b). Under the current federal structure, only the Centre has the power to impose and collect direct taxes. The Punjabi state has to wage a dual battle on this issue. First, it must explore legal means for renaming the direct tax so that it remains constitutionally valid, and secondly, it must use mass political mobilisation to force the Centre to give ground by allowing the state to impose a direct tax, even a temporary one. Whether such a tax should be imposed on wealth, property or income needs closer examination. Punjab could study the example of Scotland, which is seeking to impose an increase in direct income tax on revenue-generating activities, and use a variant of this measure. The political culture in Punjab, at this moment, is conducive to imposing such a special direct tax or levy on the super-rich, even if temporary.

Punjab also needs to explore avenues to increase exports and export revenue by creating closer and peaceful relations with its immediate neighbouring country, Pakistan. Within the existing federal structures, the states have no role in shaping Central foreign policy; at the same time, the border states need an entirely different policy from that needed by non-border states (Singh and Mann, n.d.). Punjab would need to form an alliance with other border states which are similarly affected by conflicts with neighbouring countries. The allied states would need to negotiate a change in the formulation and implementation of foreign and defence policy. If this requires constitutional changes to reflect the diverse, and at times conflicting interests between different states, those changes must be fought for.

While we recognise the government's need to search for alternatives to orthodox economic thinking and practice—a need that always arises in moments of acute economic crisis—it is equally important to challenge orthodox thinking at the institutional level, the family level and the individual level. Recognising the gravity of the economic, ecological and health crises we are passing through, institutions such as universities, colleges, schools, hospitals, religious institutions, factories and shopping centres need to learn new ways of governing themselves which reduce the use of resources and the creation of waste. Individuals and families from rich and middle-class backgrounds in particular need to make changes in their general consumption and celebrations of social occasions such as marriages. The current debates regarding the Green New Deal as a transitional path from an environmentally damaging capitalist economy to an alternative and eco-socialist reorganisation of economy and society must be studied (for contributions of this author and other eco-socialists on this in the context of COVID-19 crisis, see Red and Green Study Group, 2020a, b).

One way of highlighting the unprecedented times we are living through is to recognise that UK—which has a long history of keeping economic and social records—the current recession is recognised as the deepest ever recorded. On top of this, we face ecological instability creating an existential threat to Planet Earth. Unprecedented times require unprecedented responses, and, if a response now in Punjab requires a revision of the relations between the Centre and the states, the changes needed will have historic significance.

References

Anderson, K. (1991) *Alternative Economic Indicators*, London: Routledge

Bharadwaj, K. (1986). *Classical Political Economy and Rise to Dominance of Supply and Demand Theories*, Delhi: Sangam

Foldvary, F. E. (ed.). (1996) *Beyond Neo-Classical Economics: Heterodox Approaches to Economic Theory*, Cheltenham: Edward Elgar.

Keynes, J. M. (1936) *The General Theory of Employment, Interest and Money*, London: Macmillan (reprinted 2007)

Konzelmann, S. J. (2014) The Political Economics of Austerity, *Cambridge Journal of Economics*, 38(4): 701–741.

Niskanen, W. A. (1988) *Reaganomics: An Insider's Account of the Policies and the People*, Oxford: Oxford University Press.

Radice, H. (2014) Thatcherism and Alternatives: What Future for British Capitalism?, *Capital and Class*, 38(2): 277–287.

Red and Green Study Group. (2020a) Making Sense of the Covid-19 Crisis. http://redgreenstudygroup.org.uk/making-sense-of-the-covid-19-crisis/ [Accessed 9 July 2020].

Red and Green Study Group. (2020b) Making Sense of the Covid-19 Crisis: Zoom Meeting 25 April 2020 – Comments. http://redgreenstudygroup.org.uk/making-sense-of-the-covid-19-crisis-zoom-meeting-25-april-2020-comments/ [Accessed 9 July 2020].

Singh, P. (2008a) Contemporary Global Capitalism: Multi-pronged Crises, *Economic and Political Weekly*, October 11, 36–40.

Singh, P. (2008b) *Federalism, Nationalism and Development: India and the Punjab Economy*, London/New York: Routledge (the second Indian reprint 2019).

Singh, P. (2016) W(h)ither Federalism?, *The Tribune*, August 11.

Singh, P. (2018a) Shri Guru Granth Sahib: Understanding the Sacred Word, London School of Economics. http://www.lse.ac.uk/south-asia-centre/assets/documents/18-0550-GGS-Report-New-Version-16ppV8-HR.pdf [Accessed 9 July 2020].

Singh, P. (2018b) Shri Guru Granth Sahib: Understanding the Sacred Word, London School of Economics, podcast: https://richmedia.lse.ac.uk/dpteve nts/20180322_GGSJ_SAC_speaker3ProfPritamSingh.mp3

Singh, P. (2019a) 11-Year Window to Prevent Catastrophe, *The Tribune*, July 29.

Singh, P. (2019b) Emerging Fault Lines in the push for Hindi, *The Tribune*, September 18.

Singh, P. (2019c) The Sangh's Ideology Against Federalism Underlies the Centre's Move in J & K, *The Wire*, September 30.

Singh, P. (2019d) *Keynote Address at Federalism Conference*, Chandigarh, November 1. https://www.youtube.com/watch?v=1iZjnrdbdfw&t=154s.

Singh, P. (2020a) Zeroing in on Responses to Economic Crisis, *The Tribune*, May 2.

Singh, P. (2020b). Ordinances: Naked Circulation of Centralisation and Privatisation (translation of original: Ordinances: kendrikaran te nizikaran da nanga chitta vapar), *Punjabi Tribune*, June 11.

Singh, P. (2020c) Struggle for a Federal Structure Is the Path for Struggle for Democracy (translation of original: 'Federal dhanje lai ghol hi lokraj da sangharsh'), *Punjabi Tribune*, June 12.

Singh, P. (2020d) Centre's Agricultural Marketing Reforms Are an Assault on Federalism, *The Wire*, June 20.

Singh, P., and Bhusal, L. N. (2014) Austerity, Welfare State and Eco-Socialism: With Special Reference to the United Kingdom, *Economic and Political Weekly*, September 27, XLIX(39): 111–118.

Singh, P., and Mann, R. S. (n.d.) 'Punjab's Export Potential to Pakistan: Constraining Influence of Federal India's Foreign Policy'. Unpublished.

Singh, P., and Singh, N. (2019). Political Economy of Bioenergy Transitions in Developing Countries : A Case Study of Punjab, India, *World Development*, 124 (104630), 1 December 2019.

Singh, P., Singh, S., Thandi, S., and Narang, H. K. (2020) Did Federalism Fail Punjab?, *Journal of Sikh and Punjab Studies*, 27(1), Spring 2020.

Skidelsky, R. (Ed.). (1989) *Thatcherism*, Oxford: Basil Blackwell.

Implications of COVID-19 on the Revenue of Punjab Under GST Regime

Jatinder S. Bedi and Gayatri Prabhakar

The budgeted estimates (BE) for the revenue receipts of Punjab Government are estimated to be Rs 88,000 crore for the Financial Year ending 2021 (FY21), which is 19% higher compared to Revised Estimates (RE) for FY20. The share of revenue receipts in SGDP rose to 13.6% in FY21 (BE) compared to 12.9% in FY20 (RE) and 11.9% for FY19 as per Accounts Estimates (AE). Clearly, there is an attempt to show high revenue by the State Government in its B.E. But the gap between the revenue and expenditure was high though no initiatives were made in the State Government budget to put the economy on high growth path or to fill the vacant posts or revive demand. The rising wage bills, interest and repayment obligations together add to Rs 107,000 crore for FY21 (BE), which are much high compared to revenue receipts. Thus, despite inflated revenue receipts in budget estimates, it falls short of Rs 19,000 crore compared to the committed expenditures of the state. The shortfall increases to Rs 55,700 crore in case one also adds other revenue expenditure worth Rs 36,700 crore. Most of this other revenue expenditure is actually also obligatory as some specified percentage of contribution from states is necessary to avail these centrally sponsored schemes/grants.

J. S. Bedi (✉) · G. Prabhakar
Institute for Development and Communication (IDC), Chandigarh, India

S. Singh et al. (eds.), *Covid-19 Pandemic and Economic Development*,
https://doi.org/10.1007/978-981-16-4442-9_22

1 Centrally Sponsored Schemes

The limited maneuverability which the states otherwise might have enjoyed has been curtailed as the states in order to avail the benefits of centrally sponsored schemes have to contribute their share or forgo the benefits. Thus, this top-down policy of the Centre, floated considering that it will equally fit all, leaves no scope for adjustment according to the state specificities. Another problem of these schemes relates to the frequent changes in priorities and agendas of the Central Government without any consultations with the States. The changes vary from one extreme to another. For example, the focus in the past has shifted from one extreme, i.e. to promote the state of art technology to enhance exports and bring competition to other extremes of favouring labour-intensive technology with the intent to generate more employment. The states after such shift in focus are left in lurch and often are compelled to protect such unviable projects, which in the absence of such policies might have not existed in the first place. The states like Punjab are severely hit as they are often left with no funds to pursue their own development priorities even after routine additional borrowings.

2 Fiscal Autonomy of the States

These financial crises are not new to a state like Punjab as conditions are continuously deteriorating since the late eighties with successive State and Central Governments failing to show any resolve to take the state out from crisis. In a way, the state has given up and left it to the market forces. As a result, the financial position of the state of Punjab goes on worsening day by day. The outstanding debts of the state is now hovering around Rs 2.5 lakh crore and with likely slow down in the SGDP, the revenue to the SGDP ratio of the state is expected to be as high as 46% by the end of FY21. This is much high compared to what is projected in BE at 38.5% for FY21. The estimates of 46% are derived based on contraction in real SGDP of Punjab by (-) 7% (Bedi, 2020). However, this may be even underestimation as things are taking much longer to normalise than initially expected. The public expenditure on the other hand is likely to increase with higher and higher percentage of population falling below poverty line with decline in opportunities for livelihood. Additionally, more and more enterprises are looking for Government support to sustain their businesses.

3 Public–Private Partnership (PPP) Model

The limitations of private or PPP model have been thoroughly exposed in delivering services like health, education, and delivery of other public goods especially at critical times like COVID-19. The public sector lacks resources to invest and emphasis was placed on market forces. COVID-19, however, has exposed that the private or PPP sectors cannot substitute public sector in critical services, but can act as complimentary. But unfortunately the revenue receipts of the centre and the states have steeply fallen after COVID-19. The Centre in a way is not facilitating the states even in such circumstances and though the limit for fiscal deficit has been enhanced to 5% of SGDP, but is linked to fulfillment of certain conditions. All these are indications of curtailment of fiscal autonomy of the states on one or the other pretext and that too even at difficult times like COVID-19, when the expansionary fiscal policy is essential and should have encouraged.

4 Punjab Has Made Limited Efforts

If one look at the BE of Punjab Government over the years, it becomes clear that there is candid admission by various State Governments that the state wishes to withdraw and leave everything to market forces. Therefore, the successive budget documents of Punjab Government have not made any attempt to explore new avenues for state's own revenue. Instead, even budgeted revenue of the state from its own resources show (-) 0.9% growth in FY21 (BE). Within this, the own revenue from tax sources grew by (-) 1.6% and non-tax revenue by 1.1%.

The combined effect of negative growth in revenue from the State's resources and high growth in revenue from centre's resources resulted in decline in the share of state's own revenue. The share of state's own tax revenue excluding GST declined from 27.4% in FY20 (RE) to 22.7% in FY21 (BE). While the share of state's own non-tax revenue in total tax revenue declined from 10.8% in F20 (RE) to 9.9% in FY21 (BE). This decline in the latter is acceptable as there are limited opportunities to expand state's own non-tax revenue. But slowdown in state's own tax revenue is the cause of major worry and requires careful analysis. Because of this decline, it is expected that the share of state's own tax revenue in total revenue has fallen by 4.7 percentage points during FY21 (BE). This includes 1 percentage point decline in state's sales tax, 0.6 percentage points in state's excise duties and 2.8 percentage points in share of duties on electricity and is caused by various factors.

But the revenue and grants from the centre are shown on a much higher side than generally achieved. Clearly, the intension is to put the blame of lack of initiatives on lower transfers from the centre compared to the budget at the later stage. The state's share in central taxes has been shown growing at 35.5% and centre's grant to Punjab excluding GST compensation grew by 56.4% in FY21 (BE). With the result, the share of central taxes in the state's revenue increased from 14.0% in FY20 (RE) to 15.9% in FY21 (BE) and that of centre's grant excluding GST compensation from 18 to 23.7%.

Problems Faced by Punjab: The downfall in revenue from domestic consumption of electricity during FY21 (BE) is caused by Rs 2,267 crore power subsidies to industries and another Rs 1,705 crore to domestic consumers, including Scheduled Caste, Backward Class, and below-poverty line consumers (*Times of India*, 2020). This is major reversal compared to past pattern as revenue from electricity duty jumped from Rs 2330 crore in FY19 (Accounts) to Rs 4479 in FY20 (RE). The main component of power subsidy goes to farm sector and is amounting to Rs 8,275 crore during FY21 (BE). With the successive hike in power tariff, the burden of subsidies is rising and there is a repeated debate going on to withdraw the same to medium and large holdings (>10 acres). These farmers account for approximately 65% of the cultivable area of the state but much larger share of power pumps are installed on their land. The issue of withdrawing subsidies above 10 acres though relevant, but is hanging on because of political implications.

In case of share of excise, the downfall in the budget estimates seems to have been projected on the basis of past experience and in a way is frank admission that the state is not doing anything to reverse the pattern. The excise duty budgeted for FY20 was Rs 6201 crore, which was 23% higher compared to Rs 5072 crore FY19 (Accounts). But the RE for FY20 are estimated at Rs 5676 crore, which are 12.6% higher compared to FY19. Based on the experience of FY20, the revenue from excise duty is targeted at Rs 6250 crore, almost the same as budgeted for FY20. The projected growth, therefore, at 10.1% for FY21 (BE) is low compared to growth achieved during FY20. The cause of low excise collection during FY21 was mainly leakages and illegal trade. The FY21 (BE) accepted this pattern to continue instead of focusing on improving the Governance. The state Government however is facing huge losses due to prolonged lockdown and has raised the excise duty and additional fee on liquor in the range of Rs 2 to Rs 50 on various quantities of sale of alcohol depending upon the type of liquor with the aim to generate additional revenue of Rs 145 crore in FY21.

Punjab faces lots of challenges even to decide excise duty: After the introduction of Goods and Services Tax (GST) in July 2017, many types of excise duty was subsumed except excise duty on petroleum and liquor. These are now the prime source of state's own revenue. But there exists several problems in the face of stiff competition from neighbouring states. Take, for instance, the recent crash in international crude oil prices and both centre and states try to extract maximum share in the pie by raising their respective excise duty till the point oil companies exhaust all the margins. Presently, Indian consumers pay over 250% collectively in excise duty to the state and the centre (Times Now, 2020). The base price of petrol is at Rs 18 while over Rs 50 per litre is levied on top of it in taxes.

The Centre has comparative advantage here in the sense that any hike in rates raises prices uniformly across the country. The states on the other hand face competition and need to take into consideration specifically the policies of neighbouring states. If the neighbouring state keeps its rates lower, then the state with higher rates have danger of losing a large segment of consumers residing in boundary periphery to the state with lower rates. The duties imposed on petroleum product are the main source of revenue for the states and no state wants to lose its consumers to the neighbouring states.

Because of this comparative advantage of the Centre, it was able to raise major hike in excise duty on petroleum products twice after the recent fall in international crude price. On March 14, 2020, the Centre hiked excise duty on petrol and diesel by Rs 3 per litre each and then again on May 5 by a record Rs 10 per litre in case of petrol and Rs 13 on diesel. These two hikes are expected to raise central revenue by Rs 2 lakh crore during FY 2020–21 (Bloomberg, 2020).

Against this, the Punjab Government reversed its earlier policy of keeping petroleum prices low compared to neighbouring states as that resulted in Revenue loss of Rs 800 crore. It raised VAT on diesel from 11.0 to 15.2% and on petrol from 20.1 to 23.3% on May 6, 2020 (Khanna, 2020). A further revision was initiated on 15th June, 2020 by the Punjab Government to raise VAT on diesel from 15.2 to 16.0% and on petrol from 23.3 to 26.4%. The aim was to increase the state's falling revenue, but with the result the petroleum prices in Punjab became costly by Rs 6.6 per litre and diesel by Rs 4.9 per litre compared to Chandigarh.

Thus, fixing appropriate VAT on petroleum product require careful consideration as high rates does not merely increase/decrease per unit rate for consumers residing in periphery areas neighbouring other states, but affects the revenue from consumers residing all over the state. It needs to be also understood that though per unit rates are important, but more important is credibility and Governance as consumer want petrol free of adulteration and in appropriate quantity. The state also needs to take into consideration the other implications on economy of high petroleum prices.

The other major source of revenue for the states is VAT on alcohol, but higher rates in this case also results in higher smuggling of alcohol. Same is the issue with higher taxes on vehicles as it leads to increasing instances of registering vehicle on address outside the state. Therefore, despite fiscal autonomy to states in such circumstances, the states have to act cautiously.

Revenue loss for not having state's own capital: One of the major limitations of Punjab is to not have its own state capital as it loses to a major consumer centre. The state capital is always considered a major source of revenue, but it has assumed specific importance after GST implementation under which revenue generation has shifted from production to consumption point. Punjab, therefore, needs to either fight for Chandigarh as its state capital or set-up its own state capital and that too at geographically central place within the state to protect revenue under the new system. Delay is not in the interest of the state (Bedi & Prabhakar, ongoing work).

Goods and Services Tax (GST) has eroded fiscal autonomy of Punjab: In the absence of GST, the Punjab Government would have enjoyed autonomy on 56.4% of its revenue resources during FY20 as against 49.9% during FY21. But GST implementation has eroded the state's fiscal autonomy by 18.1 percentage points. According to FY21 (BE), Punjab enjoys autonomy only on 31.8% of its revenue resources, while it was 38.3% during FY20 (RE). But the advantage of GST implementation for the states especially during COVID-19 slowdown is that it protects 14% per annum growth in SGST revenue for five years, i.e. till 2022. However, slow growth of SGST even at normal times (without COVID-19) for the state like Punjab is extreme sign of worry for the future especially after 2022, when there will be no assurance in the form of GST compensation for any shortfall. Therefore, active debate is taking place for exploring the possibility of extending this kind of assurance beyond 2022. In the case of Punjab, the state's own GST has grown by merely 1.3% during FY20 (RE), while the growth shown is 18% in FY21 (BE) despite BE for FY21 taken (-) 7.3% lower compared to FY20 (BE). This means the revenue receipts from SGST are remaining much below the initial expectations and even by the past trend the SGST projected for FY21 (BE) would have remained unachievable without COVID-19 implications. However, this shortfall would have been matched by additional SGST compensation. But the co-operative federalism trust with which the GST concept was introduced has taken a major hit after the Centre has gone back on several of its commitments with the shortfall in SGST revenue collection expected to cross more than Rs 3 lakh crore during FY21. Some amicable solution, however, is now expected with Centre's latest proposal to opt for Rs 1.10 lakh crore, which it will pass on to the states as back-to-back loan.

5 State's Policies to Refund SGST Are anti- GST

It is pertinent here to mention that one of the main underlying objectives of GST implementation was to enforce one nation one market principle with uniform indirect taxation policy and to bring transparency. But, the way the Centre is looking the other way, the states are vigorously waiving off SGST to attract new investments. The selective reimbursement of SGST allows such units to earn extra rent and goes against the principle of uniform taxation across the country. This all is happening under the Ease of Doing Business (EoDB) initiative, which is rigorously monitored by the centre in consultancy with the World Bank. This all raises doubt about the real intent of the Centre and seriousness to enforce one country one market principle. This all is actually resulting in states to lose one of the important sources of their revenue by competing with each other in a beggar-thy-neighbour policy. The centre should have pro-actively desisted states to pursue any such policy which goes against the very intent of one nation one market principle. But the Centre instead seems more interested to find ways to intervene in the matter primarily classified as state subject such as agriculture 'mandi' tax. Another major challenge faced regarding GST online implementation is increase in fraudulent refund claims including by exporters.

6 GST Subsumed Most of Indirect Taxes of the States

The Centre has started imposing fresh cesses of permanent nature due to lack of tax buoyancy, which need not be shared. These include Swachh Bharat cess, Krishi Kalyan cess, road and infrastructure cess and the special additional central excise on petroleum products. The cesses/surcharges are, thus, becoming contentious and suspicion on this is further raised with the Comptroller and Auditor General (CAG) pointing lack of transparency in its accounts. The states are losing with shifts of taxes moving away from sharable revenue under GST and other gross taxes including the corporation taxes, which have lots of potential. The states are now pushing to abolish cesses/surcharges except its temporary use and that for specific purposes. This all explains the low share of states in divisible portion at 32.4% during FY16–20 compared to 42% recommended in the 14th Finance Commission.

7 Way Forward for Punjab

Punjab is facing severe financial constraints and things are unlikely to improve in case the state takes corrective measures in bringing efficiency in its resource management system. The challenges which the State Government faces after depletion in its autonomy after implementation of GST needs to be tackled by looking for new revenue avenues for state's own resources without compromising state's competitiveness. In this regard, the SGST refund to units should be immediately stopped and in fact the Centre should intervene to stop such bad practices across the country.

It is also essential that the state should start taking requisite steps to fix accountability at various levels of hierarchy with appropriate autonomy. The state should start thinking to tap the potential areas from which revenue can be generated as things are likely to worsen after 2022, when the states will no more enjoy shield of revenue protection for shortfall in SGST. There is, thus, a need for thorough review of state's revenue and expenditure such as various subsidies including on electricity tariff should be examined. Higher tariff can be imposed on ownership of more than one house. This will help not only to improve revenue, but also to curtail speculative activities. This will make the land and property affordable for small enterprises, which will help in improving employment and revising demand, which is very crucial for sustainable development. There is also need to expand the tax base by taxing all irrespective of sector, if combined income from various sources exceeds some limit.

References

Bedi, J. S. (2020, May 12) Economic Implications of COVID-19 on Punjab, India and the Way Forward. *Dailyworld*: E-Paper.

Bedi, J. S., and Prabhakar, G. (On going) Inept GST Implementation Hurts Composite GST Units. Manuscript in Preparation.

Bedi, J. S., and Prabhakar, G. (2019) Impact of Supply Side Policy Initiatives: Doing Business and GST on the Structure of Indian Economy and Small Scale Sector. Department of Planning, Punjab.

Department for Promotion of Industry and Internal Trade, Ministry of Commerce and Industry, Government of India. (2019) Ease of Doing Business Reforms. Retrieved from https://dipp.gov.in/.

Department of Finance, Government of Punjab. (2020) Budget at Glance: 2020–21. Retrieved from https://www.cbgaindia.org/wp-content/uploads/2020/03/Budget-at-a-Glance-2020-21-Punjab.pdf.

ET Now Digital. (2020, June 9) With Petrol Base Price at Rs 18, You End Up Paying 275% in Taxes to Central, State Govts. *Times Now*. Retrieved from https://www.timesnownews.com/business-economy/industry/article/with-petrol-base-price-at-rs-18-you-end-up-paying-275-in-taxes-to-state-central-govt/603833.

Goods and Services Tax Council, Government of India. (2020, October 12) 43rd GST Council Meeting. Retrieved from http://www.gstcouncil.gov.in/meetings.

Khanna, R. M. (2020, June 15) Punjab Increases VAT on Fuel from Midnight; Prices to Go Up. *The Tribune*. Retrieved from https://www.tribuneindia.com/news/punjab/punjab-increases-vat-on-fuel-from-midnight-prices-to-go-up-99579.

Khanna, R. M. (2020, June 1) Liquor to Cost More in Punjab as Govt Imposes Covid Cess. *The Tribune*. Retrieved from https://www.tribuneindia.com/news/punjab/liquor-to-cost-more-in-punjab-as-govt-imposes-covid-cess-92918.

Khanna, R. M. (2020, May 17) Excise Revenue Down Rs 1,820 Cr in 11 Months. *The Tribune*. Retrieved from https://www.tribuneindia.com/news/punjab/excise-revenue-down-rs-1-820-cr-in-11-months-86077.

PRS Legislative Research. (2020) Punjab Budget Analysis: 2020–21. Retrieved from https://www.prsindia.org/sites/default/files/budget_files/State%20Budget%20Analysis%20-%20Punjab%202020-21%20for%20upload.pdf.

PTI. (2020, June 21) Petrol and Diesel Prices Hiked for 16th Day in a Row. Bloomberg. Retrieved from https://www.bloombergquint.com/economy-finance/diesel-price-hits-record-high-after-rates-hiked-for-15th-day-in-a-row-petrol-up-35-paise

Randhawa, M. (2010, May 17) Terrorism Over but Punjab Continues to Reel Under Heavy Debt. *Hindustan Times*. Retrieved from https://www.hindustantimes.com/india/terrorism-over-but-punjab-continues-to-reel-under-heavy-debt/story-mk2WWlLJZcE6VCHhEHv1lI.html.

Sirhindi, M. (2020, March 1) Punjab Budget: Rs 12,000 Crore for Power Subsidies Won't Bring PSPCL Out of Red. *Times of India*. Retrieved from https://timesofindia.indiatimes.com/city/ludhiana/budget-manpreets-rs-12248-cr-for-power-subsidies-may-not-bring-pspcl-out-of-red/articleshow/74421739.cms.

Tribune News Service. (2020, October 17) Centre, States Cross Hurdle over Sharing of GST Revenue. *The Tribune*. Retrieved from https://www.tribuneindia.com/news/nation/centre-states-cross-hurdle-over-sharing-of-gst-revenue-157332#:~:text=The%20Centre%20and%20opposition%2Druled,lend%20it%20to%20the%20states.

Public Policy and Governance Reforms for Post-COVID-19 Recovery and Sustainable growth and Development in Punjab

Sukhpal Singh, Lakhwinder Singh, and Kamal Vatta

1 Introduction

Punjab economy has turned from a leader to a laggard among Indian states during the first two decades of the twenty-first century. The first and the second waves of COVID-19 pandemic have further devastated both the inhabitants of the state and the state economy itself. In Punjab, the losses due to first wave of COVID-19 were 13.6% of the GSDP and it cost Punjab 88% of its estimated revenue for the month of April 2020

S. Singh
Centre for Management in Agriculture, Indian Institute of Management Ahmedabad, Ahmedabad, Gujarat, India

L. Singh (✉)
Commerce, Management and Economics, Khalsa College, Punjabi University, Patiala, Punjab, India
e-mail: lakhwindergill@pbi.ac.in

K. Vatta
Department of Economics and Sociology, Punjab Agricultural University, Ludhiana, Punjab, India

S. Singh et al. (eds.), *Covid-19 Pandemic and Economic Development*,
https://doi.org/10.1007/978-981-16-4442-9_23

with Rs. 3000 crore were being lost every month. Further, about 10 lakh persons lost their source of livelihood due to the lockdown and Punjab exports fell by 40%. For the year 2020–2021, the total loss of revenue was estimated to be Rs. 50,000 crore (FICCI, 2020). Though the Punjab economy was seen as an iconic model of economic development in the developing world due to Green Revolution based agricultural and allied growth and development, but the development process took a back seat due to fault lines in the model of economic development and also due to change in the nature and character of the state in Punjab. The change in the direction of the development and its consequences became only more evident during the period of COVID-19 pandemic. Therefore, this chapter is an attempt to provide an alternative set of public policy and strategy mechanisms to overcome the structural problems of the Punjab economy and ensure a better and secure future for its citizens.

2 Fiscal Policy and Revival of Punjab Economy

Fiscal policy is the most dynamic instrument of economic development available to the subnational governments. The state government can use fiscal policy for social overhead capital formation that determines the pace and direction of economic development. But, the fiscal policy of Punjab has remained under siege from the last three and a half decades. The consequence is low revenue generation and low investment despite high per capita income. It is widely held principle in economic theory and policy that public investment and capital formation in the developing countries crowding in private investment.

Punjab's public resource mobilisation remains a major challenge. Its own tax revenue share in total revenue receipts has been only 51% compared with 63% in Haryana and 62% in Tamil Nadu during 2015–2021. Further, the State GST is only 42% of own tax revenue compared with 70% in J&K, 55% in Bihar, and 46% in West Bengal. Punjab's land revenue share in own tax revenue is nil compared with 5% in Haryana, and Punjab's committed expenditure as percentage on its revenue receipt is the highest in India (80%). The state spends the highest percentage (10%) on administration and police which is only 6% in Haryana and 4% in Rajasthan and Gujarat. The state's debt servicing as percentage of revenue receipts (84%) is again the highest in India which is only 40% for neighbouring Haryana and 24% in case of Rajasthan. In fact, Punjab's expenditure on human development is only 19% of total compared with

27% in Bihar and 28% in Rajasthan. This leads to Punjab under-spending on per capita basis and the gap is as high as 45% which is only lower than Goa. Compared with this, Haryana over-spent by 2% and Orissa by 4% on per capita basis. Even the rural development expenditure is only 1.1% compared with 4.2% in Haryana and 7.7% in Rajasthan. Its health expenditure's share of budget at 4.2% is also one of the lowest in India (Tiwari and Surya, 2020).

The severe deficiency in capital formation in Punjab has prevented private investment from taking place. Thus, the desired structural transformation, even in the presence of Green Revolution generated surpluses, could not happen. The most important sectors for modern economic development are health and education but expenditure in these sector has dramatically reduced over the decades. This has created a situation of deficiency in human capital. Therefore, the investment opportunities created by the Information and Communication Technology revolution bypassed Punjab economy and expectedly the ongoing fourth Industrial Revolution opportunities are likely to bypass as well. The low revenue to State Domestic Product (SDP) and low investment in capital formation have long run impact on the Punjab economy and consequence has been higher debt–SDP ratio (Singh and Singh, 2012; Singh et al., 2020). This has happened because of several reasons such as a rampant tax evasion, high subsidies and centralisation of tax collection and distribution of tax revenue by the Union government. Therefore, it is suggested that there is a dire need to revamp revenue and non-revenue collection system to plug the leaky bucket.

Another important policy change urgently required is to release the financial resources from inefficiency in generation and distribution of electricity. The high procurement rates of electricity fraudulently increase financial burden and show high amount of subsidies given to agriculture, rural households and to industrial units. When we compare power tariffs of Punjab with other states, they come out to be substantially higher and burden the common citizens and also productive economic activities. Thus, it is suggested to reduce these tariffs which would lead to lower total burden of subsidies and the saved resources can be invested in capital formation. It is important to note that during the COVID-19 period, the facility to borrow more money on the one hand and the Fifteen Finance Commission of India's new formula for devolution of resources have increased the net flow of resources to the state government. The state government can resort to more innovative borrowing by floating bonds on the pattern of Kerala government which will generate more resources for social capital formation. When we look at the sufferings of the various sectors of the economy, the Punjab government has not been able to offer any much needed package due to constraints of low revenue generation and burden of high subsidies. The resources saved from the inefficiency of electricity generation and distribution alone can be a big source of developing a new programme of employment of the youth productively and their expertise can be used to better delivery of services of various forms including generation of new social capital formation. This programme will also help in arresting the skill loss during the COVID-19 pandemic generated unemployment of the educated youth.

3 Agricultural Revival

So far as the impact of migrant labour is concerned, Punjab needs 60 lakh migrant labour for Rabi season and migrant workers account for 80% of paddy transplanting workers. The state suffered due to shortage of these workers and therefore, wage rates in the farm sector went up significantly. Due to this, there were even local level tensions between farmers and local workers on the wage rate issue. Mostly, farmers managed this crisis by resorting to more of family labour in the case of small and marginal farmers, more machines in the case of medium and large farmers besides the use of local labour by such farmers. These farmers also substituted machines for labour and 20% even stored produce before sale during the previous Rabi season. Similarly, the informal dairy milk sector suffered due to milk holidays, deferred payment, and higher cost of production due to disruption in input supply chains. The food and vegetable production suffered a similar fate as milk and similar was the case with poultry and piggery farms and floriculture because all of them suffered market loss due to COVID-19. The poultry industry suffered losses of US$3 billion due to a drop in demand and logistical challenges. The estimated losses in dairy were of the order of 25–30% due to drop in demand with many farmers resorting to distress sale. In some states like Karnataka, the floriculture farmers were given a pay out of Rs. 25,000 each (Govindan, 2021) but Punjab has not provided any such support. It was only the foodgrains sector which could withstand the effects of COVID-19 and 97% farmers could sell their wheat crop at MSP. However, the contribution of crop sector growth in the value added of the SDP is near zero.

Punjab economy, including agriculture, has been in crisis for some time on various fronts though its agricultural sector was able to deal with COVID-19 crisis relatively successfully. However, unlike in the past, Government of Punjab was quick to set up a Committee of experts to suggest a strategy for revival of the state economy in the post-COVID-19 medium and long term scenario which submitted its first report in July 2020. If this interim report is anything to go by, then the portends are very clear. The report taking a multisectoral approach to build resilience and recovery aims at opening up the state economy to private sector, especially the agricultural sector, in all possible ways (Singh, 2021). Punjab is already suffering from overdose of unregulated market forces and if similar and higher dose of such market oriented measures will be implemented without adequate regulation and oversight, that will, instead of attending to existing crisis, will only intensify it further.

4 Industrial and Trade Sectors

In the MSME sector 99% units are micro and employ 25 lakh workers and their estimated losses due to COVID-19 were Rs. 40,000 crores. The sector suffered from major problems of very high power tariff comparable with only Gujarat (10% of tax revenue in Punjab), lack of skilled local labour and missing outsourcing facilities like plug and play or rental factories. The urban informal sector which has trade sub-sector accounting for 41% of enterprises and workers with 30% workers being informal sector, accounts for 50% of value added, suffers from poor working capital availability, market knowledge, commercial prudence, lack of Unique Selling Propositions (USPs), human resource planning, and networking and technical edge. The textile sector of the state which accounts for 23% of industrial productions and 38% of exports suffered loss of export with 60% of orders being cancelled due to COVID-19 and even the domestic demand shrinking by 15%. This sector, along with food processing sector, also experienced shortage of labour during and after the lockdown.

The industrial policy, 2017 states that the state government will help identify and transfer various village common lands and unutilised government lands to the proposed infrastructure development authority for development of industrial parks, besides a land bank being maintained by this authority. It would also design a land pooling scheme for acquisition of land for industrial parks which will be in partnership with the land owners, especially in the case of village common lands where a revenue sharing arrangement will be worked out with the village panchayats (GoP, 2017). The targeting of panchayat lands is going to be problematic as there are already struggles going on in some parts of the state where marginalised sections are claiming their share of such lands for leasing these for farming as provided in the law. This would also affect the income of panchayats which supports local development work as these lands generated income of Rs. 292.7 crore across all villages of Punjab in 2016–2017. Also, there are some 20,796 acres of such land (in 2016–2017) which have been encroached upon by local powerful interests which need to be vacated and brought under panchayat control and leasing. The important question which can be asked is: why can't a revenue sharing model be used for privately owned land for its use for industrial development, as has been done in Haryana and Andhra Pradesh?

On other hand, draft state agricultural policy (2018) states:

"The Government shall make efforts to preserve and restore ecosystems and to promote climate resilient agriculture by ensuring that:

> 'Village common lands are used to provide required biodiversity to protect agriculture. The cultivation of paddy in such lands shall not be permitted. Additionally, a biodiversity reserve of about one hectare will be planned in each village'. It is important to note that under the present leasing policy for these lands, there is no restriction on growing any crop by the leasee during the period of lease which is generally one year."

It further goes on to say:

i. Make provisions to give, on a priority basis, panchayat land of the village on lease for agriculture to Cooperatives/Societies/Groups of economically and socially disadvantaged farmers.
ii. Make certain that auction of panchayat land reserved for *dalits* is for use by *dalits* only, irrespective of all other considerations (PSFFWWC, 2018).

Thus, the 2017 industrial policy of the state which proposes to take away village panchayat lands for industry is at a complete cross purpose with the proposed state agricultural policy. Even the *Vidhan Sabha* Committee report on farmer suicides and the reasons thereof, does not pay attention to the issue of leasing of common land to the SCs. The issue of access to village panchayat lands to these households for farming at

1/3rd of the going lease rates is not even mentioned. Their loans are not recommended for waiver, only for consideration (PVSS, 2017). It is sad ot state here that even after four years of the state draft policy being released, it has not even been accepted by the state government, leaving aside its implementation. That is a telling commentary on the state of affairs in the state that despite it being a state domain, the government has not bothered to make a policy for its largest sector in terms of engagement of workers, if not value added.

5 Education and Health

Even education and health infrastructure and access to health and education facilities were not spared in the case of poor households as only 2.2% of such households in rural Punjab had laptops or computers for online learning compared with 5.2% of urban poor households in 2017–2018. One new development due to COVID-19 in the school sector was that with the closing down of many small private schools, the government schools witnessed 2.1 lakh new admissions. This 'back to government school' phenomenon is an opportunity for the government schools to cultivate and maintain public trust in them. Despite this, only 13% of the budget of the state government is for education which is one of the lowest allocations (GoP, 2021).

6 Gender

Many quick surveys of the impact of COVID-19 in India have revealed that women suffered additional hardships due to pre-existing gender inequalities and restricted mobility and social norms. Though, there were fewer female casualties than male due to COVID-19 but women still experienced adverse impact of male member's death as they were main earners. Further, the domestic work of cooking and fetching water increased due to the return of male migrants and women also suffered more hunger and malnutrition due to the fact that in a rural household generally they are the last ones to eat. They were also chances of higher domestic violence due to 'husbands being at home' more of the time during COVID-19 period. In terms of employment, the return of migrants back to their home places due to COVID-19, women were crowded out from local employment, e.g. MGNREGS where women were 20% less likely to regain employment. It is also reported that 62% of the households with returned migrants had reduced the number of food items eaten per meal and 50% had reduced number of meals eaten in a day (Agarwal, 2021).

7 Migrants, Marginalised, and Food Security

The local and migrant labour household suffered higher food insecurity due to closure of schools and *anganwadis*. Though Punjab home delivered food grains to school children and even deposited cooking cost into their bank accounts (GoP, 2021), it was unlike Kerala which delivered food kits to the school children at their doorstep. The budget 2021–2022 of the state provides for night shelters for slum dwellers but there is no provision for any shelter for the migrant workers. Rather in the name of labour welfare, the shops and establishments are allowed to open 24 hours and self-certification of compliance with labour laws is allowed to the employers (GoP, 2021).

The state government, in collaboration with Multinational Corporations (MNCs) in farm input and machinery sector, and even global sustainability initiatives like Better Cotton Initiative (BCI) are concerned more about cotton growers and take farmer concerns about labour shortage or high labour costs as real problems.[1]

These agencies and projects conceive solutions like the High Density Planting System (HDPS)[2] in cotton to not enhance yields but facilitate mechanical picking of cotton, completely unaware or unmindful of the consequences of mechanical harvesting for worker livelihoods, local or

[1] BCI refers to cotton production which adheres to the following principles at farm level: minimum use of crop protection chemicals, conservation and efficient use of water, maintenance soil health, conservation of natural habitats, maintenance of fibre quality, and decent working conditions for farmers, including workers. BCI—a multistakeholder initiative (MSI) is run by global consortium of textile and readymade garment brands since 2005. India has one of the largest numbers of BC farmers and BCI trained farmers and the second largest licensed farmer share in total (92%) as it has the highest number of projects in BC globally (Singh, 2017).

[2] HDPS refers to a system of cotton sowing in which a minimum number of plants are grown per unit area (5000 as against only 2–3 thousand at present) and in a manner of spacing which makes it amenable to single or just two mechanical harvests of the crop. This is done in order to compensate for loss of yield due to absence of multiple pickings done manually at present. The mechanical picking is also supposed to eliminate the need for labour and reduce cost of picking though the harvesting machines are highly capital intensive for individual small holders to own (Singh, 2017).

migrant. The HDPS is being advocated in order to compensate the loss of yield which would happen with mechanical picking as it would be only one or two pickings over five months under HDPS instead of 4–5 pickings manually over 6–7 months. It is also forgotten that the mechanically picked cotton would have higher trash content than hand-picked cotton and would require pre-cleaning. This, in the presence of interstate migration of landless workers from states like Punjab and Haryana to as far as Gujarat for just cotton picking, exposes the so called 'shortage of labour' argument made by cotton farmers and the state government and private agencies and, therefore, need for mechanisation. The migrant labour households explain their long distance migration for this seasonal work in terms of lack of adequate employment opportunities back home and caste based discrimination and mistreatment by farmer employers besides lower earnings from the activity due to lower yields in their home states, in general.[3] Even state agencies do not think of proactively involving workers in high value crops, instead of throwing them out of work. This is also partly explained by the only farmer focused thinking of the agencies as well as lack of institutional variety and diversity in the state (Punjab) unlike other states (like Gujarat) where there are vibrant NGOs which work with farmers and workers. In this situation, any sustainability initiative in cotton or any other crop falls back on existing institutions which are rooted in conventional Green Revolution technologies and belief systems whether it is about yields or markets or social issues (Singh, 2017).

It is heartening to note that the Ahluwalia Committee report suggested many measures including extending benefits of labour laws and housing for migrant workers and even providing funds to districts keeping in view the population of migrants in each district (Singh, 2021).

But, an analysis of the policies shows that there is complete lack of a coherent thinking on the issue of landless worker livelihoods while ceilings on land holding and land leasing restrictions are being liberalised by the state (Singh, 2020a). The interests of the landless do not seem to matter much and what is due to them in law has to be claimed by them with sustained and violent struggles as the state machinery and local institutions like panchayats are generally against the *Dalit* interests as they are dominated by upper caste and dominant class representatives. Even some

[3] Personal interviews with Punjabi migrant cotton workers in Gujarat in 2015.

of the farmers unions have also opposed the land struggles of the *Dalits* in some areas of the state. Therefore, commonality of the interests of landless and landed can not materialise and would harm the interests of the marginalised, if attempted.

8 Ways Forward

The challenges for Punjab to cope with COVID-19 impacts and move on to an economic recovery and growth are multiple and need various short term, medium term and long-term strategies. To begin with the state needs to create demand by enhancing public expenditure. The agro-industrial sector needs concessions to deal with lost markets and revenues which (as recommended by FICCI, 2020) would include exemption from cesses like Rural Development Fund Cess and APMC market fee, e.g. for Basmati exporters. The Micor, Small, and Medium Enterprise sector enterprises can be given collateral free loans and their Employee Provident Fund contribution can be reduced to 10%. In the case of perishable produce, the state needs strengthening and building of new infrastructure like pack houses, cold storages, cold chains, and new wet produce markets. More importantly given the gendered nature of many sectors and markets, there is a need to design and implement gender centric intervention in the agricultural and rural domain, including agricultural markets.

On the agricultural front, the Ahluwalia Committee report has not bothered to examine the recent draft agricultural policy of the state which had proposed some more practical measures on this aspect. The committee sets the objective of crop diversification as reducing the area under common paddy by about one million hectares (out of total 3.1 million hacs under paddy) over the next 6–7 years along with a blueprint for diversification into other crops over the same period. It recommends that Punjab should target doubling of area (from about 3 lakh hacs now) under high value fruit and vegetable crops that are suitable to Punjab. But, it is sad that other crops like maize which the state has been trying to unsuccessfully promote, have not been given due attention. The recommended paddy area reduction target is a half-way approach as if the paddy crop is the culprit and Punjab is not the suitable state for it, then, it should have targeted larger area reduction from under paddy. Otherwise, it is only postponing the problem, not resolving it altogether (Singh, 2021).

The state can also leverage its advantage in maize production for diversification of agriculture as it is a low input intensive crop, by partnering with the maize consuming industry like poultry feed and promoting various types of direct linkages with the farmers.

Many relevant sustainable technologies and practices like System of Rice/Root Intensification, micro irrigation, and organic and natural farming have been ignored despite the fact that atleast some farmers in the state have attempted organic and natural farming without any state support for some time now. That is quite surprising to note at a time when many states have gone fully organic or mandated themselves to move into more sustainable farming practices like natural farming with a policy (Singh, 2021).

It is well known that farmers face production risk due to various reasons and they need to be protected from such risk. But, the report does not even mention crop insurance which is about covering production risk of the growers. Punjab never implemented the Pradhan Mantri Fasal Bima Yojana and had declared three years earlier that it would come up with its own crop insurance corporation and policy. But, the farmers are still waiting for it when even PMFBY has been made voluntary for farmers by the Union government (Singh, 2021).

At the same time, the upgrading of worker skills needs to be provided for alongside that of growers, in order to make them better workers as crop based projects are not just about value creation and capture by the dominant stakeholders but also about value sharing with other, especially weaker and smaller stakeholders like farm workers, from a livelihood perspective. There is a need for skilling of farm labour to meet quality challenges and to produce competitively which needs their creative involvement in work which can come from fair and just labour relations regimes supported by private agencies, Multi-Stakeholder Initiatives (MSIs), state, Non-Government Organisations (NGOs), and farmer and worker agencies.

8.1 Agricultural Market Reforms

On farm produce market reforms, the Ahluwalia Committee recommends going beyond the Union government enacted farm Acts to open up agricultural markets without any regulation. It says 'Legal changes for directly buying from farmers along with investments in value chain infrastructure is the best way to reduce market risk and increase the farmers share in the consumer's rupee'. It is sad that report is still stuck with farmer share in consumer rupee while focussing on value chains. If it is the age of value chains, then why use an outdated methodology to assess farmer benefit from such value chain participation? Can a potato farmer really get very high share in a potato chips and other such high value product value chain? Can s/he not be better off even getting a lower share in a modern value chain but higher returns in absolute terms than that in a traditional channel? (Singh, 2021).

There is no doubt that *arhtiyas* have been cornering a large part of the APMC mandi benefits by acting as key agents in the interlocking of the product and credit markets on the one hand and of the input and output markets on the other, by taking advantage of weak institutional credit system for marginal and small farmers in Punjab. But this interlinkage is problematic mainly for small and marginal farmers as large farmers are able to avoid it.

The *arthiyas* have a direct or indirect presence in the market for farm inputs such as seeds, pesticides, and fertilisers which are bought on credit extended by the *arthiyas* to the farmers. The *arhtiya* finances it with cash or in kind (through *parchi* or hand-written slip system) and here, there is overpricing of such products bought on credit. Thus, the *arhtiya* is able to interlock produce, credit and farm input markets and ensure the recovery when the payment to farmer is made through him. Besides making money on farm produce (both from commission as well as margins as many of them are also *pucca arhtiyas* who can buy farm produce) and inputs, they also charge interest ranging from 18 to 36% on such loans depending on the credit rating of the farmers in terms of volume of produce they bring or the land they own which (the latter) can be used to recover such loans by mortgaging it or buying it. The *arhtiya* also charges interest on interest on unpaid loan besides on the outstanding principal after every season. Thus, there are multiple methods of exploitation of the farmer by the *arhtiya*.

Though farmers have *kisaan* credit cards (KCCs) or cash credit limits (CCLs) from banks and Primary Agricultural Credit Societies (PACS) based on their land and cropping pattern, but when they are not able to repay the crop loans at the end of the crop season, it is *arhtiya* who steps in and lends to farmers to avoid defaulting for the next season. The farmers then borrow again from the bank/PACS after such repayment to bank or PACS and repay the loan to the *arhtiya*. Thus, the *arhtiya* helps farmers from turning into defaulters. After all, a public auction of the farmer's land by the bank who has defaulted is also seen as humiliation in rural Punjab. The *arthiyas* lend for even non-agricultural and social purposes and their cash credit limits for farmers is more open ended unlike that of the banks. This is also one of the reasons that *arhtiya*–farmer relations are now being projected as *nau-mas ka rishta* (nail and flesh-like relations) and not exploitative, even by most of the farmer unions.

Although there are *arhtiyas* in Punjab's fruit and vegetable mandis too and they get 5% commission compared with 2.5% in grain markets, there is no MSP or public procurement for crop produce sold in these mandis. Therefore, interlocking is not that widely prevalent in these markets as the *arhtiya*'s risk in lending would be higher in the case of sales made without public purchase. The *arhtiya* associations in the past have asked their members not to lend to *basmati* paddy growers as that would be risky without the guarantee of repayment backed by public procurement at MSP! *Arhtiyas* know that they would not be able to successfully carry on lending without public procurement of grains and that is why they are and have been protesting and not willing to make direct payments to farmer in the state over the last more than 10 years. They even threatened to boycott procurement of paddy in the past, as now, if FCI paid directly to farmers.

This business of moneylending is facilitated by the MSP policy and public procurement of grains (wheat and paddy) from APMC markets. This enables the *arthiyas* to lend without risk as their dues are recovered from the payments by buyers, including the FCI which are made to *arhtiyas*, not to the famers for their produce. The poor priority sector credit policies of the state have also helped *arthiya* as now priority sector targets by banks can be met by various means without necessarily lending only to farmers. The norms for farm lending have been tweaked so that that lending to agriculture is no longer about crops and farms alone; they include loans for agribusiness activities like cold storages, food processing, and the like. Also, if banks can't lend to meet the target of Priority Sector Lending (PSL), they can deposit the money in Rural Infrastructure Development Funds (RIDF) with NABARD and also buy priority sector loan accounts from other banks that have exceeded their targets.

Since the state is involved in permitting these players to operate in grain markets by granting licenses (both *kaccha* and *pucca*), and, since the state has not conducted elections to the APMC bodies on which *arhtiyas* have representation along with farmers and traders besides some co-operatives and the government, they are able to dominate the APMCs. The Punjab agricultural marketing board (PMB) and APMC level elected representative appointments are made by nomination for the last many years and even decades (Singh, 2020b).

To resolve some of the so called issues in direct payment like lack of land records with large number of leasee farmers, the state government should finalise the draft pro-corporate land leasing bill with adequate amendments for making it pro-small farmer. Further, the state government should amend the Agricultural Produce and Livestock Markets (APLM) Act 2017 to make direct payment to farmers actually direct and, not direct through the *arhtiya*! The said Act also needs amendment to provide for private markets even in wheat, paddy and cotton as the state can't be the only buyer. This kind of market monopsony in cotton in Maharashtra was abolished long back.

8.2 Role of Collectives

The farm sector in Punjab needs farmers' and their agencies' control in value chains which is not even thought of in the Committee report as it does not spend any space on role of farmer agencies. It does not even recognise that Punjab has been a laggard in Farmer Producer Organisation (FPO) promotion and is likely to miss the bus again. Also, the report has not found it necessary to provide for any mechanisms to protect farmer interest while suggesting opening up of farm produce markets for private players (Singh, 2021).

The Ahluwalia Committee report seems very keen on privatising all spheres of agricultural space in the state as it recommends that the Government of Punjab could strengthen or even hand over the Custom Hiring Centres (CHCs, supported with public money by the state since 15 years, numbering 1500 and operated by PACS) to a new class of agri-entrepreneurs, which have greater potential outreach and can offer cost-effective rental services. The CHCs could be availed by start-ups as well to showcase and demonstrate machines and digital solutions for improving farm efficiency. Instead of paying lip service to FPOs in the report, it was better if the report had recognised Punjab as the pioneer in setting up PACS based CHCs during the last decade when no state was even thinking of it. Rather, it has suggested their privatisation without any reason (Singh, 2021).

8.3 *Institutional and Organisational Aspects*

That the Ahluwalia Committee report is all about encouraging large scale in farming is clear from the fact that it recommends increasing herd sizes of animals to 10–15 for small and marginal farmers, (50–100 litres of milk) and 40–50 (500–1000 litres) for large farmers and commercial farms by extending loans through NAABRD, for milch cattle. Though Punjab has been already promoting large scale commercial dairy farms, but the work of agencies like National Dairy Services of NDDB in setting up Baani Milk Producers Company and even of Punjab Milkfed has been given a go by. It is often said that Punjabis like everything big! But, that is not necessarily better. There are many empirical studies which show that size of the farm is not an issue but what you do on that farm for whom, why, how, when and how much which makes the difference. One only needs to go to Malerkotla to see how small farmers can also make money from agriculture, rather agribusiness (Singh, 2021).

The most problematic recommendation of the Committee report is about opening up of agricultural land lease market. It states 'Ideally, farmers should be allowed to lease out land freely for long periods in an environment in which the rights of land owners are fully protected. However, if there is resistance to such unrestricted leasing, a graduated policy could be introduced which allows a period of 15–20 years for plantations and orchards, agroforestry and protected cultivation. A period of 5–10 years with renewable terms could be considered for any other agricultural purpose. Longer lease periods of 25–30 years could be considered for long term investments in modern agriculture based on high tech precision farming, poly houses with artificial intelligence, modern silos, cold storages, food parks, and agro-processing industry'.

Punjab known for extensive land leasing in and out and even reverse tenancy, had 80% of the leased area rented on cash basis compared with less than 10% in Gujarat in 2003. In Punjab, by 2010–2011, 55% of the operated area was with the tenants with leased in area accounting for 48% of the operated area and the average size of the operated holding of a tenant was double that of an owner operated although the owned land did not differ across type of farmers. Further, 83% of tenant farmers owned tractors compared with 55% of owner farmers and 78% had power operated tube wells compared with 61% of owner farmers. A majority of them also employed permanent farm servants compared with only 25% of owner farmers. The semi-medium and large farmers accounted for 48 and 34% of the leased in area with another 40% being with the semi-medium farmers in 2010–2011 (Shergill, 2016). This kind of approach by the Committee to farm land lease market without any restrictions can only further marginalise small and landless farmers in Punjab in the context of reverse tenancy which Punjab is known for, and which has led to marginal and small farmers operating only 8% land despite being 34% of farm households (Singh, 2021). Rather Punjab' revenue commission had proposed to open up land leasing to all kinds of players for very long periods even when Niti Aayog was not that adventurous in this in its model land leasing Act, 2016 proposed to states (Singh, 2020a).

9 Conclusion

Punjab economy has shown the weaknesses and strengths during the COVID-19 pandemic times. The most important weak link is the dysfunctional fiscal policy and its consequences in weak public health system. Due to heavy dependence on private health care that turned non-functional during the COVID-19 pandemic, it resulted into higher fatality and infection rates. The other pillar of human capital formation is the education system. Similar to health care system, the private education has prevailed and has been promoted by the state, and public education system has weakened over time. Thus, the return of the rural students to public educational institutions, which are relatively low in quality and also lacks infrastructure to impart adequate and relevant educational skills required in the emerging modern ecosystem, is a welcome trend.

The weak link in the structure of the economy is the manufacturing sector due to tiny and small in size on the one hand and highly disconnected from other sectors of the economy and thus does not create essential externalities for stable and fast economic growth of the economy. Almost no help was extended by the state government either to the small-scale industrial units operating in the informal sector or workers working in the informal sector. The migrant labour suffered the most but was neither compensated by the employers nor compensated by the state government.

The services sector also suffered a huge loss but faced the neglect of the state government. It is pertinent to add that even the most conservative governments of the western world have given high fiscal stimulus but the governments of India and Punjab missed this opportunity. Punjab, in particular, due to lack of financial resources as well as of lack of innovations in the crisis times, failed to respond and could not come up to deal with the enormous crisis faced by the economy and society.

An important resilient sector of the Punjab economy is agriculture in which the individual capital formation by the agricultural households is tremendous. This is in the form of investment in electric pump set based irrigation, tractors for cultivation, and harvesting machines. Apart from that, a vast agriculture network of markets and rural metal roads had helped agricultural sector to sustain the momentum. However, despite the several strengths, it has also been suffering from several deficiencies and weaknesses. The consequence is the environmental hazard and non-remunerative economic activity created a wide spread rural distress. Therefore, the agricultural sector deserves innovative public policy. The above suggested structural changes in public policy can provide future pathways to develop the state economy into a resilient, sustainable, and more inclusive one.

References

Agarwal, B. (2021) Livelihoods in Covid Times: Gendered Perils and New Pathways in India, *World Development*, 139. Online first.

FICCI. (2020) *A Policy Document for Reinvigorating Industry in Punjab*, FICCI PHHRAC, Chandigarh.

GoP (Government of Punjab). (2017) Industrial and Business Development Policy, 2017, Department of Industries and Commerce, Government of Punjab, Chandigarh, October.

GoP. (2021) Budget 2021–22, Speech of Manpreet Singh Badal, Finance Minister, Government of Punjab.

Govindan, S. (2021) *Covid-19 and Agriculture in South Asia*, A Policy Paper, Focus on the Global South in Collaboration with Rosa Luxemburg Stiftung-South Asia, February.

PSFFWC (Punjab State Farmers' and Farm Workers' Commission). (2018) *Punjab State Farmers' Policy*, Draft, PSFFWC, Mohali, June.

Punjab Vidhan Sabha Secretariat. (2018) Report of the House Committee to Enquire into Farmer Suicides and Economic Distress of Farm Workers Due to Indebtedness in Punjab State and Suggest Ways Out, PVSS, Chandigarh, March.

Shergill, H. S. (2016) Growth of Cash Rent Tenancy and Modernization of Land Lease Market in Punjab, in L. Singh and N. Singh (Eds.), *Economic*

Transformation of a Developing Economy: The Experience of Punjab, Chapter 6, Patiala: Springer, pp. 121–139.

Singh, L., and Singh, I. (2012) *Rejuvenation of Punjab Economy: A Policy Document*, CDEIS Policy Paper 1, Punjabi University, Patiala.

Singh, L., Gill, A., Bhangoo, K. S., Brar, J. S., Uppal, A., Khuranna, R. K., and Agarwal, P.K. (2020) *Current State of Fiscal Health and Capacity to Pay*, CDEIS, Punjabi University, Patiala.

Singh, S. (2017) "White Gold" for Whom? A Study of Institutional Aspects of Work and Wages in Cotton GPNs in India, in E. Noronha and P. D'Cruz (Eds.), *Critical Perspectives on Work and Employment in Globalising India*, Chapter 2, Singapore: Springer, pp. 15–36

Singh, S. (2020a) A Bill to 'Corporatize' Farming, *Frontline*, June 5.

Singh, S. (2020b) Punjab: Middleman's Role, *Frontline*, December 19, 2020–January 1, 2021.

Singh, S. (2021) Punjab Agriculture: Pinning Hopes on Private Sector for Revival, *EPW*, 56(2): 10–12, January 9.

Tiwari, S., and Surya, S. (2020) *State of State Finances*, PRS Legislative Research, Institute for Policy Research Studies, New Delhi.

Index

S. Singh et al. (eds.), *Covid-19 Pandemic and Economic Development*, https://doi.org/10.1007/978-981-16-4442-9

The manufacturer's authorised representative in the EU is Springer Nature Customer Service Centre GmbH, Europaplatz 3, 69115 Heidelberg, Germany. If you have any concerns regarding our products, please contact ProductSafety@springernature.com

Printed and bound by CPI Group (UK) Ltd, Croydon, CR0 4YY
30/09/2026
02225326-0014